S

| | | | |
|---|---|---|---|
| TRAV. L?. | -4 NOV 1979 | | |
| -3 APR 1979 | 15 DEC 1979 | | |
| 19 APR 1979 | | | |
| | 29 DEC 1979 | | |
| 28. APR 1979 | | | |
| | 14 JAN 1980 | | |
| 21. APR 1979 | 23 FEB 1980 | | |
| 17. MAY 1979 | -8 MR 1980 | | |
| -4 JUN 1979 | | | |
| | 19 APR 1980 | | |
| -9 JUL 1979 | | | |
| | 19 MAY 1980 | | |
| | 12 JUN 1980 | | |
| 17 AUG 1979 | | | |
| -3 SEP 1979 | -1 JUL 1980 | | |
| 28 SEP 1979 | | | |

## LONDON BOROUGH OF ENFIELD
## LIBRARY SERVICES

This book to be RETURNED on or before the latest date stamped unless a renewal has been obtained by personal call, post or telephone, quoting the above number and the date due for return.

# Padre in Colditz

# Padre in Colditz

---

*The diary of J. Ellison Platt M.B.E.*

EDITED BY MARGARET DUGGAN

HODDER AND STOUGHTON
LONDON SYDNEY AUCKLAND TORONTO

*Glossary of German words*      *page 316*

# The Myth of Colditz

> When I use *myth, mythical,* I refer to the universal in-
> stinct of any human group, large or small, to invest,
> almost always unconsciously, certain stories or events or
> places or persons, real or fictional, with an uncommon
> significance; to turn them into instinctive centres of refer-
> ence; to make stories A, B, C, D, all roughly having the
> same theme or moral, *one,* the type. Made thus typical,
> the story becomes a communal possession, the agreed and
> classic embodiment of some way of thinking or feeling.
>
> E. M. W. TILLYARD, *Some Mythical Elements in
> English Literature.*

THE GERMANS CALLED Colditz Castle a *Sonderlager,* a
'special camp', and they made it so in a special sense by
cramming it with men who, for courage, daring and ingenuity, were the cream of the Allied prisoners-of-war. The
exploits of those prisoners have become legendary, and the
records of their escapes are now classics of the Second
World War. Though the camp in its earlier and more
spectacular days contained prisoners of five nationalities, it
finally became wholly British. But there are reasons more
subtle than that why Colditz has been so thoroughly taken
into our national mythology alongside those other great
myths of the Battle of Britain, Arnhem and Dunkirk; it is
another of those stories so peculiarly attractive to the
British of moral victory wrested from defeat, laced throughout with under-stated heroism and that absurd sense of
humour which is the pride and inverted swank of Englishmen.

No other prisoner-of-war camp has been so well docu-
mented. The dramatic escape stories, notably those by

5

Major Pat Reid, have been complemented and given an unusual dimension by Captain Eggers' record of the German point of view, a view that was often flattering and appreciative of those very elements which most please the British about themselves. And the myth finally became firmly established in the popular imagination by the BBC television series which so accurately re-created the highlights of five extraordinary years in an extraordinary place that few ex-Colditz men could find anything in the picture on their television screens which jarred their personal memories.

But memories are, by their nature, selective. One ex-Colditz man perhaps summed it up for them all when he said, thirty years later, that he could only remember life in the castle as either utterly hilarious or utterly grim — there seemed nothing in between. Yet there was a lot in between. Exciting as the escape stories are, the background against which those moments of high drama are set has its own interest. If the escapes show to what heights of daring and inventiveness intelligent and brave young men could rise, the record of the day-to-day life of the prisoners in Colditz shows the strength of the human spirit in highly unnatural and at times almost unendurable conditions.

Colditz was by no means the worst of the prisoner-of-war camps, but it was still a place of severe testing for the men who had to endure there. For five years several hundred active young men were cooped together in an enclosed space on a very inadequate diet. For them the war became a daily battle against boredom, depression, and demoralisation: a battle which most of them won with honours. They were both overcrowded and hungry, the two conditions which in an experimental laboratory are said to lead to the breakdown of all social inhibitions; yet the men in Colditz maintained not only the disciplines of a civilised society (in direct parallel to that other British myth about dressing for dinner in the jungle) but also a heightened intellectual alertness, and a persistent sense of the ridiculous.

Their humour was usually of the sort that came straight from the prep schools most of them had been to; a schoolboy prankishness with a cutting edge designed to exasperate and insult the schoolmasterly Germans. They succeeded continually in both those aims, and were lectured by their captors in much the same terms that naughty schoolboys always are. But we know from the late Captain Eggers that to some of the Germans the British eccentricity and *sang-froid* when it came to taking themselves or anyone else seriously was a matter for secret envy, and after a while a few of them learned and unbent enough to join in the joke, and even to turn a joke on its perpetrators. But, true to the British public school sense of fairness about not kicking a man when he's down, once it was clear that Germany was collapsing, the jokes and insults stopped by order of the British Senior Officer. It would not have been gentlemanly conduct to make fun of an enemy who was facing defeat.

The public school moral code, with its gallantries and blindnesses, was very strong. In the light of Britain's sub-sequent social revolution, the class division between officers and orderlies when they were all prisoners together now seems unacceptable, and it is not to be wondered at that there was constant trouble with disgruntled soldiers who did not see why they should be willing servants of officers who could exert no authority over them. In a microcosm in Colditz there were the two classes of British society which, three decades later, are polarised in worker-management strife; and the more one reads of life in the castle the more clear it is that the Colditz myth is part of the great British public school myth. Had Colditz been packed with other ranks, rather than officers, there would undoubtedly have been deeds of heroism to record, but it would have been quite a different story from 'Colditz' as we know it.

Among the few officers who had *not* been to a public school was Joseph (Jock) Ellison Platt, the Methodist Chaplain. He had been captured at Dunkirk and was one of the earliest British arrivals at Colditz, sent there on a trumped-up charge of possessing escape equipment, prob-ably because he had made himself a nuisance to the Germans by constant requests to be transferred to a camp for other ranks where he could exercise his chaplain's ministry. Of all the prisoners who kept diaries, his appears to be the only one that has survived. It is an immense manuscript of nearly 800 foolscap pages closely written in fine pencil.

All but the last few pages appear to be a fair copy written from notes, and one can only assume that those last pages, small sheets of exercise-book paper on which the writing is so minute that it is difficult to read without a magnifying-glass, are typical of the original notes from which he wrote up the fuller diary. All the sheets of the fair copy bear a German censor's *Geprüft* rubber stamp, and we know from the diary itself that it was regularly read and censored — a batch of several weeks' entries at a time — usually by Captain Eggers, the German Security Officer, whose books have lent such an illuminating gloss to the English accounts of Colditz.

There are entries for nearly every day of the five years from Platt's capture in May 1940 to the liberation of Colditz in April 1945. It was only when he was suffering from really severe depression, boredom, or ill-health that he was unable to find anything to say. It is the minutiae of life, recording current rumours and speculation, lectures de-livered by fellow-prisoners, arguments, conversations, books he read, and concerts in the camp theatre. But he also wrote an account of what it was like actually to be a prisoner-of-war: the overwhelming importance of food and Red Cross parcels; the determination to keep mentally and physically fit; the frustrations and loneliness and in-evitable homosexuality; the international relationships and particularly the subtly different concepts of national honour, and, of course, those highlights of a prisoner's life, the escape attempts.

Writing of the escapes with his eye on the German censor he is necessarily cryptic and sparing of detail. On 14 October 1942, for instance, he reports mysteriously 'A very quiet, busy day. An intense, exciting evening.' It is only in the next day's entry, when the event had safely taken place, that he describes as much as he dares of the escape of four officers.

8

Even so, some of the escape accounts are much fuller than one would expect, and on some of the pages a detailed examination of the *Geprüft* stamp under a magnifying-glass suggests that it might be a forgery. Forging rubber stamps — and much else — was a highly developed art in Colditz, and it is possible that once the innocuous entries on escape days had been censored, Platt substituted pages in the diary containing a fuller account, and bearing a forged stamp. Certainly his diary was always a matter of anxiety to Rupert Barry, the British officer in charge of codes and information.

Editing the diary has been a formidable task. The simplest part was to cut it down to a reasonable book length (about a sixth of its original length) by excluding all the lectures, sermons, rumours, and second-hand accounts by other prisoners of their experiences in other camps. I have omitted almost the whole of 1943 which was the middle and most tedious year of the five that Platt was in captivity. But I do not think I have omitted anything which illuminates the picture of life in that very enclosed, international and entirely masculine community.

But much more difficult has been editing Platt's own writing. He was not a well-educated man in the sense that most of his fellow-prisoners were. He was born in the small Cheshire town of Winsford in 1900, and educated at the local grammar school. His father kept a shop and small-holding, and was a local Methodist preacher. Jock Platt, when he left school, went to work for his uncle who kept a boot and shoe-repair shop until, in his middle-twenties, he entered Hartley College, Manchester, to train for the Methodist ministry. In 1933 he married Maisie Grainger, the daughter of another Methodist minister, and they had a brief period of service in South Africa, from which they returned shortly before the outbreak of war.

Platt read widely, and he read even more widely in Colditz. But he never escaped from the self-educated man's tendency to use pompous circumlocutions instead of simple and direct language. Always in his diary he prefers 'commence' to 'begin', 'converse' to 'talk', and 'enquires whether he might be permitted to purchase'. This sets an editor the delicate task of steering a path between changing the character of the original writing, and leaving it irritating to read. I hope that by simple excision of the occasional phrase, and the very occasional reconstruction of a sentence, I have managed to edit this manuscript for publication in the way that Jock Platt would have approved.

It might well surprise the reader that this, being the diary of a chaplain, contains so little spiritual or theological matter. There is very little in the manuscript. Padre Platt was a conscientious and caring pastor with a real and loving sense of responsibility for his fellow-prisoners, to many of whom — because he was comparatively middle-aged — he became something of a father-figure. He was also, especially in later years, a popular preacher. In many ways he seems to have had a better sense of what the average nominal Christian needed than the rather stiff-necked high Anglican chaplains he found himself with. But his spiritual and theological comments rarely add anything to our understanding of Platt himself, or the situation in Colditz, and I have omitted most of them.

It is a matter of great frustration that the diary ends about thirty-six hours before the actual liberation of Colditz by American troops. Obviously by then the emotional tension was just too high to be committed to paper, so I have had to depend on other, and often conflicting sources for the end of the story. But we know from Major Reid's research for *The Latter Days at Colditz* that Platt flew home with the nucleus of men with whom he had spent so much of his war.

The next few months he spent as chaplain at the Oswestry rehabilitation camp, and his own rehabilitation, especially as far as his health was concerned, took a long time. In fact he never really recovered his health from his time in Colditz, and as he got older he suffered from increasingly severe bronchitis.

He returned to the circuit ministry of the Methodist Church, first in Sussex, and then in Orpington, where he became Superintendent of the circuit, and supervised the building of a new and larger church. But in 1950 his wife Maisie died of cancer, and three years later he married again. With his new wife, Betty, he moved to Castle Cary in 1956. But he could not go on very much longer. By 1960 his health was so bad that he was forced to retire five years early. They moved to Dorset and, cared for by his wife, his retirement was long and happy. He died of a sudden heart attack in 1973.

Jock Platt had often thought of editing his huge diary for publication, but had never found the energy to do so. It was some while after his death that Mrs Betty Platt offered it to Messrs Hodder and Stoughton who put it into my hands.

Mrs Platt was able to give me the details of her husband's early life; and Mrs Brenda Hague, who twenty years ago typed about half the diary manuscript and so made my work easier, was also very helpful. I am grateful to all those ex-Colditz men who have published their memoirs for adding so much vivid colour to the story for me, and particularly to the late Sir Rupert Barry who, though in failing health, answered at length all my many questions. The Reverend John Beaumont also supplied me with his personal memories, books and press-cuttings; and by marvellous good luck the Reverend Canon John Bown, who was taken prisoner with Platt at Dunkirk, came to live close to my home just at the moment when he could be most helpful in telling me more about the first days of their captivity. My friend, Peter Wyld, encouraged me and kept me straight on military matters, and I owe a great debt indeed to my friend, Larry Ward, for his patient reading of the manuscript and proofs with a meticulous eye for both English and German grammar. And not least am I grateful to Edward England of Hodder and Stoughton who made it possible for me — too young to take part in the war, but an envious little sister of brothers who could — to live vicariously through five years in the magnificent company of the prisoners of Colditz.

# Dunkirk 1940

DURING THE HOT May days of 1940 the roads to the French and Belgian coasts had streamed with tired and frightened women, old men, and children, as limping and bedraggled as refugees always are. Some pushed hand-carts piled high with household goods. Some drove, dragged or exhorted their farm animals along the road. The lucky ones were crammed into the few lorries left to the civilian population, and others had farm-carts with horses already staggering under their panic-piled loads.

The banks and verges along the road were littered with the clothes and the packages and the domestic bits and pieces the people had jettisoned as they became too heavy or awkward to carry. There were constant traffic jams caused by broken-down carts and vehicles that had run out of precious petrol. From time to time there was pandemonium as a diving Messerschmitt or Stuka spattered bullets along the defenceless procession, sometimes leaving one more body to lie by the road in the hot sun.

But now, at the very end of May, the civilians had mostly gone, and the evacuation of the British Expeditionary Force had begun. Every road leading to Dunkirk was choked with trucks and carriers, horse-drawn artillery from an earlier war, Bedfords and Scammels, soldiers on motorcycles, soldiers on bicycles, soldiers asleep on horseback, weary soldiers on foot. There were accidents and collisions as the faster traffic pushed its way through the slow. There were occasional shells and bombs and machine-gun fire. And always in the background the noise of battle kept the ground under their feet in perpetual vibration.

Most of the wounded who could still walk managed somehow to find transport to the coast and the Dunkirk beaches. But in the Belgian village of Krombeke nine hundred seriously hurt men lay head to foot in the village church, and more were in the cottages from which the tenants had fled. The medical officers of the 10th Casualty Clearing Station had been working round the clock, operating in the village school, and pressing every one of their personnel into medical service. Even the chaplains had turned anaesthetists, keeping men unconscious with chloroform bottle and rag, terrified that the patient might come round too soon.

By May 29th Krombeke was in the comparative quiet of no-man's-land. Dunkirk was an hour away and, from Dunkirk, a ship could be home in three more hours. But there was no option for the 10th CCS. They had to stay with the wounded, and that would mean being taken prisoner with their patients by the advancing Germans. There was a shred of hope — it would have been humanly impossible not to hope — and lorries were being held ready for an improbable last-minute evacuation. But meanwhile there was work to be done, and no time to think about anything but the shattered men to be made comfortable, and to be pieced together where it was possible.

Jock Ellison Platt, the Methodist chaplain to the CCS, straightened his back at the end of a long day spent stooping over the wounded as they lay on straw and blankets in the church, and walked out into the evening air for a breather and a smoke. He was dizzy with exhaustion. He and his two fellow-chaplains, the Anglican, John Bown, and their Roman Catholic colleague, had spent much of the last few days burying dead soldiers in a field outside the village. And when they were not doing that they had played whatever role was asked of them: stretcher-bearer, nursing orderly, anaesthetist, traffic-policeman. Now Platt was tired out; too tired to be more than vaguely aware that for him and the 10th CCS, and the wounded in their care, one phase of the war had come to an end, and the next had yet to begin.

He walked past the village cottages and up to the main road where the last British trucks had been pounding their

14

way down to Dunkirk. Earlier in the day he had collected 25,000 cigarettes from a deserted Naafi to distribute among the wounded and, as a single lorry came along the road, he tossed what he still had in his pockets into the crowded vehicle. The men shouted thanks and cheerful farewells, and he stood waving to them as they rumbled out of sight. It looked as though they were some of the last of the Allied troops to get away, for the road that in the last few days had carried so much traffic was now suddenly empty.

There was nothing for him to do but to go back to the church and the wounded soldiers, so many of whom seemed only boys to Platt, who was nearing his fortieth birthday. He had no children of his own, but everything that was fatherly in his nature came out as he comforted pain-wracked and thirsty young men, promising to write re-assuring letters to their parents, and praying as he held the hands of the dying.

There was not much sleep for anyone that night. The sky was lit with the glow of burning vehicles that the retreating troops had wrecked and fired; and several times a tongue of flame shot to an immense height as a petrol tank burst. At half-past one the last of the rearguard rattled through the village on motorcycles, shouting that they had left a few dead and wounded behind them up the road. John Bown went out with a party to bring them in. Platt stayed in the church, and dawn was not far off when he finally returned to his billet in one of the cottages for a few hours' sleep.

By the time he was up and shaved and dressed again the sun was shining brilliantly with the promise of another hot day. It was seven o'clock, and he walked across to the farmhouse that had been commandeered as the officers' mess.

The cook poured him a mug of tea. 'Any news of the Jerries, sir?'

'Not yet. I thought they would be here by now.' Platt took the tea and a bully-beef sandwich across the empty room to the window and ate in still-tired silence. It was not

15

many minutes before he saw what they had been waiting for. A German light tank rumbled into the village square. It stopped long enough for its occupants to look round, and then went off again. Platt, with the cook at his side, continued to wait. Within a few more minutes the tank was back again with two others.

An immaculately uniformed German NCO climbed down into the square. Platt walked cautiously to the door as other members of the CCS appeared out in the road. The Commanding Officer's batman had gone running for him, and the CO, usually a paragon of military correctitude, marched into the square to surrender his unit with his face half-covered in shaving-soap.

Within half an hour the village had been taken over by the German military machine with impressive efficiency, and with courtesy. The British reported that there was a wounded German airman in the church. The German NCO went to the church door and cried, 'Heil Hitler!' and immediately he was answered from the chancel. Platt watched him pick his way among the wounded and greet his compatriot who, Platt reflected, had ceased to be a prisoner the moment he, Platt, had become one. The pilot obviously spoke well of the treatment he had received at the hands of the British, and it had its effect. The Germans completed their inspection of the wounded, the ambulances, the supplies, arms and ammunition with painstaking politeness.

The doctors and other officers who had come off duty were allowed to get on with their breakfast and, with an uncertain future before them, were making the most of their bacon and eggs when a German officer appeared in the doorway. 'Gentlemen,' he said in excellent English, 'I must ask you to surrender all arms.'

Rather rudely he was told that doctors did not bring guns to breakfast, and all weapons had already been handed over. 'I think, gentlemen,' said the German mildly, 'you have forgotten the rifles on your ambulances. But we have looked at them and they are so dirty that we have discounted them.'

Later in the day the SS troops arrived, considerably less

16

gentle in their dealings with the prisoners than the front-
line troops had been. With great dispatch they began load-
ing the wounded into ambulances to be taken to the *Feldlazarett* at Ypres. The medical officers, to their dismay and
anger, were ordered to discard all their instruments and
drugs. They were to follow the wounded to Ypres on foot,
but they would not be allowed to care for them.

Platt marched with the first contingent of CCS personnel
next day while John Bown stayed behind to bury the remaining dead. They went through Poperinghe and reached
Ypres in the evening to find the town apparently deserted
by its citizens, and some of its streets a shambles. Their
wounded were lying on straw in a large two-storied school
and an adjacent cinema. There was no medical aid for
them, though some of the worst cases had already been taken
by Belgian nuns to their own hospital.

The town was waterless, which greatly increased the
misery of the wounded men. Without drugs, without the
surgical attention the British doctors could have given them
had they been allowed to keep their equipment and their
supply of dressings, gangrene quickly became an all too
familiar stench. In the following days a lasting bitterness
grew in the souls of the doctors who had to watch young
men lose their limbs and die for lack of those drugs and
instruments that had been left behind in Krombeke.

Two days later they were joined by the rest of the 10th
CCS who arrived in Ypres tired, dusty and thirsty. Platt
and Bown again went out with burying parties, this time to
look for British bodies along the canal embankment where
last stands had been made. Some of the bodies had been
lying there for nearly two weeks, and it was a revolting
task. Platt had a burying party of eight Pioneer Corps who
were some of the toughest specimens of Glasgow and Liver-
pool dockland he had ever struck, but they surprised him
by the tenderness with which they did their gruesome work.
The burial ground they were allowed to use was the St
Jean (Extension) Imperial War Graves Cemetery, full of
the dead from a previous war. As the pioneers dug the
new graves their shovels often struck the bright studs on

the soles of the boots of an earlier generation of dead soldiers.

Once Platt met a German chaplain engaged in the same duty who, as Platt read the burial service, came to the graveside and, at the end, saluted the British dead. A little later Platt went to stand at the German's side, as he read the service, to salute the German dead.

Water remained dreadfully short. The Germans were processing it from the canal, but there was never enough, and in the hot weather thirst became obsessive. Eight men had to wash and shave in half a gallon.

The medical staff had been drawing water from the well in the school-master's garden to supplement the drinking supplies for the wounded, but the Belgian schoolmaster, a little dandy of a man who had fled among the refugees at the German advance, returned one day to find them doing it. He flew into a rage of protest and strutted off to the German *Kommandantur* to complain. To the surprise of the British, the Germans upheld the rights of private property, but the unpleasantness of the incident was off-set by the generosity of a Belgian butcher who offered ten gallons of water a day for the wounded for as long as his well held out. His offer was accepted with gratitude, and the Germans provided buckets to carry the water the half mile from the butcher's garden to the school. It meant an extra half pint a day for a hundred and sixty men and, to Platt, the well seemed to take on the nature of the widow's cruse, for it never showed any sign of running dry.

After they had been in Ypres for a week, representatives of the International Red Cross arrived with promises of evacuating all the wounded and the CCS personnel to the Red Cross hospital on the coast at Blankenberge. They were greeted with a good deal of scepticism, and when a convoy of Red Cross ambulances arrived the following morning it was clear that only half of the injured — the most seriously wounded — would be able to go. They were loaded and driven off, and by mid-afternoon the news arrived in Ypres that the hospital at Blankenberge was full, but another was being opened at Ghent. Then followed rumour and counter-rumour, and a day of being paraded, kept waiting, and dismissed only to be paraded again. German ambulances came, and by late at night the rest of the wounded had been taken away. The following morning the thirty NCOs and men of the Pioneer Corps who had been attached to the CCS were marched away. Only the officers and a number of nursing orderlies remained, waiting around, officially on parade, but drifting away to doze in the sun until something happened.

In the early afternoon, to everyone's relief, transport arrived: the luxury of a charabanc for the officers, and a truck for the orderlies. They drove off, back to Poperinghe and then on to Boulogne where the charabanc driver stopped to ask the way. Almost immediately a young French woman ran to the side of the coach and, standing on her toes, thrust a quart jug of coffee through the window to the British passengers. She was followed by a boy and another woman with a long white loaf, and packets of Woodbines, army biscuits and chocolate which had evidently come from the shelves of some deserted Naafi.

They drove on through Etaples to Camiers and, late in the evening, they stopped outside the general hospital in Le Touquet. They were clearly not expected there, and the driver was advised to try what had been the British No 18 Base Hospital near Camiers where the 10th CCS had been stationed a month before. They found it and found the Nissen huts and the field kitchen still in place; but the site was deserted and, on the prisoners' advice, the driver went on to No 17 Base Hospital two kilometres away. It was third time lucky, and by 11.30 p.m. they were paraded, counted, and allowed to join the British officers already there, and to go to British beds with British blankets in a British hospital marquee.

No 17 was full of British wounded. Most of those who could walk or move at all were able to sit or lie outside in the unending sunshine looking down over the village of Etaples on to the shimmering and empty sea. The weather was proving the surgeons' best friend, and even the seriously injured cases were making amazing progress. On

Sunday, 16th June, Platt was able to take his first Free Church service since capture, and a hundred and fifty men, many of them in bandages, sang 'Fight the good fight' and 'Onward Christian soldiers'. Platt talked simply about the green fields of England, birds, bluebells, and a good God.

Next day came the rumour that France had capitulated. As there were also rumours that America had entered the war and already had a fleet in a Portuguese harbour, that Churchill had given Hitler twenty-four hours to clear out of France, Belgium and Holland 'or England would bomb Germany to blazes', and that the Allies had stirred up a rebellion in Abyssinia, it was hard to know what to believe. Churchill was supposed to have said that France and Britain were no longer separate but had combined to form one nation to be known as 'Anglo-France'. Later they heard 'on the highest authority' that he had said that every Frenchman to land in Britain would immediately be given British nationality. But so many rumours were 'on the highest authority' that doubters believed nothing, and it was another week before the last of them were convinced that France had actually signed (on 22nd June) an armistice with Germany.

On 28th June they were told that all but three officers of the 10th CCS were to leave the next day with three hundred of the walking wounded for an unknown destination. Platt was one of the three to be left behind and felt it a wrench to be parted from the companions with whom he had spent the whole of his war. John Bown was among those who were going, and though the two of them had little in common besides the fact that they were chaplains, they had shared the work of burying very dead bodies, and they had even leapt together into an open grave on top of a corpse to shelter from the machine-gunning of a diving Stuka. They had worked as colleagues and Platt, rather hesitantly, on Bown's last morning, offered to accompany him to the Anglican Communion service. It seemed a fitting way to part, and they did not meet again.

It had become obvious during the last few days that the hospital was closing down, and on the 3rd July, after a lot of waiting about, Platt and nine MOs from various units were driven to the railway station at Brussels only to find that something had gone wrong with the arrangements, and there was no train for them. The German guards became worried, for it was already past ten o'clock at night, and the local *Kommandantur* was not prepared to be interested in ten surplus prisoners. They tried the town gaol, but were turned away and finally the truck made for the artillery barracks at Malines, where there were a few other British officers and a large number of French troops. There was no food, no beds, and nothing to drink. A tiled floor in a disused saddle room was the only accommodation offered to them.

The next day a number of British wounded were brought from Antwerp and Brussels, and the medical team had to wrestle with the French for stretchers and straw to make the lying cases comfortable. It was the first of the running battles with the French troops — many of whom were Moroccan — that were going to make the next few days a fight for survival. Platt already had a full measure of the English prejudice, common at that time, against the French, and what he saw of French manners and hygiene in the period they spent in the company of those troops gave him a contempt for French behaviour that never really left him.

The first meal of the day was issued at noon, but the French mobbed the kitchen doors, shoving and pushing, trampling on each other, and trying to pass dixies full of soup over the heads of the surging crowd to friends at the rear. In disgust at the undisciplined mêlée, the British officers walked away to return half an hour later — by which time all the food had gone. They were quite unable to make themselves understood by the French cooks in the kitchen, and their appeal to the French officers was received without sympathy.

They were ready in good time for the next meal. They saw the bread and cheese cut up for distribution — but got neither. The only British to eat were two orderlies who knew how to snatch.

By now the British Quartermaster was boiling over.

Lieutenant Weekes was a short, spare and very fit man in his late forties who had risen from the ranks and could make himself understood in both German and French. He had a determination which overcame the British good manners that had proved so ineffectual. 'Leave it to me, gentlemen,' he said. 'Go back to your room, leave me four orderlies, and I will be up with your food in half an hour.'

He was as good as his word, and bread, excellent cheese and coffee were produced. After that, 'Leave it to Weekes!' became a familiar cry, and the British orderlies collected the food regularly so that the British officers and wounded could eat it peacefully in their quarters while the French continued to scramble round the kitchen door.

Weekes was no mean quartermaster. It was he who, snooping round the barracks, found a room in another building full of palliasses and iron bedsteads and, at a time when the French were busy fighting for their food, had enough brought across for every patient, officer and man to sleep comfortably.

But within a week all those who could walk were ordered to be on the move again. After a morning of the inevitable waiting about, the gates were opened and the French moved out with the British bringing up the rear.

The gates clanged to behind them, and neither prisoners nor guards were prepared for the scene that followed. The high street of Malines was crowded with women and children laden with food, cigarettes, tobacco and sweets to thrust upon the prisoners.

As the British marched out at the end of the procession it looked, from the trampled mess in the road, as though the people had begun by throwing their gifts to the prisoners. But a lot had been wasted, and now they had changed their tactics.

Though the military police tried to hold them back, the women broke through the lines again and again to push food into mouths and pockets, and to hang ready-prepared parcels round the prisoners' necks. Some ran into the road to hold cups of coffee and mugs of beer to the men's lips as they marched, and then rushed back to their menfolk and children on the pavement for fresh supplies.

Four times in the length of the street the women broke through the restraint and loaded their gifts on the prisoners. On the last occasion Platt found a huge roast-pork sandwich thrust into his hand, and a box of cigars pushed into his gas-mask.

'Are you British, padre?' asked the young woman in a clear Scottish voice.

'What are you doing here?' he exclaimed.

'I'm married to a Belgian doctor. I've been here seven years. Good luck. God bless you.' And she kissed him quickly and retreated.

'A braw wee lassie,' said the nearest German guard, and Platt looked at him in amazement. For a while they were separated, and Platt was busy stuffing into his mouth the sandwich, hard-boiled eggs, pieces of sausage, honey-cake and fruit-cake that had been pushed into his hands and pockets. But when the long straggling line of prisoners got out into the open country he learned that the guard had spent several years in Scotland and England, and deplored the fact that good personal friends were now national enemies. Platt offered him a cigar, but he refused politely. 'It is a long way to Germany, and you will need all you have!'

The weather was still hot and most of the prisoners, including Platt, were wearing their greatcoats and carrying a heavy pack. Every man still had his pockets bulging with sausages and cigarettes, packets of lump sugar and sweets. Sweat poured off them as the guards kept them marching, but very soon there was another diversion. Bicycle bells rang behind them in mad chorus, and young women and small boys came among them with baskets filled with ripe black cherries. Full of food as the prisoners were, the cherries were irresistible, and this time the Germans did not even try to stop them being given in handfuls.

The kindness of the Belgian country people persisted. In each village and hamlet that the prisoners marched through the local people placed buckets of water at the very edge of the marching lines so that men with mugs could dip them in as they passed, take a mouthful, and pass the remainder to the inner lines. Some of the MOs, with the habitual British fear of typhoid in foreign lands, tried to remonstrate as they saw men drink mugful after mugful; but most of the prisoners were too thirsty to care. Platt, middle-aged and cautious, contented himself with rinsing his mouth and spitting it out.

The sun was setting when they reached Louvain and were taken to the local workhouse. The British officers were given an upstairs room with plenty of straw, and with tremendous relief they discovered a communal wash-house in which they could sponge down their sweaty bodies. The incomparable Weekes organised a pint of hot soup each, and their good luck continued the next morning when they found a lorry waiting to take them on the next stage of their journey.

It seemed a marvellous day, and as soon as they were out of the workhouse gates they were again pelted with food by the people of Louvain. They sang as they rode, and it seemed to matter little that the driver lost his way and drove them back to Louvain again. But they set off once more, and eventually found themselves in a ramparted castle in Diest where there was straw and fresh pump-water, and cabbage soup.

The next day they were marching again, and blistered feet became a continual torture. When they stopped that night at a large council school in Hasselt the local German *Kommandant* humanely provided dressings and ointment, as well as a good meal resembling Lancashire hotpot, and plenty of coffee. He was a careful and conscientious man, and the next morning when the prisoners were due to march off again he ordered that fifty of the British soldiers should stay behind to clean up the school and its latrines. Platt had never seen anything so filthy as the latrines were that morning. They were typical school water closets, the best they had come across on their march. But the users had not flushed them and, when the lavatories were choked, had used the floor.

The British protested indignantly. This was not their

24

doing. The Moroccan troops in particular had shown no respect for latrines or for any form of personal hygiene along the route. But the *Kommandant* was adamant. He was a reasonable man, and he explained that he had no blame for the British, he simply believed they would make the best job of cleaning up. When they had done it, he promised, they would be given a good meal and transport to the next camp. It seemed a fair bargain, and the fifty British remained behind.

Marching became more painful and wearisome, hour after footsore, sweat-sodden hour. The marchers began discarding some of their belongings. Platt, with a pack on his back, his communion set in one hand and a parcel of hymn-books in the other, decided that the hymn-books would have to go. He slipped one of them into an already bulging pocket for his own use, and left the rest by the roadside.

That night they were turned into a wire enclosure in the middle of an open field, and an unofficial search by German NCOs relieved them of a good many of their more useful possessions. It was the first looting they had been subjected to. Most of them lost their blankets and rubber raincoats, and had to sleep in the long grass with nothing to cover them. As luck would have it, the long, hot drought broke in the middle of that night, and they were soaked by the first heavy shower of rain in weeks. The rain turned into a steady drizzle which persisted all the next day.

By now they were in Germany, and another day's march brought them to a railway junction. They were herded into trucks and taken a three-hour journey to Dorston where they were able to rest and heal their feet for three days. Then the officers and men were separated, and Platt and his nine companions from the hospital at Camiers were taken on to Hemere, and then to the officers' prison camp at Spangenberg. It was the night of Saturday 20th July when they climbed the steep main street of the medieval village of Spangenberg and, after a routine search and delousing (to their great relief), were taken climbing higher still to the castle set on its conical hill, overlooking a wide and beautiful valley.

They crossed the drawbridge, went through the heavy gates, and were taken to their quarters. There were already more than forty British officers in the long dormitory into which they were shown. Among the crowd clad in a strange assortment of home-made nightwear were RAF pilots, some of them Canadian, who had been prisoners since the first week of the war. All of them were anxious to hear whatever news of the war and of England the ten newcomers could tell them.

The dormitory was furnished with two-tier wooden bunks, each fitted with a palliasse, a blue-checked sheet, and a blanket. At the end of the room were twenty iron washbowls with running water. After the conditions of the last few weeks it looked almost like luxury to the footsore and weary men.

But the next day they settled into the prisoner-of-war routine that they faced for an indefinite future. Breakfast, served at long trestle tables by British orderlies in an adjoining room, consisted of three thin slices of bread and a cup of ersatz coffee. There was vegetable soup at midday; and four slices of bread, two cold potatoes, and a small piece of blood sausage in the evening.

The day was punctuated by *Appells*, the constant roll-calls and countings-on-parade that were to become such a routine feature of prisoner life during the next few years. *Appells* were the official time for communication between the Germans and their prisoners, and they quickly became the prisoners' greatest opportunity for annoying their captors. In the officers' prison at Spangenberg they specialised in finding ways — that hardly breached good manners — of confusing the conscientious Germans in their count. No German NCO, for instance, could resist a polite greeting and enquiry after his family's health from a British officer of field rank, even though he was busily muttering '*einundzwanzig . . . zweiundzwanzig . . . dreiundzwanzig*' as he moved along the lines. No matter how often he lost count, the flattering interest got him every time.

In between meals and roll-calls the prisoners spent much of their time in bed where they felt less hungry and could conserve the small amount of energy that had been fuelled by their meagre diet. They also needed to keep warm. After the hot days when they had marched in the sun in great-coats with the sweat soaking through their clothes, the weather had turned to continuous rain. Inside the medieval stone walls of the castle a damp cold chilled them, and reduced them to arm-swinging and foot-stamping to circulate warmth through their limbs.

But worst of all was the obsession with food. Hunger became a tyranny they could not escape. They thought about food and they dreamed about it. Every moment of their lives became preoccupied with it, and concentration on anything else needed superhuman effort.

The Germans at no time observed either the letter or the spirit of Article 11 of the Geneva Convention governing the treatment of prisoners of war which required that 'the food ration of prisoners of war shall be equivalent in quantity and quality to that of the depot troops (of the detaining power)'. Ten ounces of bread — soon cut to nine — two potatoes and some vegetable soup formed the bulk of the daily diet. Any additions in the way of meat and fat and more nutritious vegetables varied from small to non-existent. This meant near-starvation for active young men in their early twenties. During the periods when they had to depend entirely on German rations they rapidly lost weight and became so weak and easily exhausted that climbing stairs could only be managed a few steps at a time. Young men who should have been in their athletic prime would be reduced to sitting panting half way up a flight of steps, summoning the energy to face the long haul to the next landing.

So the food-parcels supplied throughout the war by the Red Cross to all prisoners whose countries had ratified the Geneva Convention became essential to both health and morale and probably, in the long run, to life itself. Those parcels brought a sense of psychological well-being as well as nutrition, and strong and pitiable was the contrast in the prison camps where the Geneva Convention did not apply. Russia had not ratified it, and as she did not observe its

27

edicts with respect to the German prisoners in her hands, so the Germans did not observe the rules of the Convention in their treatment of Russian prisoners. The brutal result could be that in one camp British, French and Dutch prisoners would be living in spartan decency with a diet adequate to health, and sports and study equipment to provide occupation, while, only a matter of a few strands of barbed wire away, Russian prisoners would be literally starving, without clothing or bedding, without letters from home or reading matter, without any aid to retaining human decency. And the German prisoners in Russian hands would be facing the same existence in Siberia. Such was the civilising influence of the Geneva Convention and the International Red Cross; and such could be the treatment that the same humans could mete to each other when the all-important signature had not been appended to that document.

The food-parcels weighed nine pounds, and the contents varied according to the country in which they had been packed. Those for British prisoners came from Canada and New Zealand as well as from Britain. The tins of butter, meat, fish, bacon, dried egg, milk, cheese, biscuits, jam, tea, coffee, and cigarettes provided both the protein and the essential variety that they needed for reasonable health. When the parcels were plentiful — when each man had at least half a parcel a week — the prisoners kept remarkably fit. But when the parcel supplies ran out, usually because of blockage in the transport lines from Geneva, their health rapidly deteriorated.

From time to time additional parcels came filled entirely with cigarettes and tobacco, with medical supplies, or occasionally with soap, toothpowder and toilet rolls. Later in the war the Red Cross also provided the prisoners with books, games, study material, musical instruments, and sports equipment. So did many other organisations, notably the Licensed Victuallers' Association; but more often than not they concealed escape equipment — maps pasted under book-bindings, compasses in the handles of tennis rackets — and so, though many got through, enough were discovered by the German censors to make those parcels suspect and subject to the most intensive searches. But the International Red Cross were totally scrupulous about not trying to smuggle anything to the prisoners, and so the Germans readily co-operated in distributing their parcels as they came.

In the early days after Dunkirk, when the Germans were struggling to cope with forty thousand new prisoners, it took a long time for the first supplies to dribble through. When there were only a few British prisoners in the first months of the war the parcels had been addressed by name, and the earliest inhabitants of Spangenberg *Schloss* were already getting theirs. They had agreed to pool the tea and coffee, but to keep the rest of the contents for their own private consumption and, in the first few days when Platt and his companions were on bare German rations and the old hands were eating comparatively well, this became a matter for tension. A public meeting was called at which Platt was asked to tell what he knew of the intentions of the Red Cross in England, and how the parcels were funded by public subscription on the understanding that all prisoners of war should benefit equally. The intention was to put moral pressure on the old hands to share their extra food, but the sudden arrival of a dozen parcels marked 'for general distribution' saved their consciences being put to the test.

A week later it became possible for the prisoners to buy a few small additions to their rations from the canteen. Under the Geneva Convention the prisoners received the same pay as German officers of equivalent rank. Part of it was given to them in *'Lagermarks'*, a specially printed currency which could only be used in the canteen, while the rest of it was credited to them. There was not much for them to buy. Pencils and toothpaste were almost the only stock on the canteen shelves, but in the early months a man could buy a bottle of beer twice a week, and occasionally there were a few tomatoes or apples or hardly-worth-having Polish cigarettes.

As soon as life settled down, Platt became anxious for

permission to work as a chaplain. He was a conscientious Methodist minister, and he wanted to get on with the job he had come into the Army to do: the pastoral care and Christian teaching of the Free Church men around him who should be forming his congregation. Above all, he wanted to be able to hold services; for every Sunday that passed without his minister's routine of church-going, preaching and hymn-singing was a day in limbo for him. But permission from Berlin took a long time, and all he could do in those first weeks was to hold a bible class for half a dozen Free Church prisoners who wanted to work through one of the gospels.

Joseph Hobling, an Anglican chaplain who arrived at Spangenberg shortly after Platt, suffered the same frustration. In Platt's eyes he was rather prim; a celibate high churchman who tended to get prudish about sex and bad language. The relationship was not an easy one, but both of them felt they would be more properly employed if they could be transferred to a *Stalag*, a camp for other ranks, where life would be tougher than in an officers' camp like Spangenberg, but the need for their ministry would be greater. Together they put in a formal request for a transfer, and nagged the Germans steadily, but without apparent result.

Lectures had already become a feature of camp life. The most insidious enemy the prisoners had to fight was boredom, and the demand for mental stimulation of any kind was constant. Any prisoner who could lay claim to any expertise, however recondite, was invited to lecture on his chosen subject. The inside stories of peacetime professions — anything from city finance to brewing — were always popular; so were politics and political and military history. An invaluable member of the camp was Captain Nichols, a red-haired Scottish brain surgeon with a faultless memory for miscellaneous information. He drew the largest audiences of all with a series of lectures on palaeontology, ancient history and egyptology from the briefest notes prepared from memory. 'The correlation of his data', wrote Platt in his diary, 'was as plain as a pikestaff to him, but a veritable monsoon of apparently unrelated facts to us. His bibliography was equally bewildering and of amazing length. He has promised to repeat today's lecture tomorrow, and to forget his unwarranted assumption that "I need not go into that, you will remember it from schooldays".'

Gradually the living conditions improved. Hot showers were a regular relief and pleasure, and so were the issues of clean sheets and pillowcases. The Germans were as keen as the prisoners to wage war on what camp orders delicately called 'unhygienic inconveniences', and at the first complaint of an itch the delousing routine was in operation.

And at last the old potatoes, rubbery and rotten, came to an end, and new potatoes made a great improvement in the basic diet. Their only drawback was that, boiled in their skins and various in size, they were more difficult to divide into precisely equal portions — the uncomfortable duty of the table representative, and a job which Platt hated. However careful one was, every prisoner coming to the table looked first at his own plate and then at those of his neighbours. By some sort of optical illusion, the portion on a man's own plate always looked smaller than anyone else's.

But even the basic rations were getting better. On a few occasions there was American bully beef, looking very much like that from the huge supply dumps the Allied troops had left in France; and every evening there was a spoonful of sugar. And the Red Cross parcels were coming through more frequently with food and tobacco. By taking great care and re-rolling fag-ends, the Red Cross supplies of British and American cigarettes could be made to last. No longer were the real addicts driven during blank periods to experimenting with Virginia creeper leaves rolled in newspaper.

A reassuring contact with the outside world was the daily delivery of German newspapers. Though they contained rather less hard news than propaganda, it was a relief to know that even in the German press London was not yet 'kaput', as some of the German guards delighted to tell them. The fluent German-speakers among the prisoners

31

(from whom many of the others were taking regular lessons) translated what news there was, and most of the conversation for the rest of the day was speculation about what lay between the lines.

In the middle of September the restriction on letters to England was lifted, and the prisoners were allowed to write the agreed monthly quota of three letters and four postcards. They became skilled at cramming the maximum possible number of words into a limited space, and Platt began his regular Sunday-afternoon letter-writing to his wife, Maisie, by writing in rough first, and then seeing how far he could condense what he wanted to say into the space available. He was missing her badly, and all that home meant, but so far he had received no letters, and was not sure where in England she might be. She had accompanied him to Dover when he was stationed there before leaving for France, and he had left her there. But it was quite likely that she had gone to stay with her parents.

Some mail had come, but it was very erratic, and it was not until the end of September that the first letters came for some of those who had marched with Platt from Camiers. But there was nothing for Platt among them. Day after day he stood in the crowd while letters were distributed, and watched the rapture with which the lucky ones received their news from home. It was October 13th, a Sunday morning, when he first heard his own name called. He grabbed at the two letters held out to him, so excited and anxious that even as he had them in his hand he was frightened that it might be a mistake and they would not be addressed to him at all. But they were: his name was on the envelopes, the first news from home since he was captured almost five months ago. And then the disappointment flooded over him until it was almost too much to bear: neither was from Maisie.

It had never occurred to him that it was possible that his first letter might not be from her. It had been her letter he was depending on. Those from the rest of his family, like those in his hand from his two sisters, could come later. It had been Maisie he had been writing to every Sunday

32

afternoon, two hours set aside as a precious time of communion with home and normality; and it was the response
to those letters that he wanted more than anything else that
was possible within the castle walls. His sisters' letters were
a poor substitute, and tantalising in their reference to Maisie
having 'gone north'.

Two days later his frantic impatience was appeased.
Waiting in the front row of the crowd he got a letter she
had written on 25th August. So elated that he could scarcely
contain himself, he hurried to the semi-privacy of his bunk
to read it. She had moved to Southport with her parents,
but had obviously given him the details of the move in an
earlier letter which had not yet reached him. He read and
re-read the paragraphs, treasuring her mis-spellings and all
the domestic trivia she described. Then, still inwardly gloating, his pastor's conscience made him go and commiserate
with those who had still had no letter, but he found it
impossible to utter words of sympathy in his own joyous
state without feeling a hypocrite.

The next day, 14th October, he and Hobling were suddenly told that the requests for a transfer had gone through,
and they would be leaving for an other ranks' camp the
following day. They must have their heavy baggage packed
and ready for searching that afternoon, and they would
leave Spangenberg at 3.45 next morning.

Prisoners of war were always moved at short notice, and
at inhumanly early hours of the morning. They were called
at 2.45 a.m., and were given hot coffee in the guardhouse,
and a day's rations to take with them. Then, after a very
thorough searching, they were taken out through the castle
gates, across the drawbridge, and marched through the
frosty, star-lit night down to the railway station in the
town.

It was noon when they arrived at their new camp at Bad
Sulza and found that nobody expected them. At the *Kommandantur* they were passed from one person to another,
all equally helpless when handed a brace of enemy parsons
who could speak little German. It was some while before

an interpreter could be found to whom they could explain themselves, and who could then explain them to the *Kommandant*. And it was only then that they learned that Bad Sulza was a camp for French troops, and there was no accommodation for officers. The *Kommandant* was not at all sure what he could do with them. There were some British camps in the area, perhaps they could be moved to one, or at least visit them; meanwhile, would they mind sleeping and eating with the French troops?

Platt and Hobling said they would mind very much, unless they could be assured that the French were neither lousy nor careless about hygiene. No such assurance could be given, so they were finally housed in one of the punishment cells off the guardroom. It was a single cell with a three-tier wooden bunk, and their washing facilities were in the camp kitchen among the cabbages; but the beds were clean, and they had two blankets each which were still warm from delousing.

They got into conversation with some convalescent naval ratings in the kitchen, and next morning they were told it was forbidden for them to talk to any other prisoners. In a rage of frustration, and with the aid of a German grammar, they prepared and signed a protest to the *Kommandant* pointing out that they could not possibly do their work as chaplains if they were not allowed to talk to the men. The response came through the interpreter. Bad Sulza had no accommodation for the chaplains, they had not been expected, and it was suggested that they returned to Spangenberg for further instructions. They could have three days in which to decide what they would do. They had no real choice. Three days later they went back to Spangenberg.

They got back on 24th October to find there had been quite a lot of escape activity in the short while they had been away. There had already been escape attempts by three of the Canadian airmen: Flight-Lieutenant Hank Wardle had got out from the garden and had been brought back the same night in a battered condition, having tried to escape again as he was recaptured; and Flying-Officers

Milne and Middleton had walked out of the main gate dressed as painters and carrying a ladder, and were caught the next day. The German reaction had been to increase the barbed wire round the camp boundaries and, while Platt and Hobling were away, three more prisoners, Lieutenant Teddy Barton, Captain Harry Elliott, and Lieutenant Peter Storie-Pugh had cut through the wire. Barton and Elliott were retaken almost immediately, but Storie-Pugh put fourteen kilometres between himself and Spangenberg castle, and was caught trying to board a southbound train.

All this had made the Germans thoroughly uneasy. They began calling *Appells* in the middle of the night, making the prisoners stand by their beds while they were counted. They also became very nervous about anything that might be used as escape equipment — a twitchiness that was to have an immediate effect on Platt's future. On Saturday morning, 26th October, he was told by the British Senior Officer, Major Clout, that he was summoned before the *Kommandant*.

Thinking it might be news of another transfer for him and Hobling, he went along eagerly, and at this point we turn to Platt's diary for the continuation of the story.

SATURDAY 26 OCTOBER
I imagined the interview was about the possibility of Hobling and myself paying weekend visits to the British *Lagers*. I was not a little excited as I took the steps up the wooden stairway two at a time, and sprang smartly to attention, ready either to answer questions or to give my parole for weekends.

The *Kommandant* acknowledged my salute and began at once to read a statement in German from which I picked out certain ominous words. The *Dolmetscher* (interpreter) was present, so I asked — with some internal uneasiness — for a translation.

I think I managed not to betray astonishment or alarm as the *Dolmetscher* told me, 'You are on a charge for having brought into this camp from *Stalag* IXc a house-

35

breaking instrument: a jemmy. Instruments of that nature are not permitted, and would only be possessed for one purpose — escape. Have you anything to say why a sentence of five days' solitary confinement should not be passed on you?'

'Yes. I have something to say! In the first place I have never possessed — or even seen — a jemmy; and in the second place I brought nothing back from *Stalag* IXc that I did not take with me.'

The instrument concerned, a piece of fairly stout wire turned up at one end, was produced; and I was asked if I recognised it.

'Yes, I do. It is a piece of wire I used to prop up the lid of my battered suitcase.'

'Will you explain to the *Kommandant* how you came by it?'

'Certainly. If my memory is right, I picked it up in the dormitory on the day I came to the *Unterlager*, and have used it for the purpose I have just described. It is a piece of perfectly malleable wire which, so far as I know, is innocent of any nefarious purpose. Furthermore, it has not been to Bad Sulza, for the English-speaking *Gefreite* threw it out of my case when he examined our personal luggage in the guardroom on the day we went to Bad Sulza.'

'The *Kommandant* does not believe you when you say you have never seen a jemmy. It is a serious offence for which you will begin five days in solitary confinement from midday on Monday.'

I remarked with some warmth that 'as a Christian minister I am not accustomed to having my word questioned; but since my word means nothing, I have nothing more to say'.

Major Clout, who had been present throughout the interview, intervened on my behalf, saying that he had never seen a jemmy either, but imagined it to be an instrument of considerably greater strength than the piece of wire they had produced.

I was dismissed, and walked into the exercise ground an amazed man. As for the five days in the cooler, I could do them on my head. But I was sore about being accounted a liar.

After about half an hour the *Kommandant* drove out of the *Lager* gate, and I went in search of Major Clout. We talked for a time, and finally agreed that I should prepare a statement setting out my defence. He will invite the Senior Officers' Committee to give their concurrence, and forward it to the *Kommandant*, asking for a stay of execution of sentence. I set out my statement as follows:

27th October 1940

Defence of Captain Revd J. Ellison Platt, CF, against the charge of being in possession of an instrument described by the *Dolmetscher* (*Leutnant* Helmboldt) as a 'jemmy'.

A piece of wire lay on the shelf at the foot of my bed when I came to this camp from the *Schloss*. I picked it up and used it for propping open my attaché case, and at no time has it been used for any other purpose.

I had no idea that the bent end of the wire made it resemble an illegal instrument — a jemmy.

I have never seen a jemmy.

The wire in question is malleable, and could not be used for leverage on any door or lock as it would bend before becoming effective.

When packing for my departure at Bad Sulza, I laid the wire openly in my case without any attempt to conceal it from inspection, thereby showing I was unaware that it might be construed as an escape instrument. It was removed from my case before departing for Bad Sulza, and was not brought back from that camp by me, as stated by my accusers. I was present when the wire was removed from my case, and no suggestion was made then that it was an escape instrument.

The charge was sprung on me, and Article 47 of the Geneva Convention was not complied with.*

*Article 47 of the *International Convention Relative to the Treatment of Prisoners of War*, Geneva 1929, begins: 'A statement of the facts in cases of acts constituting a breach of discipline, and particularly an attempt to escape, shall be drawn up in writing without delay...'

I am a voluntary prisoner, having chosen to stay with 900 wounded, rather than effect my evacuation, and naturally I have no intention of escaping, since I hope for repatriation under the Geneva Convention.

The sentence of five days' solitary confinement was passed upon me and committed to paper by typewriting before any explanation was required of me of the facts which show I was entirely innocent of the use to which it is suggested the wire could be put.

(Signed) J. Ellison Platt, RAChD.

In the dormitory it is regarded as a huge joke, and I come in for endless ragging. Holland says that many a housebreaker has masqueraded as a parson, while Dickie thinks five *weeks* would be no more than justice.

At the concert tonight the compère solemnly announced to the awed house that a common housebreaker had been unmasked in their midst. In response to outraged cries of 'How very dreadful!' and 'Who might the wretch be?' I was hauled from my seat to the stage while Major Ponsonby, our arch-magician, discovered a kit of housebreaker's tools hidden in my hair. From my right nostril he produced an alarm clock — said to be missing from the German guardroom; and, after searching my pockets and producing from each one some article claimed by the audience, he displayed his masterpiece by denuding me of my trousers and finding (cardboard impressions of) master keys, saws, a brace of pistols, and a vicious-looking knife.

I think I have begun to regard the affair in the same spirit. It is not the first time I have been sport for everyone, but I don't remember having my leg pulled to this extent before.

TUESDAY 29 OCTOBER
Well, here I am in jug! I came in at noon yesterday, and have almost completed my first twenty-four hours. The worst aspect of this experience is not having free access to an *Abort* and wash-house. But on the credit side is the gift of quietness: a priceless enjoyment that is utterly impossible in a dormitory shared by eighteen others. There is

real opportunity to read without being interrupted to answer someone's questions, or interrupting oneself to advise someone else to shut up if they don't want to stop a boot.

The cell I am in is not a cell at all; but a small second-storey room about fifteen feet by nine, with a reasonable window that looks out over the courtyard and, in a slanting direction, across the pine-clad hills. I have a bed and blankets; a table and chair, paper, pencil, and four books. The rules of solitary confinement are much the same as anywhere else: no talking, except to oneself; no smoking; and bare rations. The exclusion of cigarettes is a discipline I had not looked for, and one I have complained about.

My chief regret is at having been crimed. I have always sought —— in a fairly varied life — to respect the proprieties of any set of circumstances in which I have found myself. The statement of defence which the Senior Officers' Committee sent forward has neither evoked a reply, nor affected the course of punishment — unless the agreeable fact that I am in a room rather than a cell is a conceded amelioration.

I have not yet been given exercise, and I don't know the provisions of the Hague Convention concerning exercise for convicted prisoners of war. I would have washed at breakfast-time this morning, but the guard hadn't a key to fit the lock on the door. If only I had my 'jemmy', and knew now to use it, I might not have to wait until midday!

At the moment of writing the patch of hillside I can see through the window is dappled by wintry sunshine. The deep crimsons, russets and golds of autumn are past. The bracken, under the sombre green of the firs, is a sodden, dull brown; and the fruit trees that I can see are unkempt and scraggy, looking more like piles of hedge trimmings waiting for winter's tidying fires.

Now the sun has gone and left a very bleak landscape.

FRIDAY 1 NOVEMBER
I had thought to write much during these five days of isolation, but here I am, an hour before *Lichts aus* on my

39

last night, and nothing done. I have the framework of a novel with me that might profitably have engaged the whole of my time: whether it would ever be worth anything to anyone but myself is quite beside the point.

With the exception of devotional periods I have spent the time with Wodehouse, Evelyn Waugh, Gino Watkins, and D. H. Lawrence. I made tea today a longer meal than usual through having received — via the orderly — a further packet of cigarettes and Kenneth Grahame's *The Wind in the Willows*. Since moving my cup and plate to the floor, I have been sitting ruminating, and wondering among other things how a long-term prisoner must feel on the eve of the completion of his sentence.

I am tired of having no one to talk to; tired of eating my food in eagle isolation; tired of hearing the flick of the guard's key in the lock; of getting in and out of bed without a word to anyone. Mind you, I am by no means at the end of my tether, nor even approaching the middle. I am not more tired of these things than I am of mustering for *Appell* each morning and evening, or of taking exercise with a guard's bayonet within perilous distance of my bottom.

MONDAY 4 NOVEMBER

This weekend has passed in an ecstasy that had little foundation other than my own good spirits. Indeed, camp life has struck one of its dull patches. The usual concert on Saturday night was not better than moderate. Yesterday there was no service: Maclean* doesn't know why; he was simply forbidden to conduct worship. In the afternoon I spent an hour and a half over Maisie's letter. How did I live, I wonder, during the weeks and months when writing was not possible? Browsing over my weekly letter is the hour I enjoy most in the whole week.

Got my second letter from Maisie this morning! It was written on 1 September. I quickly sought the comparative

*The only chaplain (probably because he was the only Regular Army chaplain) who had been given permission by the Germans to hold services.

seclusion of my bunk and lay tasting every word — snatching and imprisoning the fugitive atmosphere of home. Frank Bibbings interrupted my magic flight by calling, 'Padre, you lucky fellow, you've got a parcel!'

At once I passed out of one state of ecstasy into another. My exultation was far higher than the coming of a mere parcel warranted — but it isn't a mere parcel! It is a mute witness to love and care seeking to express themselves while hampered by distance and war. It is a substance come direct from the place with which I most want to establish substantial contact. Home is in danger of becoming ephemeral unless months of dreaming can be confirmed occasionally by something essentially tangible, something that smells of home and satisfies the senses as a dog's instinct is comforted and quieted by the scent of his master's clothes.

The parcel was packed by hands of which I know every line, and its contents will dismiss an aching need.

'When is the issue, Frank?'

'Sometime tomorrow, I expect. I don't know any more than you.'

I go to Nick's lecture on the American Civil Wars impatient of the morrow, of censors and censoring; but as full of joy as a man can be without bursting.

TUESDAY 5 NOVEMBER
Collected my parcel at 10 a.m. None of the contents were confiscated. It was not that I had slipped through anything prohibited, such as flannel bags, civilian shirts, or pullovers; but that such weight and space as is permitted had been used for permissible things.

An hour after receiving it I am a well-dressed man in khaki sweater, new slacks, shirt, and a pair of shoes. For five months I have worn the only footwear I possessed, a pair of heavy boots made for a much larger man, and superweighted with hobnails and steel tips on heel and toe. Wearing shoes, and snug-fitting clean linen, I feel like a fairy looks.

Handling the shirt, handkerchiefs, socks, tie, pipe and

41

pouch, brought the atmosphere of home very close. They are not all new. The pipe, pouch, and shoes, for instance, have other associations, and have brought something of the otherness with them. It is an otherness which has to do with companionable days and nights, with pleasurable motor trips, and the supreme comfort of one's own fireside.

THURSDAY 7 NOVEMBER
Red Cross parcels were delivered and distributed yesterday. It is generally believed here that all prisoners should receive two Red Cross parcels in three weeks. One in five days would not be too much, but we are getting less than one a month.

Most of the junior officers, and the lads in the *Stalags,* could eat one in three days. They are growing boys of nineteen and twenty for whom the Army thought twelve ounces of beef a day not too much.

The reply to my statement of defence came at noon today. I have had our German speakers vet my translation.

> Your protest of 27 October 1940 against punishment of five days' confinement is turned down for the following reasons:
> First, your explanations about a piece of wire made into a jemmy contradict each other. On the one hand you say that the wire in question can be bent and could never be used on any door or lock because it would bend before working. It must have been known to you therefore that the subject concerned a jemmy.
> Second, a contravention of Article 47 of the Geneva Convention does not come into the question.
> Third, you come under German military laws, and in the sense of these laws you were interrogated by *Leutnant* Helmboldt before the punishment was pronounced.
> (signed) Meissner
> Colonel and Commandant

Well, I have failed to establish my innocence, and am

42

branded a potential escaper. I should not mind the brand
so much if my calling permitted me to merit it. Even though
the Germans have indicated that they expect me to escape
and have put me under the same *Militärgesetze* as the
fighting officers, the Royal Army Chaplains' Department
would not relax its hold on the vows I have taken were I to
act as a fighting officer.

The men who do escape get a double advantage. Besides
the excitement and thrill of getting ready — perhaps over a
period of weeks — they have the magnificent escapade
itself. It may be short-lived, as indeed it is likely to be —
escape from Germany at present is almost impossible. But
the night or day when the break is made, and every second
that they are free — free in an enemy land, pursued by
armed troops, hunted with dogs, and perhaps shot at if
sighted — every second pulsates with as red-blooded adventure as can be found. For only a very few moments of the
white-hot life that escapers live while they are free, ten
days in the cooler is a very easy price. The dreary sameness
and inactivity of prison makes the entertainment of escape
a priceless luxury.

SATURDAY 30 NOVEMBER
During the past fortnight *Lager* life has not deviated a
fraction from its monotonous course. Reveille at 7 a.m.;
an uninteresting breakfast; four hours to be killed by some
means or other — usually lectures; an uninteresting lunch,
and a further five hours to be killed by some means or
other — usually lectures. '*Lichts aus*', and sleep if you can;
if you can't — then listen to others sleeping.

I have no work to do. I am sick to death of the type of
literature our library provides. For days it has rained so
hard that we cannot walk in the yard and are crowded
on each other's heels in the dormitories; and though
there is neither quarrelling or expressed irritation, we
are all the time only too conscious of each other's
presence.

It says much for self-discipline and bonhomie that in
such a crowd no serious quarrels have broken out. Oppor-

tunities for personal hostility are more frequent than in ordinary circumstances, nor would they be passed by in ordinary circumstances. But — and I am certain it is so — every one here has set himself — for the duration of imprisonment — to laugh off every disagreement that is big enough to be important.

SUNDAY 1 DECEMBER
After service this morning Major Clout brought the news to Hobling and me of our impending move tomorrow. He didn't know where we were going, but had been instructed to tell us to have all our heavy baggage ready for searching at 4 p.m. today. He thought we should have fuller instructions at evening *Appell*.

I went into a flap over my diary which has not been returned to me since the search when we came back from Bad Sulza. One of the *Kommandantur* personnel came up with letters at midday and I extracted a definite promise that it would be returned and placed with the examined luggage this afternoon.

Five of us are moving: the three escapers — Captain Elliot, Lieutenants Barton, and Storie-Pugh — and Hobling and myself. My first thought is that another *Stalag* is in the offing. Then I realise, with some momentary uneasiness, that Hobling is the only unconvicted person among us, and while he may be going to a job somewhere, I am almost surely going with the escapers to a *Sonderlager* (special camp, presumably for bad eggs).

My diary is with the baggage at 4 p.m. when we are called to witness the search.

At evening *Appell* our names are called over; and instructions to be ready to move off at 3.30 a.m. tomorrow are read out. Hobling and I have talked little beyond an easy exchange of greetings since we returned from *Stalag* IXc. Now we have to confer again. He thinks he is making for a different destination and will part company from us some where *en route* or — if he does happen to accompany us to the same camp — which he deems very unlikely — it will be to serve in the capacity of chaplain since he is crime-clean. His little piece of naïveté has amused me greatly.

A little bird whispered about an hour ago that we are going to a *Strafe* (punishment) camp somewhere in Saxony. But I keep quiet.

MONDAY 2 DECEMBER

One of the night sentries called us at 3 a.m. sharp. We washed and packed our more personal things under close observation, and were taken to the *Revier* where breakfast from the day's rations consisted of coffee, which the night orderly had kept warm on his stove, and bread with *Wurst*. Then our luggage was loaded on a hand-barrow in charge of four orderlies, and we marched under heavy guard to the station.

There are many travellers beside ourselves, some of whom greet their friends with a '*Heil* Hitler' and settle back into their seats to recapture lost sleep. Sub-Lieutenant Geoffrey Wardle, RN, whom we knew at the *Schloss*, joins us. He is a tall, auburn-haired, lanky fellow, about twenty-two, who always seems at a loss for a place in which to store his long legs and feet.

Two compartments are reserved for us and our five guards. It is a pleasant but cold journey, and though we are separated — three in each compartment — we can talk over the five-foot partition without hindrance. Until daybreak, when the blackout is removed, we exchange news and views about events in the *Unter-* and *Oberlagers*. Once the blinds are drawn up we stop talking and look out over the dazzling expanse of snow-bound fields.

But for the three changes, one of which entails an hour's wait on an extremely draughty platform, we are comfortable enough. Our main direction is towards Dresden, but the last change brings us onto a branch line which meanders and winds like a rock-bound stream.

Colditz, the station at which we finally arrive at half-past six in the evening, is under the pall of blackout, and is by no means exciting to city-hungry people. There is no conveyance for our luggage, but the guards assure us that the *Schloss* is not far distant.

45

We go out of the station in twos, humping our packs as best we can through what appears to be the main street of the small town. The guards are considerate and permit frequent halts for breathing. It is fairly steep, and we are not as tough as we might be. I'm as bad as a broken-winded horse. But we stagger on. Geoff has dropped his sailor's kitbag from his shoulder, and is dragging it behind him. Hobling is in sore distress with his load. We are now only travelling about twenty-five paces between each rest, and are sweating as though it were midsummer.

After several hundred yards we fork left and, crossing the bridge over the moat, begin the ascent to the *Schloss*. We are in the intense white light of great arc lamps which is reflected from the snow. The lamps serve the dual purpose of enabling us to see our way, and enabling the guards to keep an eye on dark recesses and shadowed turnings. But in this light the grim forbidding character of the place is painfully obtrusive. A fit place indeed for a *Straflager*.

These dull stone façades with their small serried windows are not the *Schloss* itself, it appears, for we are leaving them to climb a long gaunt carriageway, spanned at two points by stone bridges. The part we are approaching looks even more dull and impregnable, and finally becomes a *cul-de-sac*. A high wall is on the left, the guardhouse in front, and on our right a pile of high grey buildings in which a huge gate is set under a heavy archway. Yes, this is a *Straflager* all right.

While waiting for the huge gates to open and engulf us I think of Dunkirk, and of British ships that positively beckoned me to England and Maisie. What good did I do for the nine hundred with whom I stayed?

'Abandon hope all ye who enter here.' I should need something a thousand times stronger than the wretched crinkly bit of wire that brought me here to get out of this place.

'Well, what about this, Padre?' asks Storie-Pugh.

I muster a smile and say, 'Oh, I shall wake up fresher here than from some of the cemeteries I know.'

While we are still waiting for this Gate of Gargantua to open, a German officer approaches.

'Good evening, my English friends.'

We spring to attention, but he waves our stiff address aside.

'You must be tired after so long a day. You will sleep well tonight. By the way, which is the Methodist chaplain? Has he come with you?'

I step forward, coming smartly to attention, and admit that I am a Methodist. I wonder what that proud fact may connote.

Any doubts I have are dispersed at once as, with an engaging smile, he continues, 'A very personal friend of mine is a Methodist minister. He stayed in my home when he studied in Germany...' Did I happen to know Mr Connell?

Did I happen to know him! Dick and I were at college together, and he was the redoubtable president of the football team of which I was the trainer. I have little difficulty in describing him to *Leutnant* Eggers' satisfaction — and, indeed, to my own. Dick is a comfortable shape to emerge out of a conversation held outside the towering gates of a *Sonderlager*.

After these friendly salutations Eggers disappears through the needle's eye set in the gate and leaves us, six very cheerful men. In a moment he reappears, and we also pass through into pitch blackness. The torches of the guards throw thin, fitful shafts of light, which we follow. I am struck dumb by the politeness of everyone.

We are crossing a courtyard.

'Mind the steps, please. There are three.' It is Eggers' voice, and he continues, 'I am sorry there is no better accommodation for you tonight, but this is only for tonight. Tomorrow you will join your English comrades. I am sorry, too, that after your journey you should have so many steps to climb, but leave your luggage here, and I will have it brought up to you. This way please.'

And up it is. A spiral stone stairway that curls on and on until we wonder if the heights of Mount Olympus are not

47

more easily scaled. But once at the top *Leutnant* Eggers assures us again that this is only for tonight and, after making sure we have three blankets each, he advises us to get to bed early since the room is not heated — as soon, indeed, as we have had the bread, hot soup, and coffee he will now send up.

'Good night, my English friends, and sleep well.' We return his salutation with equal feeling, and when the sound of his descending tread is lost we go into a huddle and agree we were never more politely used in our own country.

The room itself, half full of wooden two-decker bunks and palliasses, but otherwise distressingly cold and bare, is not sufficient to depress our high spirits. The soup is piping hot, and the coffee too. There is butter with the bread, and we have met a perfect gentleman who treated us as gentlemen.

Collars and boots only are removed before we wrap ourselves in blankets and shake down for the night. My prayers are short, but full of earnest praise. I thank God for the Methodist Church and for Dick Connell, and the inspiration — or accident, I don't mind which — that sent Dick to the home of Dr Eggers. If the world is a small place, there is no reason why my gratitude should be small.

## TUESDAY 3 DECEMBER

Hot coffee is served by a French orderly at 7.30 a.m. He thinks we shall be searched at about 8.30. He is right. Our packs and packages are carried off to the search room to await our return from the office in which our camp records are examined. I see my photograph and fingerprints which were taken at Spangenberg, and my declaration concerning myself. All are found to be correct, and we are supplied with a printed slip which lists all the objects that a POW may not have in his own keeping.

As well as the usual list of firearms, compasses, maps, dangerous knives, etc, I am amazed to find fountain pens and matches prohibited, both of which we could buy in the canteen at Spangenberg. If our stuff was gone through with a fine-tooth comb in other camps, it is gone through with two or three fine-tooth combs here at *Oflag* IVc. A bobbin of cotton is not passed as a bobbin of cotton until the examiner has satisfied himself that it is a bobbin of cotton with no false end, and nothing is hidden under the winding of cotton. Every small article is scrutinised; every bit of paper bearing marks or writing is separated from our other possessions and sent to be *geprüft*.

About none of these things do I feel disgruntled, but it is a blow that I should not be allowed to keep the extra pair of slacks that Maisie put in my personal parcel. I challenge the right of the examiner to withhold my clothes, but he assures me that his instructions are definite. No prisoner is allowed more than one suit, one pair of boots, one overcoat; but he may hand into the store room at any time the boots, coat or trousers he is using, and get the others in exchange. The arrangement presents a bit of difficulty over trousers, particularly in the winter, but there the rule is.

The search of our belongings for nefarious implements is followed by a search of our persons for 'unhygienic inconveniences', and this again lacks nothing in thoroughness. We undress in a small room, and all our clothes — even to our bootlaces — are taken to be processed while we gurgle for an hour under the soothing embrace of a hot shower. There are four rows of showers and five showers in each row. Water is really hot and in abundant supply. It is a pleasure indeed: such pleasure, we agree, as we have not enjoyed since capture.

Three Polish escapees are being deloused with us, one of whom is Vatzek Gassowski, an air pilot who is an international runner. He and his three companions have an eyewitness story of the fighting in Poland and the German occupation. We talk in French.

It is 12.30 by the time our clothes are returned to us and we are taken to British quarters. Four of the ten British officers we meet are not strangers. Colonel German is the first to greet us. He, and a Jewish orderly, arrived at *Oflag* IVc from Spangenberg a month ago. They were preceded by the three RAF officers: Flying-Officers Wardle, Milne, and Middleton, who escaped from Spangenberg *Schloss* last August. The other six are escapees from VIIIc: five captains and one second-lieutenant in a kilt. It is the first kilt I have seen in Germany.

The general atmosphere is decidedly good: a first impression that is confirmed when one after another of our new companions describes different aspects of camp life. I hate to commit myself too soon — a characteristic the Methodist itinerant system gives sooner or later to all its ministers — but if my first impression and the month-old impressions of the other fellows are true, then this is the best camp I have struck. The best not by reason of its situation, for indeed the castle is grim, almost menacing; which is perhaps the very reason why the administration is content to leave our safety to the impregnable nature of the castle instead of the usual long list of petty rules which only add to a POW's burden of discomfort.

Judging from my personal experience of seven different camps, it is evident that in matters of local rule — permissions and prohibitions — considerable liberty is enjoyed by the *Kommandant*. The refusal, for instance, to allow matches at IVc, but to allow petrol lighters — fuel for which is supplied through the canteen — is typical of several such minor differences. In broad outline, however, the administration is much the same, but the differences concern such things as might be useful to a prisoner intending to escape. Only one set of clothing allowed; all tinned food received in parcels must be opened and the contents emptied into a bowl, and the empty tins retained by the parcels officer, so that is is impossible to accrue any stores of food.

I don't know the precise date of this *Schloss*, but I judge the old part to be eleventh or twelfth century. The *Hof* (courtyard) is set at the four points of the compass, and north to south measures fifty paces, and from east to west is half that distance. At all four corners there are spiral staircases built in red sandstone, and leading to the five storeys of the main building. We are at the south end, with the Polish orderlies and the *Revier* (sick bay) on our left. At the north on the left is the entrance to the French and

Belgian quarters, and on the right the three levels occupied by the Poles.

Also at the north an old Gothic church is built into the main building, and the interior is in the charming family fashion of the middle ages. A high stone altar commands the family boxes and the two servants' galleries. These are surmounted by an organ loft and a comparatively good pipe organ, obviously a recent installation. The pews are all high, straight-backed, and too close to each other to permit worshippers to kneel. The reredos, usually so magnificent in continental family churches, is an almost life-size picture of our Lord.

The English quarters, if viewed with sufficient imagination, could be described as a self-contained flat on the first floor, reached by one of the spiral staircases, some of the steps of which are worn hollow by countless feet. The first room is equipped for use as a kitchen, with a cooking stove, table, sink, cupboard, and platters. On the right a low wood and glass partition shuts off six taps and four WCs. At the far end of the kitchen a door opens into a dormitory which is the larger of the two rooms at our disposal. It has a combustion stove, five lockers, and the customary two-tier bunks. The next room, exactly half the size of the dormitory, with a window at each end, has been chosen as the dining, reading, writing, class and games room. A small room adjoining it is occupied by Colonel German and three captains, but is always referred to as the Colonel's room.

Hobling and I, by reason of our cloth and all it might connote in two unknown chaplains, have been awarded — to state it kindly — a small rectangular room built over the old entrance porch to the main building. It is ten feet by seven, and has windows looking on to the *Hof* on three sides. It will be pleasant enough when summer comes — if its coming finds us still here — but at present the glass is heavily frosted. The old window fittings let the hoar get through and, with the interior condensation, form into streaming icicles and clots of ice on sills and walls. Hobling, who has never lived in an old country house in rural England, is aghast at the prospect, and feels like asking for accommodation in the dormitory.

### FRIDAY 6 DECEMBER

From the *Kommandant* down, there are at least twice the number of German officers and three times the number of other ranks here that there were at Spangenberg. There are three *Lageroffizieren* who are directly concerned with us, who take *Appells* and have general control of our affairs: *Leutnant* (Dr) Eggers, who in happier days played host to Dick Connell; *Hauptmann* Priem; and the *Rittmeister*, a Cavalry officer of captain's rank.

The *Rittmeister* is senior of the three. He speaks English with fair fluency and a decided accent. At a few minutes to noon today he saw me tramping round the *Hof* for exercise and took the opportunity to tell me of the Camp Orders for church worship.

'No one may hold a speech unless permission has been granted. You must write out your speech and give it to me tomorrow morning. You will be holding a speech, yes?'

'No,' I said. 'I shall not preach on Sunday. I have arranged a communion service at which there won't be a sermon.'

'I see. Then at all other weeks you will give me your speech on Friday morning. You understand?'

'I understand.'

This morning Hobling and I got down to copying out a few sets of hymns that are generally known. There are only two English hymnbooks in this camp, his *Ancient and Modern* and my *Methodist Hymn Book*.

The total British strength here is sixteen officers, seven other ranks, and one civilian — Howard Gee. Two officers, Pat Reid and Teddy Barton, two orderlies, and Gee are Roman Catholics. Four officers are non-worshippers, one of whom is anti-church. So the thirteen that remain — if they do remain — when divided into nonconformist and C of E, will form our respective congregations; and the three non-church and the one anti-church will be our wide field of missionary endeavour.

52

If, as is extremely probable, fifty per cent of the basic congregation are indifferent, and others who are careless forget the time of service, our rock bottom number to be divided may not be more than six. If, on division, four of the six are Hobling's and two are mine, we need not expect the choral aspects of worship to touch top notch. In priestly and prophetic conclave tonight we agreed about the advisability of uniting our forces.

Among the orderlies I have discovered three Presbyterians — Scots laddies from the Clyde — and two officers are nonconformist, one of whom, Don Middleton, is the son of an Ontario Methodist manse. The sturdiest denominationalist — which I certainly am not — would be hesitant to discourage united services with such a field of restricted activity.

## SUNDAY 8 DECEMBER

The Communion service was at 10.30 a.m. Don Middleton presided at the organ. Seven were present. We had neither wafers nor wine, but used German rye bread and water. Later in the day I discovered that Postrach, the Polish chaplain, had some unconsecrated wafers and wine he would have given for our use.

I wonder if it was brown, black or white bread that Jesus broke with his disciples at the Last Supper. Perhaps in our simple poverty we were nearer in kind to the simple elements that he used than we knew. In spirit, at least, we were graciously near.

The church was bitterly cold, but we had not expected it to be heated; and those who were fortunate enough to possess them wore greatcoats, scarves, and gloves. The service lasted twenty-five minutes, by which time we all sought to control chattering teeth and to ignore stone-cold feet. But no one complained. And my Presbyterian laddies were filled with rich joy. It was the first act of corporate worship they had taken part in since capture.

A pale wintry sunshine smiled thinly on the snow for half an hour this afternoon. We trooped into the *Hof* and mingled with the tramping, surging throng of Poles, French, and Belgians. Polish is the only one of the five languages here I am completely ignorant of.

Wrote a letter to Maisie telling her of the change to *Oflag* IVc, and of such first impressions as are likely to pass the censor.

### WEDNESDAY 11 DECEMBER

Had a gala day today! Five letters from Maisie! They were dated August and September. I read them in order of writing and reached the third, still with no little jubilation, only to find it contained news of my father's sudden death. That he died instantly in no way mitigates the shock, but there was no tedious illness. 'Dust thou art, to dust returnest.'

### THURSDAY 12 DECEMBER

The Dean of Peterhouse staggered in to our winter resort through a driving snow storm today. He was taken prisoner on his third day in France, never once having conducted worship with the Expeditionary Force. Richard Heard is of a distinguished Irish family, and when his tunic and slacks were made to measure he would be a pretty striking figure. His service dress now looks as though it had been made for a man exactly his height but just twice his figure.

From *Oflag* VIIc at Laufen he asked to be transferred for work as a chaplain to a men's camp. He was being sent to a group of *Stalags* in Silesia, but for some reason has made a forced landing here. He had news of John Bown and some of the 10th CCS MOs who are at VIIc. It was the first I had heard of them since waving goodbye at Camiers. Bown, it appears, has been in the *Revier* under medical care since arriving in early July. Forty chaplains have collected at VIIc, three of them Methodists.

Today was our weekly bath day. The hours are 1.30 to 3.30 p.m. I haven't yet recovered from the shock of delight at having so commodious a bath house, and such an excellent supply of hot water. We stood under the streaming roses and sang songs — some of them of typical army sentiment which makes it difficult for chaplains to share them. The dressing room, through which hot pipes pass, was pleasantly warm, and in various stages of undress we sat and talked.

Dick Howe, Captain in the Royal Tank Regiment, is a great personality. He regaled us with stories of his boyhood among the Inca Indians a few thousand miles up the Amazon. Being the only British boy for hundreds of miles through that vast forest and swamp country, the friends of his childhood were all Incas. He learned to walk Inca fashion, and this afternoon had us roaring our applause at his demonstration of Incas picking out forest trails. His full six feet of wiry muscle was no hindrance to this contortionist feat.

Since he was made prisoner he has been awarded the Military Cross for the brilliant capture of nine enemy tanks. He is modest, even shy about talking about himself. But with all the lack of self-consciousness of a schoolboy (though he is nearly thirty) he loves to illustrate verbal description with characteristic sounds, as of an animal, a gurgling stream, the whizz, whistle and crash of a bomb, or a Stuka's roar and the rat-tat-tat of machine-gun fire. Few people I know do it so naturally or so well.

FRIDAY 13 DECEMBER
Hobling's worst fears materialised last night. We were almost frozen in bed. The temperature must have been 20° below zero.

Our German class is temporarily suspended while Second-Lieutenant Peter Allan recovers from a mild form of 'flu. Peter is twenty-two, and wears the only kilt I have seen in Germany. He is a brilliant linguist, and in peace time conducts parties of tourists to Europe from America for his father's travel agency.

Copied out more popular hymns today. When seven of us, three of whom will be padres, swell our voices on Sunday in 'Lord, we are few, but thou art near', it will certainly tell the Lord something he ought to be informed of.

Last week I wrote to the Berlin branch of the YMCA inviting them to provide us with a parcel of American or

English hymnbooks. That, so far as I can see, is our only hope; or else the weary duty of copying will have to continue. One thing is certain: the singing of hymns is so refreshing, and has proved so great a blessing to those who gathered for worship last Sunday, that a hymnless service is unthinkable. Hobling has the ambitious idea of writing out and pointing some psalms and the *Te Deum*. I shall not discourage the idea in the least — providing he doesn't expect me to do them.

One of the highlights of this camp is the installation of a radio speaker in our general purposes room. The main set is in the guardhouse and the programmes are selected there, but we have a switch in our room to switch it off if we want to. There is a lot of music, and we get the German news broadcasts, and Lord Haw-Haw in the nightly propaganda broadcast in English. This afternoon a first-class Italian soprano reminded me how pleasant a woman's voice can be. Until *Signora* brought the want out of my subconscious into broad daylight, I had not known how great the want was. How many more unconscious wants have I got that will only be revealed when the need is partially satisfied? A strange life this; and it conditions strange states of mind.

Last night the radio programme was interrupted to allow a British broadcast, evidently for our special benefit. It was a question and answer programme from a coastal battery. It is not surprising that we were all dreadfully homesick. After the first realisation — for it came on without any announcement — we sat on chairs and benches with eyes closed, transported back to what different surroundings! Few of us — except perhaps the Canadians — could have answered a test paper on the substance of the broadcast; but when it was over it was as much as the most matter-of-fact among us could do to return without a sigh to the life of a *Kriegsgefangene* after that short leave in England.

SATURDAY 14 DECEMBER

A monotonous kind of day. One of the Spangenberg variety

concerts would prove an acceptable diversion tonight, but our numbers are far too small for any such effort. Only a moderate-sized cast would engage the lot of us and leave players without an audience.

Chess and bridge are our chief pastimes; and apart from reading and the radio there is simply nothing else to do except listen to plans for escape.

## SUNDAY 15 DECEMBER

The *Rittmeister* visited our quarters betimes this morning and found us all in bed. He was very annoyed; demanded that we got up at once, and hinted that a punishment to fit the crime would be decided upon. The most obvious punishment is the suspension of the beer privilege. Two bottles per prisoner per week are available in the canteen at a cost of 50 *Pfennigs* a bottle. Half a dozen of our number are tee-total, so the hardship — if such it may be termed — will fall on those who have regarded their beer as the week's sole luxury.

Burning incense may raise the spiritual and mystic temperature of a church, but it doesn't touch a thermometer. We followed the Poles and French into the church this morning. The place was redolent of the burning censer. I don't recall having conducted worship before with the presence of a scarlet draped crucifix on the communion table, images at two kneeling benches, and an atmosphere charged with spice. There were eight present, three of whom cannot sing in tune. It is something of a misfortune that out of a grand total of eight there should be three croakers.

Three of the RCs, two officers and an orderly, have excellent singing voices. But had *they* been croakers it could not have mattered to their Mother Church with her hundred Poles and fifty-odd French. However, it is not for me to suggest to the Almighty that his Protestant praise would be more pleasing to us for the addition of a few Protestant nightingales.

At the close of morning worship Heard, Hobling and I discussed between chattering teeth the advisability of an evening service. The Anglican Church was not prepared to say in the present circumstances it was not desirable. The Methodist Church refused to be accommodating and furnish the desired judgement. Hence it was strategically left that anyone of us may revert to the matter if at any time he should feel the urge to do so. Very prettily dismissed, and none of us with a troubled conscience.

TUESDAY 17 DECEMBER
A thorough-going bronchial cough has given me a rough time for the last few days. The French MO who, under the German *Arzt*, is responsible for our health, has supplied bronchial tablets which, when dissolved in hot water, are quite an agreeable dose. He wants, much against my own wish, to put me in the *Revier* for a period. The patients in the *Revier* are excused *Appell*, and the ward is kept at an even temperature. No doubt it is the wisest thing to do, but I have no hankering to be jabbered at in Polish, French and German all day long and, quite apart from the racket and jangle of languages, a prison hospital is a prison within a prison. So I shall try another day or two before agreeing to be put to bed.

Mid-life is not the best period in which to learn languages, but it is something to do. Most of the officers are working at German — little or much — and occasionally some burrowing student emits a wisecrack. This afternoon a translation back from the German produced, 'You to the marines can it tell'. Yesterday Geoff Wardle translated rat-trap into *Grossemausgefangenapparat.**

WEDNESDAY 18 DECEMBER
Spent the day swotting German, coughing, and reading Wells.

THURSDAY 19 DECEMBER
Spent the night coughing, and the day reading Wells, coughing, and swotting German.

*Literally translated 'large mouse prison appartus'.

FRIDAY 20 DECEMBER

Bronchial tubes clearer; cough *petit mieux*. After listening with his naked ear pressed close to my body, back and front, Dr Leguet straightened himself and said, *'La prescription est une vacance en Egypte'*. No patient ever concurred more entirely.

Dick is sitting on the table this afternoon in tailor fashion, twisting odd bits of newspaper and coloured paper into grotesque shapes. The camp authorities have promised us a Christmas tree, and he has started on the decorations. Could there be anything quite so incongruous as Dick Howe, Tanks Captain, sitting cross-legged making paper posies? The paper twists successfully two or three times, and then tears at a crucial turn. He remarks with some heat on the dissolute character of the wood pulp which begat this immoral paper as he adds one spoiled bit after another to a largish pile. We don't hesitate to offer him suitable encouragement and advice, which in a moment will bring a stool or a bottle hurtling towards us.

Pat Reid throws with a better eye than most of us. One can never be sure whether he is aiming high or low or solar-plexus-wards; though because he always gets his quarry his choice of projectile is less savage. A Captain in the RASC, he is an Indian-born Irishman, as full of mischief, good humour, and laughter as only 'the broth of a boy' can be. A brogue would put the final touch to his characteristic charm, but in speech he is as English as the rest of us.

He studied engineering at King's College, and pre-war followed that avocation with, I should say, considerable drive and tireless patience. In this society he is extremely popular, and possesses that dangerous gift of being lucky. In his case, as with scores of other 'lucky' people, the smile of fortune may mean his undoing. He trusts his luck in games and in most other things further than many men would trust reason.

The social side of his character is a fountain of pure bubbling delight. He has a penchant for parties. The possession of a mere couple of bottles of beer is sufficient for

59

him to throw a party to half a dozen Polish or French or Belgian officers. Where will he get the other five bottles? He trusts his luck.

With Dick Howe and four other officers (Rupert Barry, Peter Allan, Kenneth Lockwood and Harry Elliott) he escaped from *Oflag* VIIc at Laufen in September, and made his début in non-*Lager* Germany dressed as a woman, and via a tunnel with an outlet into an old lady's garden. They managed to evade capture for a week.*

## SATURDAY 21 DECEMBER

Admiral Unrug and General Pishkor visited us in our quarters this morning to invite us to the Polish Christmas Eve celebrations. If they found pleasure in our almost too eager acceptance, then their satisfaction was great indeed. We have no parcels or food, other than daily rations, to make a Christmas for ourselves, so this extremely generous gesture is a gift from old Santa Claus himself.

The Admiral explained — in good English — how, on the day before the collapse of Poland, he dispatched his fleet to Britain, but himself remained with the land forces in their last desperate resistance. Few men have been taken prisoner in that gallant fashion, but again the age-old question crops up: could he not have served his cause better by going with his fleet to continue the battle from another base? He is a fine upright gentleman, sixty or more, who was born in Germany and fought for them in the last war. Will war ever be a sensible thing?

General Pishkor has no English, and as yet none of us has any Polish; but he handed his cigarette case round, and we communed in the manner of men who have no medium save that of mutual pleasure in a cigarette.

At noon our Christmas tree was brought into the day room to the grunted accompaniment by the orderlies of 'Good King Wenceslas'. Dick has 'withdrawn according to plan' from the paper-posy position, and is now cutting out of a piece of cardboard a flat model of a medium cruiser tank.

*See *The Colditz Story* by P. R. Reid, published by Hodder & Stoughton 1952.

The walls of our dayroom are covered with paper and cardboard representations of military escutcheons, regimental arms, and badges; and all the Allied flags are gathered on the north wall round the Union Jack, surmounted by the prayer, 'God save the King'.

SUNDAY 22 DECEMBER 1940
We sang of shepherds and flocks and the manger this morning, and were blue with cold while doing so. We meditated on the New Testament story of the birth of our Lord, and thought less of Bethlehem than of home.

After the service I went to speak to some of the forty French orderlies. They too were thinking of home. Human feeling is very near the surface at Christmastime, and in the absence of a French priest I ministered to their spiritual poverty, and am now left wondering if they knew of my Protestantism. If they did know, it has made little difference. They were insistent that I visit them on Christmas Eve.

CHRISTMAS EVE
Really Christmas morning! An extension of lights is allowed tonight until half-past midnight — it is now ten minutes past.

Our negotiations to hire a piano came to a successful issue last night. Our hireling is an iron frame *Bretschneider*. Don Middleton is our only pianist, and his skill is chiefly in jazz. The piano arrived within half an hour of lights out, so he spent the remaining time in swinging a few carols mixed with once-popular dance tunes.

The day's menu, written in chalk on a blackboard which stands at the kitchen entrance, showed a Christmas addition to rations: sweetened *Nudeln* in generous supply which we added to the evening meal. I think that *Wehrmachtsuppe* was also issued, but our evening rations were drawn by the Poles and served with the many good things their Christmas parcels from home had contained.

My Christmas present was a packet from Mrs Marshall in Lisbon. I don't know the lady, but I am indeed grateful for her goodness. My packet contained four two-ounce bars of milk chocolate, forty Diana cigarettes and a hand-kerchief. Within ten minutes of receiving it seventeen officers and six orderlies were smoking to Mrs Marshall's health, and wishing her such a gay and merry Christmas as she had not enjoyed before.

The 'reception' in the Poles' quarters was at 5.15 p.m. The medieval severity of the room had been softened by festive artistry. A Christmas tree stood in the deep window recess, and the gloom was illumined by the soft light of five wax candles. The national emblems of all the Allied nations, crayoned or pencilled on paper, studded the massive walls on three sides of the room, while a second window recess accommodated a superb cardboard model of St Peter's, Rome, standing ten feet high. A small glow from its altar threw a faint gleam throughout the model, just sufficient to catch the colour of the stained glass windows — an exquisite effect achieved with crayon and coloured paper wrappings from sweets.

A small alcove provided the setting for a Nativity scene, done like St Peter's in cardboard, but representing a grotto. Outside the shepherds waited while the Magi presented their gifts. French, Polish, Belgian and British officers removed their hats involuntarily, and stood bowed for a moment before a scene of such tranquil beauty.

Short speeches of welcome were spoken in Polish by General Pishkor and Admiral Unrug. The French and British colonels replied, each in his own language; the guests replying to the welcome they did not understand in two languages that were double-dutch to the hosts. But there could be no misunderstanding the essential sentiments.

The next incident is memorable for its unique and splendid simplicity. The Polish priest, Fr Postrach, stood by the grotto and offered a Latin prayer. He then took a plate full of wafers — about three times the size of altar wafers — from a small table in front of the grotto, and handed it to the General, with a second plate to the Admiral. Together they distributed them to all and sundry. Then came the ceremony of pledging fidelity and friendship. The Admiral tapped my right shoulder and bade me take a piece from his wafer; and he pinched off the tiniest bit from mine. Then, with right hands clasped, we ate together. The pledge of fidelity and friendship was made, and sealed with the exchange of a kiss on each cheek.

It was no new ceremony to the Poles. Its significance was evident in their profound sincerity. If it was as new to the French as to us, they proved the more apt pupils. We of the British community were a little uneasy over the kissing, and in exchanging pledges with our own company we were content to eat and clasp hands.

When every officer had pledged every other, irrespective of nationality, a score of Polish voices broke into the British national anthem. Every person in the room sprang to attention. The *Marseillaise* followed, and then the Polish national anthem. Only a conquered people could sing of home as they did!

Dinner consisted of rations and the contents of their Christmas parcels. It was an excellent satisfying meal, finished off with cakes and wine. I sat next to the Chief-of-Staff of the Polish Navy, with Colonel Schubert on the other side. Lord! But the language problem is colossal! Scraps of German, French and English were all brought to the elucidation of one simple sentence.

An impromptu concert concluded a perfectly marvellous evening. The Poles are a gallant, friendly and generous people. I shall learn a bit of Polish in the next few weeks. It is stupid not to be able to talk with such a fine crowd.

Two German guards came into the dormitory a moment ago on their midnight rounds. They offered us Christmas greetings with true sincerity, and wished they and we were spending the happy festival at home.

CHRISTMAS DAY
The day began with an acute attack of nostalgia. It is a worse complaint than bellyache, lumbago, or cramp. One can grouse about those when the pain is sharp and thus get at least mental relief. But nostalgia battens on grousing.

The other fellows in the dormitory were dressing in dead silence. Their outlook was no brighter than my own. We were browned off, and a pretty dark brown, too! I knew I ought to start a carol. I tried, with the result that there were sounds in my throat reminiscent of a cat's purring. I argued with myself that I needn't try again, and anyway singing before breakfast was *verboten*. In a minute I tried again. No one threw boots at me, or told me to shut up, so — thus encouraged — I broke into another verse: 'Yea, Lord, we greet thee, born this happy morning.' It says much for the goodwill this day inspires, for not a boot or pillowsack came my way; instead a dozen voices were upraised, the lumps disappeared from our throats, and the standard for the day was set.

I am at a loss to understand how the Church of England makes the celebration of holy communion foot the bill for almost any and every religious festival. A week ago, when we discussed the Christmas services, both Heard and Hobling were agreed that Holy Communion was the only suitable celebration. I contended, if not for something else, at least for something more. They were adamant, and so was I. So our union went by default today.

High Mass was sung at midnight, and mass was said this morning at 8 a.m. Holy Communion was celebrated at 9.15, and a usual type of nonconformist service with Christmas hymns and sermon at 9.45. I am rather glad we had this showdown today, and they, I fear, are sorry. Attendances showed with perfect plainness which kind of service interpreted the layman's mind. They will perhaps aver that the layman is not the best judge of what is good for his soul; but I have found in practice it is the layman who decides whether he will come to church or stay outside. And I think he not infrequently stays outside because he disagrees with what the priest thinks is good for his soul.

As a concession to Christmas, *Appell* was put back to 10.30 a.m. After the parade was dismissed, the Poles and British fought a desperate snowball battle. There was some excellent throwing, and for over half an hour the *Hof* echoed to shouts and laughter. It was simple unselfcon-

scious enjoyment which had the added virtue of making us
tingle and glow with warmth.

At lunch Dick Howe, who is kitchen officer, had a surprise for us. He had saved several tins of meat roll from
the last Red Cross parcels, and had made a stew of them.
The day's potato ration was generous, and we were eating
with appetite and relish when he cried, 'Hold your horses,
boys. There's Christmas pudding to follow!'

Though it needed some little disguise, it did not look
unlike Christmas pudding. Actually it was bread pudding,
for which he had reduced our seven slices a day by two.
Two packets of dates and a handful of prunes — the gift
of a Belgian whom Dick knew — completed the illusion.
Honest-to-goodness Christmas pudding was never eaten
with greater relish.

The ration of *Wurst* was doubled at the evening meal,
and jam was also issued. In the early evening we gathered
round the piano and sang songs of home as only exiled
men can sing them. This has been no mean or unhappy
day, but it has left much still to be desired: the whispering
deep down of wife, sweetheart, children, home. Truth to
tell, the whispering calls refused to stay deep down, for
every now and again someone would drift out of the day
room into the dormitory to spend a few minutes alone.
Everyone knew the significance of these brief excursions,
notwithstanding the muttered falsehoods about a book,
knife, or a handkerchief. 'Letter', would have been nearer
the truth.

And so to bed where, for an hour or two before sleep
comes, social obligation ceases, and one may enter the
privacy and seclusion of one's own thoughts of family
circles, of party-chatter at the supper table — and wish,
and wish, and wish!

BOXING DAY

Red Cross parcels arrived this morning: fifteen of them!
We are twenty-four officers and men, so the division worked
out at rather more than half a parcel each. A few representatives of the other nationalities were invited to share

our riches, and together we accounted for pretty much everything that was edible.

As a mark of appreciation of our excellent kitchen officer's endeavours, we hoisted him — struggling and protesting — shoulder high and sang 'For he's a jolly good fellow', and 'Why was he born so beautiful?' We were in the frame of mind to enjoy a party, so he was carried down into the *Hof* and rolled in the snow. It was at Pat's suggestion that Dick was so maltreated, so we caught Patrick after a smart chase round the *Hof*, and well and truly rolled — indeed buried — him in soft snow. In the general mêlée that followed no one escaped a snowy immersion. Honour was satisfied, and we all glowed and tingled with what is surely nature's most pleasant warmth.

Lord Haw-Haw was at the top of his form tonight.

### SUNDAY 29 DECEMBER

My *Oflag* IVc *Lagernummer* — 240 — appeared on the parcels list again today. It was a second parcel from Mrs Marshall containing two tins of sardines, a pair of socks, and a handkerchief. The socks were two sizes too small for me, and exactly what Peter Storie-Pugh needed. The sardines formed a tasty welcome addition to our evening meal.

The division of them gave us two sardines each. Teddy, soliloquising aloud, wondered if our wives would find us easy or difficult to cater for when the war is over. He said the question that had flitted through his mind concerned the two sardines. Would he, when back to post-war normal, be content with small quantities or, instead of two, would he think twenty-two sardines 'only a taste'? We assured him that his unhappy wife would spend her remaining and declining years in an unsuccessful effort to eliminate his *Kriegsgefangene* complex.

### TUESDAY 31 DECEMBER

The Poles have produced a marionette show for tonight and have invited us to attend the first performance. It is scarcely my taste for New Year's Eve, and seldom — if ever — have I spent the fugitive moments in a like manner. But 1940 has no special claim on my goodwill so far as I know. Do men make years or do years make men? I have never before felt myself to be so completely at the mercy of events. But please let me delude myself into believing that I had little or nothing to do with the begetting of 1940. Was it Bernard Shaw, in his capacity as scourge to the smug conscience, who wrote 'one must either share the world's guilt or go to another planet'?

# Colditz 1941

## NEW YEAR'S DAY

THE NEW YEAR'S party was a roaring success. An extension of lights until 12.30 a.m. made it possible. Our hosts were in great form. A special allowance of beer had already lighted up one or two of the younger officers. Song and laughter greeted us as we were conducted to the central table as guests of honour. It was a perfect *Beggar's Opera*, for we were the most ragged and out-at-elbows people in the room.

For the space of half an hour I sat by a cousin of Joseph Conrad. We made heavy weather of conversation for, unlike his illustrious author cousin, he speaks no English. Neither is he literary-minded. He had not only not read his cousin's books, but had no intention of doing so, though their personal relationship has always been cousinly.

At midnight we made rings along the room like a piled-up column of figure eights, and sang *Auld Lang Syne* in the three languages represented. I left after this and went straight to my bunk. As we are one hour east of Greenwich my own people — Maisie particularly — would not be celebrating the New Year for another hour. I watched the time and followed their movements in imagination until the moment struck. Then I knew that they were thinking of me, and I knew that they knew I was thinking of them.

## SUNDAY 5 JANUARY

After service this morning we sprinted round the *Hof* to restore circulation. My blood seemed to have given up all idea of travel, but ten minutes smart sprinting lighted the internal fires again.

Worship must have real meaning before a man will sit in a completely unheated church with the temperature outside twenty below.

**MONDAY 6 JANUARY**
Approached *Hauptmann* Priem with a view to getting possession of the pages of my diary which were detained with all other personal memoranda when we arrived at IVc.

Chess, chess, and more chess! The two sets we possess have been in constant — almost uproarious — demand since morning *Appell.* Conversation about anything but chess is impossible.

**TUESDAY 7 JANUARY**
Thirteen Red Cross parcels arrived and were issued this morning. Dick and I made a bully beef goulash for dinner. *Klippische* was on the menu, but *Klippische* is *Klippische* — a coarse-grained fish that has been dried, and in the process has lost most of its natural fat. Even in our hungriest days it was loathed. I have never seen, smelt or tasted anything quite its equal.

**WEDNESDAY 8 JANUARY**
Spent the morning — as indeed most normal mornings — working alternately at German and French until 11 o'clock when the newspapers arrive. Peter usually reads out the front page news, then the papers are divided and, with a dictionary, we spell out the remainder of the news.

At two o'clock Peter went hopefully to wait on the post officer. Today was a good day, not one on which hope was deferred. There were letters for several of us, and I have two from Maisie. But post time brings disappointment and elation without discrimination or care. Some of the RAF fellows have been so long without letters — Hank twelve weeks, Don fifteen, and one of the orderlies only one letter since capture — that they have been allowed to telegraph via Geneva: an excellent gesture.

SATURDAY 11 JANUARY

If this is a *strafe* camp — as it is — my chief regret is that I was not strafed from the first day of capture. during my period of detention in Germany I have had nothing that is better and much that is worse than *Oflag* IVc.

The British community in this camp are here because they are of bolder spirit and larger initiative than their fellows in other camps. An escaper is always in danger of being shot like a rabbit, and I think the German authorities — who would be proud enough of any of their officers who made an escape — honour these fellows for their daring and their refusal to be nice comfortable prisoners who give no trouble.

In all other officers' camps that I know, certain élite sets have segregated themselves and have lived in indigent but pompous isolation. At Spangenberg (where, of course, our numbers were counted in hundreds rather than tens) the 'Regulars' were exclusive to a degree. Most of them were bitten badly by the bug of which the Regular Army has never been deloused — Territorialphobia! A Territorial is some incredibly low form of life, always to be spurned *coûte que coûte*. I quite willingly confess to a preference for working with Regulars. Generally speaking they are less officious, and of course they know their stuff. But so they ought, otherwise there is no justification for the Regular Army! The assumptions of knowledge, etc., of Territorial Army officers can be intensely irritating, but so, to an adult, are the assumptions of adolescents. But wisdom as well as good manners forbids the shunning of adolescents.

The Eton set — Army or civilian — were another separatist coterie. They ate together; paced the exercise ground in twos, threes, or fours; attended the same lectures; and went to the *Abort* together. They were not offensively separatist, but sufficiently exclusive to be noticeable.

There is no hint of that in this camp. We are seventeen officers. No two are alike except in good comradeship. Some of England's top public schools are represented; while some of the RAF officers would make no wider claim than an intense willingness to serve their country. My present judgement is that there are none who regard themselves as being of different clay from the rest. Regulars, Territorials, Emergency Reserve, *et al.* take each other for what they are worth; and it seems to me that their worth as men and soldiers is pretty high.

At *Oflag* IVc we have been mercifully preserved from that arch-tormentor of prisoners-of-war, the organising genius. May his type always remain mild enough not to be sent to a *Sonderlager* — or anyway not to IVc. What little liberty is accorded to us we enjoy in this camp.

I know two officers' camps where a high priest of organisation has succeeded in getting every prisoner into a strait jacket of ridiculously petty regulations. There is no hint of that — thank God — here.

The Poles and the French are also excellent fellows. They are all 'difficult' prisoners. But difficult prisoners make interesting prison companions. There is always something going on: planning escapes, putting those plans in execution, swapping war stories. So, though monotony is almost inescapable in these conditions, it is by no means as prevalent as in non-difficult-prisoner camps.

The final reason why IVc is better than other camps is the attitude of the *Lager* authorities. By and large they are the best German officers I have met since the 10th CCS was overhauled by their front-line troops. To maintain discipline they don't resort to a weak man's refuge, petty tyranny; but treat us — after they have taken every precaution to prevent us escaping — as gentlemen who know the meaning of honour, and possess a gentleman's dignity.

Lieutenant-Colonel Schmidt, the *Kommandant,* and Major Menz, the second-in-command (who went to school in Eastbourne in his boyhood) strike me as wanting to do nothing that even an enemy prisoner could regard as unfair. When either of them comes into the *Hof* or our quarters, and one of the accompanying German officers gives the command *'Achtung'*, they scarcely wait for us to make the initial effort to rise before waving us back to whatever we were doing. Needless to say, we are more meticulous about military etiquette in their presence than might otherwise be the case.

If the crime for which I was indicted at *Oflag* IXa had come for trial before *Kommandant* Schmidt, my word of honour as a chaplain and a gentleman would not, I am convinced, have been derided; nor would reflection have been cast on my truthfulness. It was my firm intention to report the matter to the American Embassy, and open up the affront to my honour in Berlin. But lest an acquittal would result in my being returned from this *Straflager* to one of the non-*Straflagers* I have been in, I prefer to let matters stand.

I wonder if one has a right — even in prisoner conditions — to let such ethical questions go by the board in favour of personal comfort? However, I know when I am on a good wicket.

### TUESDAY 14 JANUARY
Have decided to spend my accumulating fund of *Lagermarks* on an upper denture. My present plate is far too small, and in consequence is cracked in two places. A dentist attends the camp on Wednesday afternoons, and *Hauptmann* Priem has promised to put in an application through the *Kommandantur*.

We were marched out for an hour's exercise today. The enclosure was thick with snow, and more was falling. Our standard of football in these conditions wouldn't get us into the First Division. We make our own rules, and a player is loudly cheered when he is able to tackle an opponent and roll him in the snow and get away with it.

Of greater interest to me than the football was the emergence of a great spotted woodpecker. He didn't announce his coming with the usual woodpecker squawk, but alighted on the naked trunk of a beech tree and began his machine-gun search for food. Hunger was not only keen enough to make him regardless of our presence, but it had also ruffled his plumage until every feather stood on end. The long weeks of snow and frost have reduced him to near starvation. If he can manage to hold out another five or six weeks, then spring, food, and mating will reward his tenacity. If I wait rather longer, then peace, home, and the unrestricted opportunity to do my job will be my reward.

I asked Dr Pfeifer, the *Dolmetscher*, about my diary. He explained that it had not yet been returned because of the description of the escape of Don and Keith from the *Schloss* at Spangenberg. At my request he promised to delete the offensive portions and return to me whatever remained. I am not a little amazed, for I thought I had written with extreme fairness and without prejudice to either the escapers or to their captors.

A new camp order in force today prohibits prisoners of one nationality from visiting quarters of other nationalities. Most of us regard it as an unnecessary hardship, and all our inter-language classes will have to cease or be carried on *sub rosa*.

### FRIDAY 17 JANUARY

A US Embassy representative paid the usual bi-monthly visit today as the official representative of our Protecting Power. He receives our 'moans', they are examined in relation to whatever conventions the two countries concerned have signed, and representations are then made to Berlin, and a report made to London. A frivolous or groundless complaint will evoke a pretty sharp letter of rebuke from the Secretary of the Embassy.

Our chief moan today, after the regulars about food, exercise, clothes etc., was about the German decision to confiscate all Penguin books on arrival. After the interview in the evidence room the Colonel gave us a report about it. It appears the German cause for complaint was about certain advertisements and comic art drawings which appear on the notice pages of many books of the Penguin series. London has agreed that confiscation, as a wartime measure, must be conceded.

After the evening meal Don sat down at the piano and we gathered round and roared ourselves hoarse. About halfway through the dreadful hullabaloo some one called for solos, and it caught on. When my turn came I sang 'In Amsterdam there lived a maid', and to almost drunken applause (but it was a teetotal party ) sang 'Any old iron' for encore. An accident befell me which was a source of unutterable delight to everyone but myself. My far too small dental plate shot out as I chopped off the phrase. 'You look dapper from your napper' etc. Teddy Barton fielded it in mid-air, and I had to sing 'Old Iron' again without them as the price of their return.

I have told myself a score of times in the past hour that I ought to forget two rather more than risqué songs sung by Dick and Pat. But if I, a seasoned man and a padre to boot, find myself mechanically repeating snippets of song, the morals of which are at all times to be deplored, what may I not expect from the boys in the Stalags whose sex urges burn with the all-consuming passion of youth?

SUNDAY 19 JANUARY
Lord Haw-Haw provoked our mirth in an impassioned broadcast in which he ripped the pants off 'his sartorial elegance, the Right Honourable Anthony Eden'. One of the astounding things he had to disclose was that 'in the last resort President Roosevelt was now empowered to buy the British Navy'. Pat expressed great indignation and said, 'Churchill might at least have given Eire a chance instead of selling it to those foreigners'. In the spirit of his own remark we rolled him on the floor and demanded an apology. He apologised by saying he would have liked to buy it himself as a ninety-first birthday present for his 'pore ole grandmother' who had never owned a navy in her life.

FRIDAY 24 JANUARY
A clothing parcel from the Swedish Red Cross warmed several backs today. Shirts, pants, vests were drawn for, since there were insufficient to go round. I didn't draw, for I had a clothing parcel from home two months ago. Many have not yet received a stitch of clothing from the day of

capture. It has been a case of the poor helping the poor, and of giving one shirt out of two. At Spangenberg there were the well-dressed and the naked, and some of the well-dressed were Priests and Levites. There is nothing of that at IVc.

Applied for and received a pair of German *sabots*. I have never worn them before and do not find delight in them now. But the thick wooden soles do make for dry feet, and, alas, for holey socks.

An amusing story today. German air bases in France and Belgium received more attention from the RAF than was desirable. In several places decoy bases with wooden planes and all the paraphernalia of a new base were built. When completed, the RAF flew over and dropped wooden bombs!

### SUNDAY 26 JANUARY

Wrote my last card for the month to Maisie this afternoon. It is a year today, by the date, since I saw her for a day — the last time before embarkation. A wretched day it was! Euston Road, usually drab and depressing at any time, ran through banks of discoloured snow three feet high. In Trafalgar Square it had been built into blocks which looked like bases for a score of new monuments.

We had our midday meal in the Strand Corner House, and sat there for an hour watching the tide of city business life, and wondering when we should meet again. I don't remember wondering 'if' we should meet again. The parting seemed to be quite natural, but with the dull pain of many of life's natural things.

Saying goodbye in the racket of London life was the most difficult of many difficult experiences of our married life. How could one avoid being fuller of emotion than was comfortable? Neither of us spoke of it. We grinned at each other, said 'Cheerio', and she went to the tube, and I to number 12 platform.

### MONDAY 27 JANUARY

Dick is receiving extensive Californian sympathy mail these

days. He wrote to Ginger Rogers' Hollywood address in July, at a time when letters could not be sent to England. Miss Rogers herself has not replied, but her publicity agent made front page news of the letter in the *Los Angeles Observer*.

A largish number of aspirant stars saw the notice, and at once wrote to Dick furnishing details about their height, weight, figure, colour of eyes and hair (monotonously blue and blonde) and stating their fixed preference for this, that, and the other. 'Please don't think me fast or husband-seeking because of this letter. I am a career woman (age 17) and have told Mom and Dad a score of times that I shall never, never marry' — and so they all end. In nine letters out of ten a pretty photograph of the 'career woman' is enclosed, showing her in a devastatingly attractive bathing costume, or in trousers and silk shirt. We hope for lots more. Their entertainment value is high indeed.

However, from a practical point of view the whole thing is a wet squib. The original letter was one of many written by officers to people they thought might be good for a monthly food and tobacco parcel. Of course the ulterior motive was not openly avowed in the letters, but there were some who received letters who thought immediately of a parcel. Dick drew a blank. Letters yes, parcels nary-a-one. Still, the letters are of unspeakable value; they give our forcing-house of humour a much appreciated rest.

THURSDAY 30 JANUARY
Last night the escapers, who have planned a tunnel, began work. Their kit of tools contains one six inch nail, several pieces of stout wire, a wooden marlin spike, and a table knife. It will be necessary to cut through the foundations when they are reached, and in the meantime to dispose of the rubble. The line they are following passes right under the canteen, and will eventually come out under the eastern ramparts. It will occupy three months, working two or three hours a night after lights out. Having to work in darkness increases the difficulties. The necessity for silence, lest a night sentry should become suspicious, adds to the

other complications. At present there are two watchers who use a system of signals to indicate when the sentry on his beat is near enough to hear unusual sounds.*

SATURDAY 1 FEBRUARY
During exercise this afternoon I stopped a hard kick on my right shin from a Polish naval officer. The skin was broken and a fierce swelling soon started.

It is three days since I shaved. There is no reason for not doing so except slackness; but after a full day's chiding about 'an anti-social excretion' and 'a disgustingly dirty chin' I have decided to grow a beard. Rupert Barry and Pat assure me that it will be forcibly removed.

SUNDAY 2 FEBRUARY
Because of my leg I had to ask Hobling to take the service. Until midday I lay in my bunk, and since then have sat in the day room with my throbbing leg raised on a stool.

Sunday afternoon is usually devoted to correspondence, but at 1.30 today a serious international chess match began. Spies were posted at different points to prevent a surprise visit from the Germans. It would have been with extreme difficulty that we evacuated our visitors had the emergency arisen, slick as the British are at this particular form of warfare.

MONDAY 3 FEBRUARY
Had my shin examined thoroughly by the German MO this forenoon. He would be better satisfied if I stayed in my bunk all day, but he finally agreed to my sitting up in the afternoon if I kept the leg raised to body level.

WEDNESDAY 5 FEBRUARY
Kept an appointment with the *Zahnarzt* to arrange for an upper denture. Kenneth and Stanislawski helped me down

*On minute inspection the German censor's *Geprüft* stamp on this page of the MS diary looks as though it could have been forged, so perhaps this rather surprising passage was added at a later date after this section of the diary had been censored and approved.

the staircase to the infirmary where the tooth-doctor has a room. The process of explanation took an amusing and much laboured quarter of an hour — one does not learn dental technicalities in a grammar. My old plate, made in 1921, has a gold foundation; the new one would be steel, but the price is about M200. At the pre-war rate of exchange that is £16.13.4. I decided not to have the plate made. Perhaps my present one will see the war through, and anyway I would much prefer a gold base.

Just how painful cracks over the shin can be I had forgotten since college days. Discoloration has travelled to several places too distant from the contusion to be original bruises. 'Sympathy' is the word, it seems, but it feels more like a cracked tibia.

The moles went to their tunnelling in fine fettle. Progress is slow.

THURSDAY 6 FEBRUARY

Geoff Wardle, who is always referred to in the third person as 'The Navy', disturbed our peace after lights out by developing acute stomach pains. He got short shrift for the first ten minutes, being advised it was only a touch of naval flatulence and he would shortly fart like fury and all would be well. Someone suggested it was the beginning of labour. Everyone but the Navy was facetious. He became more serious as the pain grew more acute, and something had to be done. It seemed the obvious symptoms of appendicitis.

Now how could we get hold of a doctor? All exits are locked, bolted and barred. There are no bells to ring, or telephones to use. Night sickness is not provided for. Finally we decided to risk a shot by opening the window and shouting to the sentry on the eastern rampart. If the sentry didn't understand our English, at least he was a wise lad. He communicated with the guardhouse instead of pointing his rifle at us, and was soon round to see what all the shouting was about.

By that time Peter was fully awake, and explained the need for a doctor, and the sentry went in search of Dr Leguet. It took a full hour. Acute appendicitis was authoritatively diagnosed, and by 2.30 a.m. an ambulance had arrived, and The Navy had docked for repairs.

This morning I attended the infirmary for examination by the German MO and am no longer excused *Appell*. My leg is considerably better, but another few days' leave from lining up would have been easier.

### FRIDAY 7 FEBRUARY

A report in this week's issue of *The Camp*\* deals a severe blow at the escapers. In POW camps in Canada, German senior officers are required to furnish a note with the senior officer's signature and the number of prisoners on *Appell*, and the number sick. In the POW camps in Germany the same system will come into effect tomorrow by way of reprisal. A German senior officer in Canada has been punished with twenty-eight days' *Stubenarrest* for not reporting an escaped prisoner as absent. Similar punishment may be expected here for similar failure.

In the good old days *Appells* could be worked, sometimes for several days, while the escapers put a good distance between themselves and their captors. Now the few hours between Appells is as much as an escaper can hope for.

Our moles have recently added a few useful tools to their tunnelling kit by methods of appropriation which would cause a civil judge to comment caustically on the inadequacy of six months' sentence for such as they. I think it is my job as padre to help them remember that this military necessity is an attitude of mind that should be temporarily employed rather than permitted to become absorbing.\*

### SATURDAY 8 FEBRUARY

We are in great form today! The German High Command announces that Benghazi has fallen into British hands after severe fighting. It is perhaps the first British success of any

\**The Camp*, a newspaper for POWs in their own language, produced by the German Ministry of Propaganda.
\*The page on which this entry was made also bears a *Geprüft* stamp which could be a forgery.

importance, and indicates, we think, the turn of the tide.

My diary and three *Geprüft* books were released today. None of the diary has been confiscated, for which I am extremely glad. It would have disappointed me — after the extreme carefulness with which I have written — if the censor had thought my entries unfair.

It has been washing day, too. I washed my pyjamas and dried them over the kitchen stove. They haven't quite a schoolgirl complexion.

SUNDAY 9 FEBRUARY
A Polish orderly, who has spent several days weeping the tears of the demented, went completely bats this morning. I woke up to shouts of angry protestation coming from the *Hof*, and saw the poor fellow pacing wildly about, stopping to strike a menacing attitude, and then pacing more wildly than before. Some of the Polish officers tried to calm him, but he flung them off and finally had to be overpowered. Poor devil! He has now been removed to a mental hospital.

Richard Heard conducted worship this morning. His Irish wit flashes out like his gems of learning. A private conversation with Heard could change a young man's life. His charm and logic are well nigh invincible.

MONDAY 10 FEBRUARY
Woke up feeling very browned off. I took myself in hand, failed in the process, and by midday was worse.

Played football during the exercise, and at one point threatened to break Harry's neck. 'I wish you would, old boy,' he replied, and I was shocked into the realisation that he must be feeling ten times worse than I. I talked to him like a Dutch uncle, which didn't make me feel any better. My own inner hypocrisy filled me with self-loathing. A few minutes later Harry whispered, 'You've done me good;' but actually I was the debtor, and told him so.

TUESDAY 11 FEBRUARY
Am browned off and will not write. I would be ashamed of any entry I made. I know I would.

**WEDNESDAY 12 FEBRUARY**
Am nearer normal again. I ought to be on top of the world for good has favoured me.

An English gentleman in Bucharest had a hunch that a parcel of pyjamas might fill a need. It was a 'sure good hunch' as our Canadians say. There were twelve suits, and nine of our number were entirely without night attire of any kind. Their needs were supplied first; then the remaining suits were drawn for.

Aces were low, and I drew the deuce of diamonds, and am therefore possessed of a spotlessly white sleeping suit. There were also seven blankets. I suggested that the blankets should be given to those who had not drawn pyjamas, but draws were in the air. This time aces were high, and I drew a ten of spades. It was the fifth highest card, hence I have a good blanket also.

Though the luck of the draw has been greatly in my favour recently, I strongly disapprove of it as a method for distribution. A roster would be more just. But in most of my fellow-prisoners' minds an equitable distribution is the last thing to be desired. They will lend and give as freely as the rain watereth the earth; but let no man attempt to socialise or rationalise life!

**FRIDAY 14 FEBRUARY**
Geoff, The Navy, returned to camp this morning. His appendectomy was done in a military hospital for which he has nothing but praise. Doctors, nurses, treatment and food were all excellent. He seems to regret his return.

**SATURDAY 15 FEBRUARY**
Geoff came from the *Revier* to resume normal camp life. Pat seized upon the occasion as a suitable opportunity for a party. Had anyone any left from the last issue?

We have become wary of Pat's parties, and no one but Pat was dismayed when there were no volunteers. The evening resolved itself into a singsong.

———— dragged me out of the singsong to talk about

81

prayer. This must be the thirtieth time he has told me he has been 'praying like mad and nothing happens'. I talked with him for half an hour going over the old ground again and again. He is now annoyed that I responded to Pat's call to rejoin the party and sing 'Old Iron'. He feeds voraciously on the personality of stronger people, but is not a bit stronger for having weakened them.

SUNDAY 16 FEBRUARY

Pat's welcome party to Geoff developed as the night wore on. Some of those who had beer produced it, and Patrick produced a bottle of *Kölnischwasser* (eau-de-Cologne) bought in the canteen. Mixed with the beer it quickly produced different degrees of drunkenness.

At lights out Hobling and I went to bed, but the piano jazzed on in the darkness, and the song became more uproarious and less tuneful. At about a quarter to midnight Pat, followed by half a dozen others, stumbled across the dormitory towards our small room. They got lost several times among the bunks before reaching us, and suitably addressed each other on turning down the wrong avenue between the beds. Finally they reached us and demanded that Hobling sing 'McNamara'. Hobling lifted his voice with little enthusiasm, for he was half asleep. They at once grabbed our wooden double-decker with the purpose of carrying us into the combined lavatories and washroom.

Sleeping on the bottom deck I found it comparatively easy to bring them down one after another by jabbing them in the back of the knees. After a time they tired of picking each other up in the dark, and falling on one another in the process. The application of a stiff straw-filled pillow in no way added to their pleasure.

By 12.30 the escapade was at an end. The Church Militant, sober and united, had succeeded in keeping its double-decker within two feet of its original position. Herein is a parable.

WEDNESDAY 19 FEBRUARY

One of the privileges in this camp is that of celebrating

birthdays. By application a few days before, arrangement has been made to buy two or three bottles of wine.

After morning *Appell* I asked the *Rittmeister* if I might thus celebrate my birthday on the 21st. He didn't reply directly, but reminded me of certain camp orders British officers were in the habit of observing in the breach, and then asked if I would drink the wine myself. I said I had no such intention, and he forthwith refused permission to purchase.

FRIDAY 21 FEBRUARY
Five letters yesterday anticipated my birthday; and this morning there were thirteen Red Cross parcels. Teddy presented me with a very fancy shaving set bought through the canteen.

The gift that touched me more deeply than the little extra chocolate awarded me from the Red Cross parcels was an offering brought by an orderly, Johnny Smith. For quite a time he has suffered severe stomach pains, and in an effort to give him a little relief the German MO yesterday put him on white bread and butter. This afternoon I was sitting writing in the 'Bishop's Palace' when Johnny knocked and came in with a piece of his white bread, buttered and sprinkled with sugar. It was a present far above price, for he is little over nineteen, and possesses the appetite his years suggest. I said, 'No thank you, Johnny. It is awfully good of you, but ...' His face dropped like a thunderbolt, and I saw that by refusing I was trampling on an altar it had cost him much to build: putting my foot — as it were — through a sunset. So I accepted his gift with gratitude. I gave him my last cigarette, one saved specially for a birthday smoke. He asked if it was my last, but was easily reassured.

But I am now smoking a marvellous pipe of tobacco, lighted forty minutes ago and still going. A Pole who received an American parcel gave Storie-Pugh two pipefuls, and Storie insisted on giving one to me. Some men give ten per cent of what they possess to others; but few give fifty.

SATURDAY 22 FEBRUARY
Dick has see-sawed at his piano-accordion nearly all day. Musical instruments became available through the canteen two months ago, and Richard has had the accordion a fortnight and has spent some part of each day shivering and practising in the wash-house — the same old exercise over and over again. We are all agreed that his progress in a fortnight is terrific, and — further — that a man is deserving of success who will sit practising in an almost icebound wash-house.

Cottage pie stood for all courses at supper. The innards of the pie were such Red Cross excellences as 'Aberdeen roll', 'Farmers' dinners', herrings, and Heinz beans in tomato. The fusion of such diverse flavours may be regarded by people of mild palate as altogether too bold, but bold flavours don't scare us. Anyway, none of the foods gathered tenderly together in our cottage pie was in sufficient quantity to be eaten alone, and a hot meal at night is a virtue in itself.

At 8.0 p.m. one of the orderlies carried in the three pies and in his excitement dropped one on the floor. The bowl crashed and the pie spread out like a smashed egg. He apologised and hurried back to the kitchen to get the orderlies' pie. But Pat and Rupert got a soup bowl and were on their knees scooping up pie and dust with a spoon. Pat triumphantly showed us the retrieved pie, and it was seen to have lost little. We decided to draw for the non-dusty ones rather than penalise the orderlies, and it was Pat and Rupert's table who ate dust with their pie.

MONDAY 24 FEBRUARY
A tobacco parcel! A pound of Cut Gold Bar and two hundred Player's cigarettes. What a birthday present! I divided the cigarettes between tables, and gave some pipe tobacco to pipe smokers. Maisie was toasted at supper — and what a supper, too! Red Cross bacon and half a sausage, with fried potatoes.

TUESDAY 25 FEBRUARY
The French appear to do exceedingly well for food. The parcels from France are regular, and contain roast pork, beef, and ham in generous quantities. Many of the officers belong to the old French aristocracy, so most of their meat supplies come off their ancestral lands.

WEDNESDAY 26 FEBRUARY
The Poles began their Lent services this morning. I wakened to the Te Deum sung to the old, old Latin tune. Kenneth, who has developed a close friendship with Podporucznik Mikusinski, attended the service and observed that the worshippers were sprinkled on their heads with oil and ashes.

We met for prayer at 11 a.m. Heard led our thought, but for me the path led nowhere. In some remote age those prayers may have stimulated faith and vouchsafed a vision, but I fear I am too concerned with faith and vision in this age.

Beer is stopped this week as a punishment for a light being seen at 11 p.m. on Monday night.

SATURDAY 1 MARCH
Have just completed my share of the hymns for tomorrow. Weariness to the flesh was compensated each time I came to the verse:

> Take up thy cross, let not its weight
> Fill thy weak spirit with alarm.
> His strength shall bear thy spirit up,
> And brace thy heart, and nerve thy arm.

Life as a prisoner of war makes one thrice thankful for an inner consciousness of invisible things: but belief in everlasting rightness does not make unappetising food more appetising, or crowded communal life a joy. Grace suficient for the day! Grace sufficient to enable one not to add to the general discomfort by showing irritation, or losing one's temper unnecessarily. Yes, all that. But don't tell me that such self-disciplines are anything to laugh about. And I wonder if there might not be a touch of priggishness about the satisfaction one feels at the end of a more or less successful disciplinary day.

After a *Klippische* lunch I was appealed to by the orderlies to settle an argument that had arisen out of the lunch. Doherty, a strapping young Irishman, can see nothing wrong about settling a friendly argument with his fists when he is rendered speechless.

The subject of the immediate argument was what Doherty would do to a hypothetical wife for certain cooking offences. All but one of the boys are between 19 and 24 years old, and the argument had resolved itself into the straight question: Is a man ever justified in striking a woman?

Doherty had Clydeside support from Munn, who is well over six feet and as rough as a wild horse. Munn said it always rattled him as a youngster when he saw his mother chastised, 'but the woman next door deserves a bonny wee whacking, but her husband is scared stiff of her.' I listened to his savage description of the old termagant, and discovered that her daughter is a bonny lassie (nothing like her mother) who is likely to become Mrs Munn as soon as the war is over. Munn and Doherty are amazed at the unsophistication of the others who have never seen a woman thrashed. 'Phew, Jim,' said Doherty, 'they must have lived in a field!'

### SUNDAY 2 MARCH
Fencing foils, ordered through the canteen, were delivered this morning. A condition of purchase is that all foils must be delivered each night for custody in the guardhouse. All afternoon duels have been fought as vigorously as chess was played six weeks ago.

Ludo now holds the affection of a small but noisy group. It is extremely probable that the Ludo sets will shortly be used for fuel.

### WEDNESDAY 5 MARCH
Storie-Pugh, who sleeps very soundly and gets an occasional

nightmare, fell out of his bunk with a terrific thud which caused Teddy — who talks in his sleep all night long, every night — to yell 'Earthquake! Earthquake!'

Dick, in his usual soporific savagery, shouted, 'Shut your something mouth, Barton, and let a fellow sleep,' and awakened everyone who had survived the other rumpus except Teddy, who cried, in perfect Hollywood style, 'Goodbye, my darling! Z-o-o-o-m!' And in a moment he broke out again — well above the turmoil of earth — with, 'Well, old boy, this is the first time I've played bridge at over seventy thousand! Three no trumps.'

This aerial adventure woke Dick's sense of humour, which invariably oversleeps him by half an hour on nice mornings and longer on not-so-nice mornings. I'm sure I heard him laughing.

The air resounds with the clash of steel all day. Everyone has become a fencing expert in five minutes, and everyone demonstrates less skill than the advice they give would seem to augur.

FRIDAY 7 MARCH
Twenty-seven Red Cross parcels, delivered at 11 a.m., added substantially to our rations.

SATURDAY 8 MARCH
The arrival of Red Cross food is evidently the signal for a disturbed night. Peter Allan had us all out of bed at 1.30 a.m. He was in a heavy cold sweat, and shook and shivered for all the world like an ague. It was a full hour before the doctor arrived, by which time Peter had stopped shivering and felt better. None of us was feeling over grand, and the sight of Peter vomiting had directed several on a somewhat hesitant course to the *Abort* where much good stuff was lost.

MONDAY 10 MARCH
Our bread ration is six slices a day. For a long time past odd slices have been missing. Yesterday Teddy was two short. I have frequently been one short. We caught one

member of our table today, having had two slices for breakfast, one at midday, still having four slices left for the evening meal.

Miscounting one's bread slices to one's own advantage is a heinous crime in *Gefangenschaft*.

TUESDAY 18 MARCH
When climbing back to the *Schloss* after exercise we were able to see the dogs that are intended as sleuth hounds for escaping prisoners being put through their paces. I was by no means impressed. In spite of the success of certain isolated dogs, I have never believed Alsatians to be suited to police work. They follow sight more readily than scent, are impatient and sharp-tempered and, while quick to attack, are just as quick to shy off a quarry. For long-distance trailing, even on a hot scent, they are very second-rate.

The French quarters were searched this morning and quite a bit of escape material was found and confiscated. A little later two French officers were caught working a tunnel leading from the church. They were marched off to the cooler.

WEDNESDAY 19 MARCH
Every nose in the place is running, and handkerchiefs are as scarce as food. The four I received in my clothes parcel were drawn for when they arrived, since I already had one. Strange that most people have forgotten to include handkerchiefs in personal parcels.

THURSDAY 20 MARCH
After the cold came the cough. Dr Leguet prescribed what to me is an entirely new treatment for bronchitis. It consisted of the use of half a dozen small glass jars which were brushed inside with an alcohol rag, lighted, and pressed on my back while still aflame. The vacuum thus created pulled hard at the flesh, almost half filling the jar. After fifteen minutes they were pulled off with a sharp pop, leaving me with half a dozen clearly defined brand marks

on my back. Just what the treatment has done for — or to — my lungs I have no idea. It has done no perceivable harm.

Instead of going to work last night the escapers went into conclave to explore the possibilities of other means of escape. Keith made a fantastic proposal which on examination seemed less fantastic, and is now under serious consideration.

FRIDAY 21 MARCH
A black Friday for the escapers.

The evidence of their earnestness has been emphasised by the fact that, though food is desperately scarce, a little store has been laid by — and it was intended to add more — against the need of two or three weeks' trek to the frontier. Alas and alack! For all the self-denial! This morning it was found and confiscated. It had been buried in a suitcase under the floor. Not a terrifically good hiding place, and all too readily discovered, as we observed when *Feldwebel* Gephard and the *Rittmeister* bore it away.

The tunnel is almost complete. Before going to work tonight the moles held a longish discussion on whether to go within the next day or two and take their chance of getting food *en route*; or whether the better policy is to wait until the hedges are in foliage and provide some sort of cover, and another store of food has been laid in.

My own judgement is that they are in no condition for a three hundred kilometre march, sleeping out and going short of food.

SATURDAY 22 MARCH
The show started at lights out. Goldman let up the blind to open the window in the orderlies' dormitory and sprang back smartly as two close shots rang out. We heard the ping, ping of two bullets, and knew at once that something unusual was afoot. From a different vantage point to our usual one we watched the proceedings, and saw the sentries all keyed up at their posts instead of evincing their customary boredom. Further along on the east side, below the

ramparts, officers and soldiery could be seen engaged in what we believed to be escape practice.

Pat, Dick and Rupert were working in the tunnel — tonight would see it finished. Their scouts, Geoff and Storie-Pugh, could only see and hear what happened in the *Hof*, and we couldn't tell them what we could see on the eastern ramparts.

Everything would be all right — as it had been several times before — if at midnight the visiting orderly officer did not examine the beds too closely; and there was no reason to suppose he would. The dummies were tastefully arranged: Dick curled up with his knees under his chin, Pat lying full length with the sheet over his head, Rupert lying pretty straight with a fairish size protuberance at his rear, Geoff and Storie hunched up, Storie making rather less hunch than Geoff. The stage was all set, and we hoped for the best.

The worst occurred a few minutes before midnight when the *Rittmeister* and a few soldiers came into the *Hof* through the small door set in the main gates. Why the *Rittmeister* was on duty it was difficult to understand, for *Hauptmann* Priem is now Senior Camp Officer.

He made a bee-line for our quarters, and at once the steady tap, tap, tap of the tunnellers ceased like breathing ceases at death. Having unlocked his way through two doors, the *Rittmeister* began to enquire for the person who opened the window in the orderlies' room. Goldman acknowledged having done so tonight as on all preceding nights except when driving rain or snow made it inadvisable. The *Rittmeister* was not satisfied with the answer, and seemed determined to carry the matter further.

The officers' dormitory was next. He switched on the lights as he entered, took a quick glance round, and passed through to the day room. But one of the guards in his wake stopped to examine the one window, set in a deep recess, which looks onto the eastern rampart. He brushed past Geoff's bed, and Storie's, to reach the window, and — returning — bumped into the head of Geoff's bed. When no one stirred to answer his apology he looked closer.

'*Rittmeister!*' he cried; and we knew the game was up. Everyone was ordered to assemble down the narrow centre of the dormitory. Lined up there, twelve in all, we looked at the recumbent effigies of the five moles. An Old Testament miracle would have redeemed the situation for us, and the presence of a ventriloquist could have provided a bit of first-rate fun. Alas! Both the miracle and the ventriloquist were absent, not to speak of the moles.

The Colonel was invited to say where they were, but of course he did not know. Neither did he; for knowing — as they already must have done by reason of the rumpus — that their absence was discovered, they might easily have completed the tunnel and bolted.

Orderlies were called out and numbered; and Wilkins, the senior was asked if he knew where the five missing officers were. His answer was the same. We asked to go back to bed, but were refused. We asked to go to the day room, but were refused. Someone lighted a cigarette, but had to put it out immediately.

*Hauptmann* Priem had been notified by this time, and when he arrived he was his usual calm, good-humoured self. He asked for information about the escaped five. 'Were they on evening *Appell*?' He had a suspicion that the Colonel may have given his signature to their being present when it was otherwise, and added 'if that is the case you will be shot, and I will send a wreath to your funeral.' He then said '*Hauptmann* Howe' (pronouncing it 'Hover' in German fashion) had been seen escaping and had been shot. He observed our reaction to this announcement, and probably deduced from our merriment that an actual escape had not taken place. In any event his face showed marked relief, but at that time I did not realise how shrewd a thrust he had made. We would have evaded direct answer to a question designed to discover whether they had actually escaped or were still working in preparation for escape, but our laughing told him much that he wanted to know.

The *Rittmeister* now appeared with the Alsatian dogs and dogmen. This part of the proceedings — the *Schnüffel-*

*hunde* in action — interested me tremendously. Notwithstanding the dogmen's encouraging '*Such! Such! Such!*', and their gentle thrusting of the dogs' noses into bedding and clothing, the dogs appeared to have little idea of what was required. I watched them leave the building and cross the *Hof*. To do so they passed the point at which the moles turned to enter the tunnel, and within three feet of a hiding scout, but they never swerved. I am more convinced than ever that what Alsatians are fit for is to be good servants to a shepherd.

At this point *Feldwebel* Gephard, wearing a sword and well lit up after an evening out, arrived in great fettle. It is the first time we have seen Gephard smile. Usually he is of dour temperament and gives the impression of being permanently browned off; but tonight he was in a riot of laughter, and his tongue unusually loose. 'He who laughs last laughs best,' he said, and laughed uproariously. The *Rittmeister* rebuked him twice, for which we were sorry. Gephard was good fun.

When, by about 1.30 a.m., the investigations were complete, and all clothes, bedding, and personal effects of the missing five had been removed, attention was turned to our comrades of other nationalities. The obvious question — have any of them escaped with the British? — was asked, and an *Appell* called to supply the answer. The *Hof* was garish with the fierce glare of three powerful arc lights. The Poles chanted a dirge as they stood and shivered. It was the first midnight *Appell* since our coming, and we — the culprits — did not have to stand shivering in the *Hof*, but were locked in our quarters under guard.

How mouselike the moles lay was evident from the fact that by 3.45 a.m. the *Schloss* had been searched from end to end without success. The other nationalities were dismissed from the *Hof*, and we were ordered to bed. Colonel German had to appear for a few minutes in the evidence room, but they were the same questions, and the same answer: '*Ich weiss nicht.*'

The *Hof* was patrolled by three sentries for the remainder of the night, and not until 7.30 a.m., when some show of normal camp life began, were the moles able to leave their burrow unobserved and get back to our quarters. Washing and brushing up occupied half an hour.

A German *Unteroffizier* came up the spiral stairway and saw The Navy completing his toilet. We had hoped to keep their presence secret and spring a surprise by producing them at *Appell*. But events in which Geoff is concerned are fated to go contrary to plan. The crime which put him in the cooler at Spangenberg and sent him here was not his own affair in any way; he was only holding the stolen horses — so to speak — when the long arm of the law descended on him, and the real criminals were never detected. And the submarine on which he served was depth-charged on her first mission after firing only one torpedo which completely missed its target. The nickname 'Stooge', with which he has been affectionately dubbed, fits his luck perfectly.

And so it was this time. Last night was his first association with the tunnel. Actually it was Don's turn to go to work, but he was tired and wanted to go to bed. The other moles were a bit browned off about it, for it was the third successive working night he had refused. Pat turned to Geoff and asked him if he had recovered from his operation sufficiently to do a night's watching, if so he, Pat, would arrange it with Rupert who would not mind in the least whether he worked or watched. Geoff is a fellow who would never shirk a job because of its being unpleasant, back-aching, and monotonous. He agreed like a shot, and we hailed his gallant acceptance with 'Good old Stooge; something is certain to crack up now!'

The *Unteroffizier* ran for *Hauptmann* Priem who came at once, quizzically looked Geoff over, and left just as hurriedly. In a moment he announced over the loudspeaker that *Appell* would be put back for an hour.

The five miscreants came on *Appell* at 10 a.m. wrapped in blankets. Everything except the light covering in which they had been working had been carried away last night, and none of us had a change of clothing to lend them.

During the morning the British quarters have been searched again. The food cupboard has been denuded of all tins, the contents emptied into soup bowls. Cigarette and tobacco tins from all lockers and cases have gone. The search for the tunnel has been going on all day with dogged persistence, and shortly after 2 p.m. we had a nasty moment when a *Gefreite* who is rather good at smelling things out, actually stood on the tunnel entrance looking satisfied and triumphant. But the search continues in further and more distant parts, so we have decided that his look of triumph must have sprung from a purely personal source. Manholes and drains in the *Hof* have been explored; and chimney stacks and windows, but without success.

While we were having our evening meal *Hauptmann* Priem and three guards arrived, bringing with them two short pieces of iron railing and two half-empty tins of British sweets. With a twinkle in his eye, Priem asked Pat and Rupert, who were sitting together, if they found it cold in the church. Rupert flashed back, 'I don't go to church,' and the Colonel and Pat followed with, 'Yes, it's very cold on Sunday mornings.' A good-natured argument about the escape rights of POWs lasted about fifteen minutes, and ended in Priem promising the return of clothes and personal effects tomorrow.

It is unfortunate that the church tunnel has been discovered; it is not a British venture at all. The incriminating sweets, we suppose, were once on NAAFI shelves, abandoned for any gatherers who might come along.

We learned that the moles themselves first knew of their absence having been discovered when the two scouts no longer tapped out messages, but bolted underground and told of the search. The tramping of searchers in the *Hof* and dormitories could be heard, but they could see nothing.

They were pretty tightly packed, lying not cheek by jowl but head by foot. When Rupert shuffled his feet he caught Geoff a kick on the ear, to which Geoff suitably replied. One of the funny bits occurred when the floor from which they had made ingress was under examination. Pat hung on for dear life to an underside grip he had recently attached to the tunnel entrance roof. One of the searchers did observe a square patch in the floor and tried to prize it up, but the weight of Pat, with the addition of Rupert pulling his legs until he was almost dismembered, gave it the impression of being a fixture. For over six hours they sat tight — or rather lay tight — before deciding that there was sufficient normal camp life going on to cover their reappearance.

Dick and Rupert amused themselves while lying in the tunnel by a whispered conversation on how we were behaving during the events in the dormitory. Kenneth would be going from one to the other muttering this and that; the Colonel would be looking perfectly bland and amazed; Peter Allan, as interpreter, would be surrounded by German officers . . . it was just as they imagined.*

SUNDAY 23 MARCH
The service at 10.30 was almost defunct as far as numbers were concerned. A mock funeral put on by the Poles and French was far too strong competition for us. It had occurred to someone that a funeral purporting to bury Dick would be a diversion, and Peter Allan because of his kilt, was invited to become the mourning widow. He was suitably draped in black silk taken from the lining of a greatcoat.

The moment *Appell* was over a procession started from the entrance to the Polish quarters. It was a mournful procession, moving with slow and measured tread round the *Hof*. The coffin — a dormitory locker — had been draped with a blanket that had been chalked into a rough resemblance of a Union Jack, and bore a giant red, white and blue wreath. It was preceded by two piano accordionists who drew purgatorial groans from unwilling instruments.

With them were the banner-bearers, carrying on two broom handles a window blind on which had been drawn

*The tunnel entrance was in the canteen, and a rather different version of this episode appears in *The Colditz Story* by Pat Reid. A very different version appears in *Colditz: the German Viewpoint* by Reinhold Eggers published by Robert Hale in 1961.

an enormous skull and crossbones. Peter staggered in blind grief behind the coffin, supported by two Poles. It was a terrific show, and *Hauptmann* Priem, whose statement about Dick's being shot had inspired it, stood in the *Hof* watching with all the good humour in the world. The cortège came to a stop, and a funeral oration was made. Then a French officer stepped forward uninvited and began a further oration which did not stop short at personal references. Priem at once put an end to what had hitherto been a perfectly good joke.

When we returned from service, Priem came to the Colonel to present a letter. He was so solemn and martial that we thought it would be an official raspberry for our share in the mock funeral. But it turned out to be a letter of condolence. The joke was now being turned on us, but it was a good one which commanded our appreciation.

After lunch the five escapers were called to the evidence room to answer questions. None of us know the name of the German officer who conducted the examination. His questions were through an interpreter.

'Were you in the castle on the night of the 21st?'
'Yes!'
'Did the alarm hinder your escape?'
No answer.
'Did the alarm hinder your return?'
'Yes.'

When Storie-Pugh was called in he was given to understand that the others had answered so he might as well tell the truth. 'Oh well,' he replied, 'in that case there is nothing for me to say for we were all together.' When questioned further he said, 'I got as far as Leipzig, and decided to return.'

MONDAY 24 MARCH
At morning *Appell*, *Hauptmann* Priem carried the funeral farce a step further by announcing 'In future no funeral shall take place without twelve hours' notice having been given.' A few Poles laughed, fewer of the French, but it

tickled our perverse sense of humour, and we laughed out loud. We did more than laugh half an hour later when it became known that two Red Cross cigarette parcels were to be issued at once — one hundred and twenty-two Gold Flake cigarettes each.

Workmen are bricking up the tunnel leading from the church, and carrying out repairs to the walls, floors and foundations. The roofs have all been under close inspection; evidently they are anticipating a roof escape.

Our tunnel has not been found. It is complete but for fifteen minutes' working holing out. The ten officers concerned in this scheme believe it will still be a good way of escape unless some German soldier steps on the exact spot at which the tunnel runs out: two square feet covered by not more than two inches of soil. It is hoped that after the first ten have gone, and the outlet has been carefully concealed again, the remainder of the British and a good number of the other nationalities may get away through it. The enthusiasm is terrific. For days now the only conversation has been some branch of escapology — food, money, direction, maps, frontiers, etc. Some have fond dreams that one morning shortly the three padres will be the only Britishers to appear on *Appell*.

WEDNESDAY 26 MARCH
We were out of bed at 2 a.m. On Sunday two of our most junior subalterns decided to play a joke on the night sentries by putting a dummy in an unused bunk and thus increasing the total number by one. When nothing happened their disappointment was great. Then their interest lapsed, and the dummy was forgotten.

At 2 a.m. today, however, he had a resurrection. The night sentry evidently decided it was time for the joke to mature, and called everyone out of bed to be numbered. None were more chagrined or discomforted than the two humorists themselves. The personal advice thrust on them by their fellow subalterns and some of the captains will stop their humour laying traps for night sentries upon whose goodwill much depends.

THURSDAY 27 MARCH
Twenty-four Poles were removed today. Their destination is not known, but a guess indicates Spitzberg in the Sudeten mountains. It is said to be utterly unbreakable, but I doubt if any *Lager* is quite that! All those who are being removed are prominent members of escape groups. They left amid loud cheering and shouted good wishes.

FRIDAY 28 MARCH 1941
Sentence of seven days' *Stubenarrest** was passed on the five moles for being absent from their quarters on the night of the 21st, and for attempting to tunnel out of the camp from the church.

Their immediate reaction was to refuse punishment on the ground of a false charge — they were not tunnelling from the church. A non-escaper pointed out that it is better escapology to accept punishment for a discovered tunnel than to tell the Germans there is yet an undiscovered tunnel. That appeared to be good reasoning.

SATURDAY 29 MARCH
The 'church-breakers' went into confinement smilingly. In Dick's absence I am acting as kitchen officer, which means cutting the bread ration into six slices each per day, dividing other rations and Red Cross food, and managing the orderlies.

Two of the orderlies are in open rebellion as far as work is concerned. The Colonel could report them to the Germans and get them punished, but they know very well that he will do no such thing, and that as a POW himself he has no power to punish beyond stopping part of the pay (RM5 a week) they receive from us. So they are openly rude to us and to the other orderlies who do the work.

*Stubenarrest* was the punishment a German officer received, and by the terms of the Geneva Convention it also applied to Allied officer POWs. It was confinement for a specified period of not more than thirty days in a room with the bare essentials of comfort — mattress, chair, table etc. — on standard rations, and with books, writing materials and cigarettes allowed.

SUNDAY 30 MARCH

After *Lichts aus* last night, Goldman, the Jewish orderly, crept up to my bed and asked if I would speak with him in the kitchen. I went out and listened while in rapid Cockneyisms he opened his heart.

The *Rittmeister* has been calling him to the evidence room almost every day since the night he opened the window and sprang back because of the two shots. The *Rittmeister* thinks he was spying for the moles, and has suggested that he will be sent to a concentration camp unless he confesses to his part in it.

Actually he knows nothing of it, nor indeed do any of the orderlies beyond the obvious fact that something is going on. Goldman is more than usually unhappy today because the fear of a concentration camp is added to this being an early anniversary of his mother's death. Could I as a Christian pray for him, a Jew? Jehovah! the All Highest was the Name! I had to minister to the Jewish wounded and dying a year ago, and used a Jewish Book of Offices. Now I prayed with him to his satisfaction and joy, and to my own amazement I never prayed more truly in my life.

MONDAY 31 MARCH

Drew five tins of salmon from the store. While doing so I heard from a Polish kitchen officer that one of their number is under suspicion. They think it impossible for their escape groups to have been so successfully broken up last Thursday except by the betrayal of a stool pigeon.

SATURDAY 5 APRIL

A terrific clatter in the *Hof* at midnight sounded to my slowly rallying senses as though the whole German Army was on our doorstep. Actually there were not more than twenty officers and guards engaged in a search of the canteen and *Revier*. We are without even a rumour to explain a search so urgent.

Have submitted my diary from 30 May to 18 October, rewritten on foolscap, to be *Geprüft*.

The gaol-birds came out at 2 p.m. I put on a celebration supper — tinned steak, peas, and cherries. Dick will have to take over again tomorrow. I'm tired of his job — at least, of his orderlies. With the exception of Smith and Goldman, they do nothing willingly or well.

## SUNDAY 6 APRIL

A representative of the American Embassy, whom none of us has seen before, set all the escapers by the ears, and left them dumbfounded.

In the sacred name of escapology every crookedness is made straight, every lie has the virtue of truth, and even treachery is transformed into honour by association with that sacred science. And today the visitor profaned it.

In spite of his six-foot, fourteen-stone figure, a pea would have bowled the Colonel over when, in reply to our 'moan' that five hours' exercise a week is not sufficient, the American said, 'You would get more exercise, and other privileges too, if you gave up the idea of escaping. Anyway, it is quite impossible to get out of Germany, no matter how you try.'

He could not have said a more blasphemous thing to out-and-out escapers. Our two groups regard him as the most outrageous fellow since court jesters went out of fashion.

## WEDNESDAY 9 APRIL

We — non-combatants included — had our photos and our fingerprints taken. The fingerprint expert is from the Berlin Criminal Investigation Department. There were amusing scenes when several officers proved thoroughly obstructionist, pulling faces before the camera, smudging fingerprints, and what not.

## SATURDAY 12 APRIL

At morning *Appell* the French Senior Officer, notified the absence of a French officer. The Germans wondered if he was still somewhere in the *Schloss*, perhaps trapped in a tunnel he could not leave without revealing its whereabouts.

They brought out the *Schnüffelhunde*, but with luck he was a good distance away by that time. The day's exercise was cancelled on his account, but no one grumbled.

EASTER DAY
'A search!' In a trice the escapers were out of bed, hurriedly hiding maps and clothes. The ingenuity is astounding. I had never dreamt of such hiding places: nor had they until one thing led to another.

At the end of the search honours were about even. The Germans had good finds and big misses.

MONDAY 14 APRIL
In the French quarters last night they still had their lights burning at 10.45. The night sentry reported them to Hauptmann Priem who came up to see what it was about. Hearing his approach on the stairway, the man who had been entertaining in his birthday suit hurriedly switched the lights out, but failed to make his bunk before Priem's torch picked him up in his nakedness.

'Where was the light coming from?' asked Priem.
'It radiated from Me!' said the French officer.
'From you?'
'Yes, from Me!'
'All right, take up thy blanket and follow *me*!' commanded Priem, and the path they followed led to the cells where the Luminaire smothered his light for the night with a blanket.

Lieutenant Josef Just, a Polish officer who left here a week ago for hospital treatment, escaped over the hospital boundary wall a couple of nights ago, but was recaptured and brought back in the middle of this afternoon. He had evidently hurt his feet, for they are bandaged and he walks with two sticks. The first report is that he dropped in the dark from a great height on to loose rubble which sprained his ankles and cut his feet.

WEDNESDAY 16 APRIL
A day crammed with interest and enjoyment. Three of the

six new arrivals are good companions of the Spangenberg days.

They were all members of a company of British officers sent to a reprisals camp at Thorn in Poland. According to a report in *The Camp* a few weeks ago, the reprisals were because of the crowded and bad sanitary conditions of German officers at Fort Henry, Ontario. The judgement of the six who escaped from Thorn, and are now here, is that the reprisals were at least adequate. All the rooms in which they lived were underground, and exercise was very restricted.

The three RAF officers, Flight-Lieutenant Donaldson and Flying-Officers Thom and Flynn tried to escape from Thorn by passing as German air mechanics and stealing an enemy plane. The other three are Lieutenant Hyde-Thompson, who escaped from Thorn and was free for eight days; and Lieutenants Cheetham and Davies of the Fleet Air Arm who were strolling round the moat embankment at Thorn, making a reconnaissance, when they saw a tunnel running through the embankment, and crawled in to discover what they could. Davies was the first to pop his head out and, doing so, looked straight down the muzzle of a machine gun. Neither of them had the faintest idea of the identity of the escape team who had made the tunnel, or whether they intended using it at an early date. Such is the secrecy attached to these things.

## SATURDAY 19 APRIL

The *Gefreite* who is usually in charge of the half-dozen *Posten* who keep a wary eye on us when on exercise is a most trying fellow. He is a short, wizened man, fortyish, with a rasping voice, and for days past he has done his utmost to provoke an incident. On several occasions tempers have been severely ruffled by his insulting manner, but the Colonel has consistently jumped on any sign of rebellion.

This afternoon, matters came to a head. The French officers lent us a football and, having been without one for some time, we were more exultant than usual. Our number is increased by six, so we picked new teams and set about as good a game as the ground permits.

No matter how well managed, the ball is sure to leap the eight-foot fence several times during play. Rupert, in a brilliant defence, kicked it over in the first two minutes. I was in the near goal and, as on a score of previous occasions, I opened the gate and ran out of the enclosure to retrieve the ball and put it back into play. The *Gefreite* became very offensive, and refused to let me pass, but fingered his revolver and tried to thrust me back into the enclosure minus the ball.

So we dropped into line, and marched back up to the *Schloss* where we could ask to see Priem and enter a protest. The *Gefreite* disliked the turn the events were taking, but we refused to be cajoled and deflected from our purpose.

The day's fresh air and exercise were lost, but the Colonel has put in an *Antrag* complaining of the impossible situation that had arisen, and mentioning several previous unpleasant incidents about which no complaint had hitherto been made.

TUESDAY 22 APRIL
Since the beginning of March homosexualism has occupied an increasingly large place in contemporary prison humour, and jocular references to masturbation are freer than is usual among healthy-minded adults. The arrival of a quantity of Oscar Wilde and Frank Harris literature has given a certain piquancy and openness to the discussion of perverse sexualism.

There are, of course, other contributory reasons for it. There are the essential inhibitions of camp life, and the presence of a young officer who is attractive to men — that is, to men who in these conditions are susceptible to homosexual inclination.

It is safe to say that among the British at the moment its worst manifestations do not amount to more than coarse humour. Erotic discussion among the junior officers is much the same as — but perhaps a little grosser than — the usual Varsity common-room talk.

## SUNDAY 26 APRIL

In obedience to a common urge we all gathered round the piano at 9 p.m. last night and sang until we were breathless. Remembering that my now ill-fitting denture always fell down when I sang 'Any Old Iron', and that the company finds entertainment in my misfortune, I was dragged forward and mounted on a stool to do my turn. When, in response to encouraging yells to make it snappy, I made it snappy, the denture dropped out; but the official catchers failed lamentably. My teeth hit the floor and were smashed to pieces. In RAF parlance it is a 'gi-normous' nuisance, for I can't chew my food, or hold a pipe, and — worse still — I have a lisp that is variously described as 'coy', 'fetching', and 'cissy'.

After *Lichts aus* there was still much roistering which might have continued for some time if the disorderly house had not been suddenly shocked into sanity. Storie-Pugh was standing at the dormitory window holloa-ing as though he were with a puppy pack in a spinney on a November morning. Suddenly a bullet splintered the glass and buried itself in the ceiling while Storie ran for cover. I have no idea what the sentry on the eastern ramparts thought it was all about, but he evidently felt drastic measures were necessary.

The Colonel will make a proper complaint about the shooting.

## THURSDAY 8 MAY

At a few minutes to eleven the British quarters were in a fever of excitement. A working party of French orderlies was carrying shavings-filled palliasses down our stairs from the store immediately above. There was a guard on the stairs, and another on the horse-drawn lorry in the *Hof* on which the palliasses were being loaded. Where the palliasses were going was of small significance; sufficient that they were passing out to the other side of those gates.

The parable of the wise and foolish virgins had come to

life. Anyone whose escape gear was complete, who had made his maps and managed to lay hands on some German currency and a civilian disguise, had a speaking knowledge of the language, and — what was more important — could be ready in two minutes, had golden opportunity by the forelock.

Some who could manage a bit of German, but had lost vital items of gear in the last search and had failed to make the loss good, were in a frenzy of despair and self-reproach. Others, like the foolish virgins, tried to borrow from officers who were less careless over hiding, and more industrious over making. But half a dozen fellows were ready in the proverbial half minute, the attention of the guard was sufficiently distracted, and a palliasse on its journey down the spiral staircase was diverted for a second into our quarters.

Peter Allan was thrust in and covered up among the wood shavings, and bundled down the stairway and on to the lorry. The *Posten* decided the load was sufficient, and the orderlies roped the load on the lorry, the driver clicked to the horses, and Peter Allan escaped! ... Always provided, of course, that the palliasses have gone to some place from which he can get out and away. He had next to no food and very little money. It is to be hoped he has plenty of luck.

The lorry arrived again at 2 p.m. Hyde-Thompson possessed the necessary qualifications in largest degree, so he was the next to go. The French orderlies refused to cooperate, thus decreasing the chances of success. But it had to be tried, and Hyde-Thompson was palliassed.

Rupert and one of our own orderlies carried him down, and would have hoisted him on the lorry but that there were six feet and about twelve stone of good British manhood in that palliasse. A push in the middle from a French orderly would have supplied just the little bit needed to lift him the necessary five feet. Alas! The two Germans who were superintending the operations observed the unusual weight of the palliasse, and made them put it on the ground by the wall. If only they had turned their backs for a moment it could have been whipped back up the staircase and Hyde-Thompson extricated. But they stood obstinately in the way; and when an *Unteroffizier* came along he groped among the shavings and found a man.

Hyde-Thompson crawled out covered with shavings and dust and grinned sheepishly. He was taken to the evidence room where presumably he was examined and searched. He had been pretty slick, for though he had come out of the palliasse like a shot once he was discovered, he had had time to conceal his escape gear — except his clothes — in the shavings, from where Rupert later recovered it.

An emergency *Appell* was not called until 5.15 p.m. We borrowed a Belgian officer to make up our number, hoping that he could slip back to the French ranks — where Belgians are numbered — to put their count right also. It proved impossible, and the whole show blew up. Identity card files were brought out and the French gone through first. Each officer was compared with his photograph, and all were found to be correct. We followed in turn, and Peter Allan's photograph — one of the first alphabetically — was without an original.

Tonight we are wondering how far he has got, and wishing that he had more food and money. It has been an exciting day for people for whom even simple excitements are rare. How does one settle down to the dull monotony of *Gefangenschaft* after all the exaggerated living of the battlefield?

SUNDAY 11 MAY
Service as usual at 10.30 a.m. Three of the six freshers swelled our number to ten.

Pat and two of the moles seem to be contemplating suicide. Pat's faith in his stars is leading him and his coterie to underestimate German diligence, and to think anyone dim who disagrees with his latest notion.

There is no change in the situation of the tunnel, except that the whole *Schloss* is now floodlit. That, however, is a sufficiently large and insuperable difficulty in itself: so large indeed as to make the tunnel quite useless unless work

106

is resumed and carried on under the floodlights — and that would mean an entirely new scheme at a much greater depth.

It seems to me, as an outsider, that the soundest policy would be to regard the whole thing as a dead loss and think of something else. But now a spice of intrigue has crept in which has thrilled Rupert to the marrow and made Pat cock-a-hoop — and left a few others of us in gravest doubt. A night sentry, whom they engaged in conversation when he visited our quarters a few nights ago, professed himself to be very browned off. He indicated that he would gladly put his rifle in the combustion stove, and said that he wanted to go home to his mother with whom things were very bad — little money, little food, and so on. As a result of this conversation, and a later one which left the impression that he was not averse to helping their escape for a price, they are considering — have considered — buying his assistance and his honour as a German soldier for a few hundred marks. It is a wild hope which leaves me stone cold.

This particular sentry has not been on inside duty before, and it is amazing that on his first visit he is able to slip away from his companion and be left alone with British officers. It so happens that for the next fortnight he will be posted for night duty at the exact point at which they would cross the eastern ramparts after leaving the tunnel. Let him know the time, and he will engage the only other sentry who might see them in conversation so as to enable a clean getaway.

These things could only be regarded as coincidental by very credulous people. If I were in charge of a special camp for escapers I should be extremely careful of the character of every soldier of the guard. But no matter how careful the selection might be, one or two unworthy fellows might escape the first scrutiny, but they would be so afraid of the consequences of disloyalty as to make a few hundred marks a very insufficient temptation. I have no reason to believe the Germans have been careless over their choice of guards for a *Sonderlager*, or that they would err on the side of leniency with a soldier who helped the enemy in time of war. Furthermore I don't think that a fine strapping young fellow like the *Posten* concerned (he looks as though in civil life he might be a policeman) is likely to be fonder of enemy officers than of his own country and people.

MONDAY 12 MAY

Midnight *Appells* are no longer a curiosity, but this morning's 5.30 *Appell* was a new and unwelcome one — until we discovered what had happened.

Lieutenant Michael Surmanowicz and another Polish officer were serving a sentence in the punishment cells for being caught on the *Schloss* roof prospecting for ways to escape. Last night they broke from the cells, and before leaving tapped on the door of a cell where Flight-Lieutenant George Skelton, a South African who went straight into cells when he arrived last night, was sleeping. Skelton woke suddenly to the questions, 'Who are you? Do you want to escape tonight? We are just going.'

Skelton didn't want to escape. Apart from having neither food nor gear, he hadn't physically recovered from his last escape for which he was completing his sentence. (This information we got later in the morning from a clandestine conversation.)

Surmanowicz and his friend then made a very enterprising attempt. After letting themselves out of the cells, they scaled the wall of the guardhouse — a height of forty or fifty feet — crossed the roof and, by means of a sheet rope, let themselves down on the other side. At least, Surmanowicz did, but his friend scraped the wall with his boots and raised the alarm which led to their capture after about two hours' liberty. The *Appell*, I suppose, was to discover how many people were involved, and whether any had got away.

WEDNESDAY 14 MAY

There were five new arrivals yesterday, four of whom are British: Lieutenant-Commander Stevenson, Squadron-Leader Paddon, Flying-Officer Forbes, and Lieutenant

Neave.* Neave, a barrister, was at Spangenberg. They have all come (post escape) from the reprisals camp in Poland. The fifth officer, a Belgian major, is an incredible fellow, and his crime is as incredible as himself. I was so astonished at his story that I asked him to show me a copy of the charge for which he was punished and sent here.

Oflag VIIb
Punishment

Kmdtr.                    Eichstadt 12.3.41
Camp Order no. 341

I punish POW Major F——— with ten days' confinement because on 2.3.41 he captured a cat, not belonging to him, and on 4.3.41 did share in the unnatural consumption of the same.

2) — POW Lt W——— with fourteen days confinement because he killed a cat, not belonging to him, in a way cruel to animals, cooked the same, and together with Major F——— consumed it in an unnatural way, although the menu for POWs is excellently prepared and abundantly apportioned.

Signed Feuerheerd, *Oberstleutnant* and *Kommandant*

The bi-monthly American Embassy visit occurred today; an old man suffering from some kind of paralysis which made the lifting and lowering of his legs and feet, and indeed his arms also, a very uncertain and slow process. His idea of helping to ameliorate our lot was expressed in the momentous enquiry: 'Have you any difficulty here over getting married by proxy?' He was obviously displeased with the mirthful answers he got, but a question more remote from our immediate needs it would be difficult to find.

The camp is rapidly filling up. The French contingent numbers a couple of hundred, and the British increase by ones and twos daily.

*Lieutenant Airey Neave (whom Platt refers to as 'Anthony' in subsequent diary entries) made one of the few successful 'home runs' from Colditz. As a military barrister he played a significant part in the War Crimes Tribunal at Nuremburg, and later became Member of Parliament for Abingdon.

**THURSDAY 22 MAY**

The Germans opened another room to serve as a dormitory for the new arrivals. Several officers of field rank now add their dignity to our company, and the first evidences of their presence are a) a wish to organise everything and us; and b) to separate the sheep from the goats by making the new dormitory not a new arrivals' room, but a room for subalterns.

Truly the way of subalterns is hard. A search was sprung on us at 2 p.m. Teddy had been careless enough to have seventy *Reichmarks* in his pocket, and Stevenson and Paddon lost some in the same way. Other officers are not a little angry. *Reichmarks* are difficult to come by, and that officers should carry them on their persons instead of depositing them in one of the two safe hideouts is unpardonable.

Much of the tunnelling kit and a quantity of escape clothes were found and confiscated. The camp authorities had a fairish day.

Our only source of consolation tonight is Peter Allan's escape. It is twelve days since he got away, and with reasonable luck he should have crossed the frontier. We are pretty certain he has made it, otherwise the news of his recapture would have been told to us with immense satisfaction.

**MONDAY 26 MAY**

Nervous tension and excitement are in the air, and in every preparation that is made. Even those who are not of the actual escape party are caught up in a whirligig of emotion. It is more intense because we must maintain a calm exterior.

**WEDNESDAY 28 MAY**

We began the day's excitement with a cinema show at 8.30 a.m., an innovation by Dr Eggers. Eight-thirty on a spring morning scarcely suggested a cinema show without violence to natural desire, but violence has long been done to our natural desire, and since none of us had seen a film for over a year we trooped up to the top floor of the *Saalhaus* carrying stools and benches. We watched the process of life from the word 'go' of a garden pea in one film, and a dragonfly in another. We then had a film of peasant life in the Austrian Tyrol.

A mess meeting was held in the late afternoon to fill the jobs that will be vacated tonight by the moles. I refused to be appointed kitchen officer.

THURSDAY 29 MAY

Royal Oak Day, and the day for which the moles have worked all winter!

They had hoped that the cleaning and painting of our quarters which was started a week ago would have been finished by now, but it began again in real earnest this morning, and the guard who accompanied the workmen — there were two today — was far too amiable to be entirely ignorant of the day's significance.

Ten British and two Poles are due to make a break immediately after evening *Appell*, but the plans for the day have carried far too smoothly, I fear. To begin with, all escape gear, clothes and food, had to be in the tunnel before noon. To get it there, packs and rucksacks made from old trousers, tunics, or any available material, had to be carried through the room where the *Arbeiters* were arbeiting and the *Posten* postening. But the *Posten* was a most accommodating fellow. Each time one of the ten was ready to pass through the room with his pack bulky under a greatcoat which was thrown over his arm, the *Posten* walked over to the window and looked out at the rain. The moment the carrier and pack were through, he tired of raindrops and returned from the window looking as bland as the Colonel manages to look on set occasions.

Downstairs Dixon Hawk allowed them to pass right under his keen nose as though he had been nick-named after that famous detective for nothing. In the middle of the morning the 'bribed guard', who is already in possession of Rm100 and will receive the remainder once they are out, came up to our quarters to change the time of the getaway

111

from 9.30 p.m. to 9.50. He affected to be nervous and stood behind a bookcase, sheltering from the eyes of the guard with the workmen. But I saw an exchange of glances as he came into the room, and the workmen's guard became intensely absorbed in the rain again.

I went into the dormitory to Pat who was just ready to take his pack to the tunnel and said, 'Pat, the Germans know!' and told him what I had seen, and what I was sure it meant.

'Oh, go away,' he said angrily. 'You're trying to put the wind up us. We've got to see it through now.'

I said no more, for it is not my business. But one of the original moles has resigned and Flying-Officer Forbes, a recent arrival who speaks German with some fluency, has taken his place.

Two of the escapers have been in the tunnel since noon, putting each man's pack in the order in which they will leave the hole. They are due to be let out at 4 p.m.

FRIDAY 30 MAY

At four o'clock yesterday it was raining hard, and the sentry who usually strolls about the *Hof* stood sheltering within a few feet of the tunnel entrance. He was relieved at five, but his relief took up the same position.

How to get him away was debated in hurried council, and in a few moments British and Polish officers were taking exercise in the *Hof* in the pouring rain. After a round or two, several of them drew alongside the offending sentry. He just couldn't stand for that, so he pushed off into the rain and strolled to the other side of the *Hof*, giving just sufficient time to release the entombed and close up the mouth of the tunnel again. So far so good. But the growing fear that those two were not going to be released in time had filled one or two of the team with sickening apprehension.

We said our goodbyes while they fed just before *Appell* — the Colonel, Harry, Dick, Rupert, Kenneth, Hank, Pat, Storie-Pugh, Geoff The Navy, and Norman Forbes. When I shook hands with the Colonel and Dick, and told them they would be in London in a month, they both smiled and winked. Evidently their reactions to the scheme are similar to my own. It would be interesting to know just what they do think, particularly since they are going through with it. For it seems to me that, if one really means to escape, a scheme that has only one chance of success in a million is a waste of two or three valuable months unless the millionth chance comes off.

Everything appeared quite normal at *Appell*. But immediately it was over, and the moles were due to disappear, another sentry took up position at the tunnel entrance. He had to be crowded out as his predecessor had been; and while everybody in the *Hof* made the deuce of a distraction with noisy sideshows, boxing and wrestling bouts, the ten slipped away, one by one, taking Lewthwaite with them. Lewthwaite's role was that of stooge, closing up the mouth of the tunnel after they were gone, and making everything appear as unsuspicious as possible in anticipation of another exodus later.

They were to be advised by signals from our quarters when the coasts were clear; the 'bribee' would appear on the ramparts at a point visible from our windows, and would adjust his hat to indicate that his stage was set. I watched all this from another window, saw the bribee's signal, and knew that the 'all clear' had been passed on.

In the meantime a small group was engaged in making an infernal din round the piano. Through the open window the familiar strains of 'It's a long way to Tipperary' were to echo while they picked their devious way across the brook and through the several barbed wire barricades they would encounter before reaching the boundary wall.

Immediately after the bribee had given his signal there was just a clear minute in which to transmit it to them before the floodlights blazed up a full ten minutes before schedule. A frantic warning was tapped through, but it was too late. They were at the end of the tunnel and coming out.

Pat was first out, and I could see him bent over the hole pulling up his pack when, in a flash, he was surrounded with German officers — from the *Kommandant* down —

and a troop of soldiery. I had been watching carefully, but I hadn't seen where they came from. I only knew that my wretched fears had materialised. Pat was as black as a miner with muck and dust, and down his forehead little pink runnels were plainly visible where the sweat had run down to his eyes. He stood there, smiling as ever, but obviously shocked and mystified. Rupert was following Pat, but he saw what had happened, and he and the rest all scrambled back to the tunnel entrance. They were trapped in the canteen.

Later, perhaps half an hour later, while they were under interrogation in the evidence room, Priem came up to our quarters, counted us, and put us under guard. He was in great form. He had reason to be. Had I been in Priem's position with a coup like that I too would have been on top of the world. He chatted laughingly with us about Pat's black face, and how he thought the Colonel could not possibly have wriggled out of the tunnel.

By midnight they were safely under lock, key, and guard; disillusionment sitting heavily upon them.

When we crawled down to *Appell* this morning their faces were pressed close to the barred windows of the room in which they were locked. We chaffed them sleepily as we passed, and their replies suited their condition. When they were searched last night their escape clothes were removed, and now they all stood in shirt and underpants except two who, being minus the latter, were girt with towels. After *Appell* we were held in the *Hof* for two minutes while they were hurried up to their bunks to dress in the uniforms they had thought to leave behind. Later in the day as many as there was accommodation for were transferred to the cells.

SATURDAY 31 MAY
Peter Allan was brought back this morning. I saw him go into the delousing shed. He is desperately thin and walks with an obvious blister — rather than a gunshot — limp.

Began the manufacture of a pair of shorts this morning. The only materials available are remnants of two khaki shirts and a Portuguese woollen vest.

WEDNESDAY 4 JUNE

Sentence on the escapers was promulgated this morning. Since it was their first break the Colonel and The Navy received only seven days; the others got fourteen.

An amusing situation has arisen over their confinement. Of the half dozen cells the camp boasts, three are already occupied, so the ten escapers will have to do their solitary confinement in company. At present the Colonel and Kenneth are together in a double cell; Harry, I think, on his own; but Rupert, Dick, Pat, Hank, Storie-Pugh, Geoff and Lewthwaite are all together in a largish room immediately under our kitchen. When everything is quiet after *Lichts aus* we are able to talk with them in morse.

This is the seventh day of perfect sunshine, and the *Hof* is agleam with shining, sweaty bodies in various stages of sunburn, rawness, and sun tan. Sunbathing in these conditions is a sweaty, smelly, sticky, gritty pastime from which, after a couple of days, I have excused myself.


SATURDAY 6 JUNE

One of the most miserable affairs during my imprisonment has been the business of the orderlies at IVc. For weeks past matters have gradually become worse. They finally came to a head last week-end.

Lieutenant-Commander Stevenson became senior officer while the Colonel was in cells. It was a pretty difficult task to get the orderlies in any kind of shape — rooms were dirty, insolence was frequent, two of them regularly talked for our benefit about revolution, parasites, etc.

If, when Stevenson stepped into the arena, and by methods honoured by long usage in the Navy, he made matters worse instead of better, it was not entirely his fault. Having drawn up a list of times and duties he called the orderlies together, and addressed them as though speaking from the bridge with the authority of the Admiralty behind him. But the orderlies declared they would take orders from no one but the Germans. With his bluff called in that fashion, there was just nothing more to be done. He has no power to punish disobedience other than by appeal to German authority, and they have made a pretty shrewd guess that he will do no such thing.

He or Colonel German might — indeed, ought to — report the three ringleaders for court-martial at the end of the war; but I suppose the orderlies have banked on a widespread feeling of goodwill once hostilities have ceased, and imagine that an unwillingness to be unpleasant will let them off. So at the moment only three orderlies are doing anything at all (Goldman is sick and in hospital). The job is far too big for three, so officers are compelled to share the work of laying and clearing tables, sweeping floors, and so on.*

Among the officers there has at no time been any lack of discipline. Colonel German has no more immediate authority over officers than over the orderlies; but, apart from an officer or two who loves to appear 'terrible fierce' and whisper in corners, there is an intelligent appreciation of the position, as well as an affection for the Colonel himself. He is precisely the right type of senior officer for a POW camp, and though there are the two 'terrible fierce' ones, there is not one British officer who does not trust his administration.

An immediate consequence of Stevenson's effort to deal with the wretched orderly position came this afternoon. As from noon the orderlies are quartered on the other side of the *Hof* with the French and Polish orderlies. That will at least save us from suffering their insolence, and from their monopolisation of the WCs and wash bowls. And instead of sharing food with us they will draw separate rations and receive Red Cross parcels and other communal parcels on a strictly numerical basis.

*It was taken for granted in the Geneva Convention of 1929 that officers were entitled to servants. Article 22 reads: 'In order to ensure the service of officers' camps, soldier prisoners of war of the same armed forces, and as far as possible speaking the same language, shall be detached for service therein in sufficient number, having regard to the rank of the officers and persons of equivalent status.'

116

The three who have declared themselves ready to continue work will come over to these quarters at specified
times. The others are forbidden to enter the officers'
quarters at any time. The *Kommandant* has been officially
requested to return the malcontents to a *Stalag*, and to bring
other British soldiers to replace them.

SUNDAY 8 JUNE
At noon Flying-Officer Don Thom went into *Stubenarrest*
for five days. He was caught three days ago by the *Rittmeister* smoking while lying in his bunk. This morning the
*Rittmeister* was again walking round when he saw Thom
sitting by a window. He went up to him and said, 'I'm
sorry, but the German soldier who was with me was witness
to the offence and I had to report you. But I hoped the
*Kommandant* would not punish you.'

MONDAY 9 JUNE
The Colonel and Geoff came out of arrest last Friday, and
Peter Allan came out today.

Peter reached Vienna on the sixth day of his flight and,
weary, footsore and hungry, he waited about in the streets
hoping to catch the sound of an American voice. In this he
failed. It was three days since he had eaten, but he would
not have given himself up and abandoned the attempt if his
feet had not been in such a bad state. In the hurry to escape
at only two minutes' notice, he failed to change out of his
light rubber-soled shoes into heavier marching boots, thus
inviting the unkindly Nemesis all foot-sloggers know too
well.

Lieutenant Mairesse Lebrun, a French cavalry officer of
courtly appearance and manners, and the most lavishly
dressed officer in the camp, escaped this morning. His
debonair Don Juan air gave a number of us the impression
that he was at his best in the *Bois de Boulogne* and the
*Champs Elysées*; but his bold bid for liberty has raised his
stock by fifty per cent.

It was an unsuccessful effort, for he was recaptured on
a village railway station ten kilometres away.

## THURSDAY 12 JUNE

The large increase during recent weeks of French and Belgian officers made a rearrangement of quarters necessary. They changed places yesterday with the Poles, and within a couple of hours two Polish subalterns — as agile as cats — were exploring the roof. It was a stupid prank for, being day time, they were quickly spotted and the guards were ordered to shoot. They were through the skylight in a jiffy.

Our escapers finish their fourteen days tomorrow. This morning they were visited by the Berlin CID official, who is now in the uniform of an army officer, and told they would be released at 10 p.m. tonight. They objected strongly, saying that their sentence did not expire until tomorrow, but if the room was required for another purpose they should be released at the proper hour today. A compromise was finally reached, and they came out at 5 p.m.

## SATURDAY 21 JUNE

We stood astonished, wide-mouthed and goggle-eyed as load after load of food for the French was deposited in the *Hof*. Nineteen tons! That is almost a hundred-weight each. It is a gift from the Vichy Government and was not, therefore, subjected to the sedulous examination given to British and Polish parcels.

A gift of 900 packets of Gauloises cigarettes and a large quantity of French army biscuits was made to us, and presumably to the Poles and Belgians also. It was indeed a generous gesture.

## SUNDAY 22 JUNE

What a day of emotional excitement this has been! Rumour was rife before morning *Appell* that Russia has declared war on Germany. Several Polish officers claim to have heard the announcement over the radio at 7 a.m. The atmosphere was electric. The German *Lagerstaff* would go no further than to admit the radio announcement.

All afternoon the *Hof* was full of standing and promenading groups obsessed with the one topic. Promenaders bumped into standers, and standers obstructed promenaders. Most people (especially the British) forgot to be polite, except the French whose social manners, now they are no longer marching and have accustomed themselves to the idea of being a conquered nation, are utterly irreproachable.

The Poles are our only source of information about the type and quantity of war equipment and the immediate war potential of Russia. We sent out a news agent to collect and collate such information as was available. It was read out to us at supper, and followed by discussion, prophecy, and bets on how long Russia can withstand the might of the German army.

### MONDAY 23 JUNE

All yesterday the atmosphere was charged as though it was heralding an electric storm. It began immediately after *Lichts aus* when, from the other side of the *Hof*, a carolling voice breathed into the still, confined air the strains of the 'Volga Boatmen'. I grinned, as did scores of others. It was a good joke. Within a trice a score of voices wailed the lugubrious 'Yoho heave-ho', and within seconds more several hundred songsters leaned from the windows and joined in a dolorous crescendo which reverberated round the walls.

The guards on duty are of a new detachment which took over a few days ago and are not yet *au fait* with the drill of an officers' camp. Perhaps on such a day a Russian song made them feel hot under the collar. One of them pulled himself to his full height and in the interval between the singing of patriotic songs of first one nation then another, told everyone in plain *Deutsch* to get to bed. In response the voices rose and fell in lively imitation of an air raid siren.

Then the storm broke. The whistle of falling bombs, the roar of dive bombers (what lungs some of these fellows have!), with — in the background and heard only at intervals — the song of the Russian river-folk. For twenty

119

minutes it was pandemonium in which everyone shared. Then someone, with the idea of adding realism to the show, bomb-whistled loudly and from a great height sent a beer bottle crashing on the sets below. It was followed by a second in which the beer had been well shaken, and the crash was appropriately louder. Cries of protest went up from almost every window, and no more were dropped, but the *Hof* was gay with newspaper-folded gliders which shot gracefully across the fifteen or twenty paces to the other side, and then petered out on the ground like falling stars.

Most of us were uneasy about the bottles. They were capable of the worst interpretation. But I am persuaded they were not meant to intimidate the guards, and did not drop near them. One of the Germans, however, went to the guardhouse to seek advice and help. An *Unteroffizier* returned with him, and after examining the smashed glass shouted something that was lost in the infernal din of battle songs, war-machine noises, and screams as of terrified women.

Then three officers and several NCOs arrived, and Priem, after looking at the mess of the broken bottles, called for what was presumably silence, though his voice was lost in the hideous noise. He tried again, with no better result. Then the order to shoot was given and, quick on the draw as the guards were, we were out of the windows and crouching on the floor a good deal quicker. Rifles cracked and bullets ricocheted, spattering the walls and splintering window panes. Silence! It was as still as a grave. POWs, more than most men, know the respect due to active fire-arms.

*Appell* was called, and we all trooped down to the *Hof* and fell in. Instead of being harangued as we expected, Major Menz, the second-in-command, called upon the senior officer of each nationality to line up before him. Then he said, 'Throwing bottles at sentries is not gentlemanly behaviour. In future you should not expect to be treated as gentlemen.'

He did not address us, the rank and file, but dismissed

the parade forthwith. Once back in our quarters the Colonel addressed us and, the typhoon being spent, no one was sorry when ordered to his bunk. The net results so far today are: radios disconnected, no newspapers delivered, all exercise cancelled.

Some time about noon Micky Surmanowicz, who has just finished his punishment for breaking out of the cells and scaling the vertical wall of the guardhouse, rather than have the whole camp strafed vicariously, confessed to Priem that he had dropped the two beer bottles. Courtyard gossip has it that the real culprits have failed to come forward and Micky has done so *pro bono publico*. Courtyard gossip, however, is worth little.

WEDNESDAY 25 JUNE
It is amazing how narrow the line is between successful and unsuccessful escapes. A French officer, Lieutenant Boullet, hit upon an audacious scheme to get out of camp. He is a man about fifty years old with a fresh complexion and a bald head. Perhaps his fresh complexion was the father of the idea.

He fell in for exercise with the British-Polish contingent at 2.30 p.m. We saw he was a French officer but, if he passed muster with the Germans who number and look over the parade before we leave and when we return, we were content.

Half way down the path to the exercise enclosure a middle-aged woman passed along the edge of our lines, walking briskly and branching to the left down the cause-way as though she would go out of the *Schloss* grounds into the town of Colditz. We thought her to be a soldier's wife or mother who had been allowed to visit the *Schloss* and was now returning. In crushing past us as we were marching double file in the narrows of an archway she dropped her wristlet watch almost under Paddon's feet. He was march-ing next to me and he stooped to retrieve it and called after her, but she took the left fork and disappeared down the causeway. The guards evidently thought as we did, that she was a visiting *Frau*. The *Unteroffizier* in charge detailed one of them to follow after with the watch.

When we reached the exercise ground those who had marched in the middle of the column told us how, at a blind corner in the path Boullet changed his dress and sex in a split second. He was just behind one guard (they usually march on our flank at a distance of seven paces) and, before the other turned the corner, Boullet was facing him and walking briskly in the direction of the causeway and the main gate.

We, from the rear, were able to furnish the miserable tidings that one of the rear guards had been dispatched hot-foot after him with the watch. Paddon was desperately sorry for his unwitting part in the matter, but if any of us had been aware of the enterprise the wretched watch would have been ground to powder under someone's heel.

This is not the first occasion on which a too well guarded secret has proved to be the flaw in an otherwise perfect plan. Within ten minutes we were paraded for a count, and needed no further intelligence of Boullet's capture.

Since Micky's confession the radio is on again, and the newspapers restored.

My upper denture came today: it is neat and very comfortable.

### WEDNESDAY 2 JULY

Lieutenant Mairesse Lebrun, who is still undergoing punishment for his last escape attempt, escaped again this morning while on exercise. He was walking round the exercise enclosure quite normally with his five fellow-prisoners when, without a second's warning, he flashed over the nine foot fence and ran like a stag for the boundary wall. Bullets ping-g-ged about him and thudded in the fence, but he reached the wall and cleared it in safety.

By the time one of the guards reached the wall and clambered to the top, sitting astride it with his rifle at the ready, Mairesse, with the instinct of a wild thing, had manoeuvred to put a hillock with a clump of trees between his own flying figure and the line of fire from the guard. He had evidently learned much about the lie of the land

122

and the barbed wire traps from his last attempt.

The guards, fortunately for him, had other prisoners to shepherd and march back to the *Schloss* before the alarm could be given. That gave the fugitive a few minutes in which to operate any decoy plans he had in mind. He would not have taken such risks if he had not believed his plan to be a pretty sound one. It was a brilliant piece of daring for which the Germans are bound to feel admiration.

### SUNDAY 6 JULY

The church, which has been closed since a Polish officer was found working underground, was re-opened for worship this morning.

### TUESDAY 8 JULY

Received a tobacco parcel. The tobacco situation has greatly improved in the last five weeks. Most smokers have a store of twelve or sixteen ounces of good Virginian pipe tobacco, and a reserve of 200 cigarettes.

The book situation is also better. We have a library of about two thousand volumes covering most subjects of general interest.

### WEDNESDAY 9 JULY

Perhaps a morning cinema is to become a regular feature of camp life, but if the war lasts too long the supply of films suitable for the entertainment of POWs may peter out. This morning's pictures were Life in Friesland, and Life Aboard a Trawler.

A rumour that Mairesse Lebrun was caught yesterday some sixty kilometres away has filled everyone with dismay.

Early this evening an iron bar about three feet long was stolen from the spot in the *Hof* where two *Arbeiters*, under the surveillance of a guard, are laying a drain. Both workmen were giving their undivided attention to making a sound union between two drain pipes. The guard too was engrossed when suddenly he missed the crowbar and saw someone — whom he took to be 'Errol' Flynn — disappear suddenly up the British staircase. Errol was shaving when the guard appeared, and the search was fruitless.

Earlier in the day someone had remarked what a useful bit of tunnelling kit a crowbar would be. At the moment of its disappearance there was such a crush of prisoners pressing in to watch the union of the pipes that it would be difficult to say where the crowbar went unless one actually saw it go. I think the *Arbeiters* and the guard were the only ones who didn't witness its disappearance. And it is amazing how soon a crowd loses interest in the high art of laying drains.

MONDAY 14 JULY

At the 'Bishop's Palace Night Club', an informal gathering of about half a dozen after lights out, every subject on earth is brought under weighty review. Hobling, who is a bachelor, and careful of what subjects he lends an ear to, sleeps (both of us are in our bunks during the sessions) when topics of which he disapproves come up for examination.

Rupert uttered a very mild blasphemy — a part, indeed, of his regular speech, and certainly milder than scores of army epithets and expletives that have gone unchallenged — but Hobling took exception to it and rebuked him as though it were a big and bad thing. Several rejoinders were made, mostly in Rupert's defence, and the session came to an abrupt end.

FRIDAY 18 JULY

Micky Surmanowicz is attending a courtmartial in Leipzig today. The charge, I am told, is of the attempted injury to guards by throwing bottles. A defence fund, officers contributing five marks each, was raised last week to secure the services of a local Colditz solicitor to watch Micky's interests. The solicitor is rumoured to have been a POW in England in the last war.

TUESDAY 22 JULY

Micky has not returned from the trial at Leipzig. Yesterday

his clothes and personal belongings were gathered up and taken away. There are three conflicting stories about his punishment: that he received four months; that he got two years; that he got four years. Admiral Unrug, the senior Polish officer, has not yet had the official report of the result of the trial.

Paddon received his notice of court martial this morning. His trial is fixed at Leipzig for the end of August. The charge is of insulting a German *Feldwebel* by calling him a *Schweinhund*. Paddon's defence is a complete denial. He did not, he claims, call the *Feldwebel* a *Schweinhund*, but rebuked him for treating him, Paddon, as though he, Paddon, was a *Schweinhund*.

THURSDAY 24 JULY
Sixty odd Dutch officers arrived here this morning. We welcomed them heartily but — goodness knows — there are sufficient of us already to make the *Hof* like a theatre queue. Almost six hundred officers and orderlies promenading a *Hof* measuring thirty-five paces by twenty.

SUNDAY 27 JULY
Forty of the Dutch officers were present at the service this morning, and the body of the little family church was filled to overflowing. About half a dozen of them have Methodist connections. They were more or less familiar with the psalms, hymns and tunes, but the majority were unable to share the words of worship. We must make an effort to find some common ground by next Sunday.

The British congregation has increased substantially with the continual arrival of new officers.

TUESDAY 29 JULY
Attended the initial lecture of a series on the history of Poland. The lecturer's jumping-off date was 1500 BC: a month or two early, I thought.

WEDNESDAY 30 JULY
At *Appell* the Colonel was told that the church was closed for a fortnight to the British and the Dutch because last

Sunday a prayer was offered for the Dutch Queen, mentioning her by name, and desiring that her enemies may be driven from her land; and at the close of the service the British national anthem was sung.

The singing of the national anthem has never been in question before; it has been our custom to sing it after every service other than the communion service. Nor, indeed, has the mention of royalty by name been questioned; It would probably never have arisen now but for Hobling's addition concerning the Queen's enemies. Poor old Hobling! He will suffer to the end of his days for his lack of tact.

## THURSDAY 31 JULY

At two o'clock this morning the British quarters were full of the noises people make when they are trying to be as quiet as possible. They were the echo of the success a team of junior officers had met with in the making of an escape hole. It is a hole which goes down the centre of one of the wide buttresses on the outer wall of the subalterns' dormitory, and the breakthrough on the ground floor comes out in one of four lavatories in the German quarters. The team had thought another fortnight's boring would be necessary, but they unexpectedly struck ground level and, while testing the wall where they were to break out, applied more pressure than was necessary and actually burst through before they meant to.

Their escape gear was by no means ready but, since a hole was now made that would be obvious to anyone going in to the lavatory, they had to escape quickly or the scheme would be lost. So the door of the lavatory was bolted on the inside in the hope that anyone finding it bolted would assumed it to be occupied within the sphere of its rightful use. It was rather a lot to hope for — as anyone who has shared a set of men's lavatories well knows. The general talkativeness when men so foregather — if they are not reading books — is only matched in a common room or bar parlour. But the team needed at least ten hours to finish their part-made escape clothes, so they planned the escape

126

for noon, hoping that everyone except the guards on duty would be at lunch.

The team was composed of Peter Allan, Don Middleton, 'Errol' Flynn, Hyde-Thompson, Teddy Barton, Tommy Elliott, Alan Cheetham, Lieutenant Verquest (a Belgian), and two Poles; and at twelve noon the first pair were lowered into the hole. The schedule provided a space of ten minutes between each pair because getting clear from the lavatories would need a reconnaisance in stockinged-feet (boots slung over shoulders) of the German quarters until they found a room with a bar-less window which did not open immediately under a sentry's nose. Meanwhile we leaned unconcernedly against the window-bars in our own quarters and saw first one figure and then another dart furtively away until, by one o'clock they had all got away.

It looked as though a scheme which most of the older officers had described as hare-brained had, right under their very noses, worked with the smoothness of a good watch. The original team of ten had gone and seven opportunists were now going to follow. Some more of the old hands were beginning to collect their gear. Hurried counsel was taken about getting away as many as possible, and bringing in some of the other nationalities.

Well, the original ten are back with us now, feeling a little chastened and worn out. We heard their story when soon after two o'clock, *Herr Inspektor* brought them trailing back through the main gates like sheep that had strayed from the fold.

The first pair, it appears, once at the bottom of the shaft listened intently for sounds of hostile presences and, deciding that none of the lavatories was engaged, crawled out and made their way into the fortunately empty corridor. Hurriedly but stealthily they crept along and took the turning at the end. In a flash a posse of officers and guards appeared behind and before, and they were hustled into a room and divested of their escape gear.

Two of the guards dressed rapidly in their clothes and went out to show themselves fleetingly in our line of vision: hence our conclusion that they had got away. It was quite impossible for those first escapers to warn other members of the team to hold off, so each ten minutes saw another pair arrive, baffled and bewildered, and the Germans going through the same procedure, until the whole team stood in the room.

Rather more than ten minutes elapsed before those opportunist escapers — who were deceived by the apparent success of the scheme — were ready to take advantage of it. So this longer than the customary interval led *Herr Inspektor* to leave his hiding place and take a peep up the shaft to see if any others were following. Two were just on the point of descending, but when they saw the colour of a German uniform they withdrew from the hole with the speed with which other burrowing fauna usually descend.

The ten who were caught would have gone into punishment immediately if that accommodation was not already so grossly over-booked, but there were already advance bookings. Some of today's adventurers will do their punishment in a couple of months' time unless they make a successful escape before then.

## Monday 4 August

A dull day with lowering skies, but the British quarters were full of animation.

Lieutenant 'Bertie' Boustead, a six-foot-four-and-a-half Harrovian, and Flying Officer Don Thom, a full foot shorter, were putting the final touches to their escape gear.

In this instance the Nazi salute was part of their equipment, and the drill was highly amusing. Bertie is a delightful but extremely sensitive fellow, fresh down from Oxford, and far too ready to divide his attention between half a dozen people at once. So many were gathered about him giving him conflicting advice on the angle of the upraised arm and the disposition of the wrist and so on that Bertie, the only one in deadly earnest, was producing something that crossed between the Soviet clenched fist, the Nazi salute, and the *bonhomie* wave of a French peasant.

Their get-up was the easy sportswear of a German soldier on leave: an open-necked shirt on the right breast of which a Swastika had been carefully pencilled, shorts, boots and stockings. The idea was quite well conceived, particularly since the actual break was to be made while on exercise this afternoon.

They broke rank at the point where Boullet had suddenly changed sex, and turned to walk back, as he did, while the main column continued to move forward. They negotiated that bit all right and were making for the causeway when Bertie foozled a salute to an *Unteroffizier* who became suspicious of so hybrid a greeting, and engaged them in conversation.

Now they are back with us, but on the preferred list awaiting private accommodation.

TUESDAY 5 AUGUST

The outstanding events of today were, first, an order from the *Kommandant* forbidding exercise to all British officers, non-combatants included, except in the crowded *Hof*. The reason given is that the walk to the enclosure is used for escaping. Second, an order forbidding Hobling to conduct British camp worship. This is because of his prayer for the Queen of the Netherlands, and that her enemies should be driven from her lands. Heard is now appointed Church of England chaplain for Oflag IVc. And the singing of the national anthem is also forbidden.

WEDNESDAY 6 AUGUST

The *Rittmeister* gave Colonel German notice this evening to provide sleeping and living space in British quarters for twenty French officers who will arrive on Friday morning. They are also to be awarded two of our four lavatories.

We are now forty-nine in number, and thicker-on-the-clod than is comfortable. Everyone is highly incensed about it, and the Colonel has prepared a telegram to send to the American Embassy.

THURSDAY 7 AUGUST

The *Rittmeister*'s twenty French officers turned out to be twelve British officers who arrived this morning. They are

E                          129

all young men who tried to escape by jumping from a moving train when *Oflag* Vb at Biberach was being conveyed to Tittmoning. They have the distinction of contributing the camp's tallest man in the person of Lieutenant 'Rex' Harrison who stands six-feet-six-and-a-quarter inches in stockinged feet. Two of the others, Lieutenants Lace and Price, are a mere six-feet-four.

In a recent search my packet of copying leads* was confiscated. I was not aware of this until this morning when I threw away a stub and went to the locker to get a new one from a packet I bought in the canteen about a month ago. Of course I knew at once what had happened. Copying lead has proved a very popular dye for making pyjamas into dungarees for escape purposes.

I saw Dr Eggers in the *Hof* and went down to ask about them. He laughed, and so did I. The *Rittmeister*, who was also there, asked how many pencils of that kind I had possessed. I said, 'About a dozen.' 'Oh,' he said, 'So you are one of them!' I was about to answer, 'Well, you treat me as one, so why shouldn't I be?' but I trapped the words before they were out. They would not have helped the purpose I had in mind which was to reach an agreement whereby I could get a supply of copying leads to continue my diary. An arrangement was finally made which permits me to get a new lead on production of the stub of an old one.

The rumour that Mairesse Lebrun had been captured sixty kilometres away was entirely without foundation. Instead he has the distinction of having made the first (so far as I know) successful escape from this camp. A letter bearing a Swiss postmark which arrived from him today merely said he had arrived and would write later.

SATURDAY 9 AUGUST
The repatriation of a number of French officers left two rooms in the *Saalhaus* unoccupied. Our two colonels and a

---

*Most of the MS diary is written in what was commonly called a 'copying' or 'indelible' pencil.

dozen majors were moved into the more palatial quarters at noon. It has left us with considerably more space, and has given us a new senior officer, Major D. W. A. Cleave, acting for the Colonel.

## SUNDAY 10 AUGUST

An interesting situation arose this morning apropos Heard's and Hobling's attitude to religious practice. A week ago yesterday, when von Linden came to enquire about the non-conformist service, I explained that the British denominations had joined forces, and introduced him to the C of E chaplains. Their first enquiry, after saying welcome to the services, was about the Dutch Reformed competence to partake of Holy Communion. Von Linden replied that it was the practice of their Church to take communion about once a year. That was very evidently a heresy that needed correcting.

The Dutch again offered the hospitality of their quarters for the church service (this is the last of the two Sundays on which the *Schloss* church is closed to us) at no small inconvenience to themselves. We gladly accepted, knowing well how great the difficulty would be of fixing our own room and our own non-church-going officers.

It was the C of E day, and Heard and Hobling talked together and decided that Holy Communion would be very fitting. Since it was neither the first Sunday in the month, nor the last, I can only think the decision was one of two things: a way of escape from preaching a sermon in un-usual surroundings; or an attempt to correct the Holy Communion heresy.

The net result was: five British officers were present, all of whom communicated; forty Dutch officers were present, none of whom communicated.

## MONDAY 11 AUGUST

The first production of the International Entertainments Committee took place last night. It was 'an instrumental concert' and proved exceedingly popular. A Dutch guitar quintet was recalled again and again for their Hawaiian music. The more classical contributions, Mozart and Wagner, were from French violins.

I am feeling very confined, and hungry for a freer view than the stone walls of the set-paved *Hof* provide. To me, at any rate, the prohibition of official exercise is a great hardship.

SATURDAY 16 AUGUST
A *Sonderappell* was called at 5.15 p.m. The absence of six Hollanders has been discovered. They have been absent for three days to my certain knowledge. The *Rittmeister* took the first *Appell* from which they were absent, and we were all on our toes watching for any signs of suspicion. But he dismissed the parade, and all was well.

Three of the six are reported to have escaped, and one of the three to have been recaptured. The other three are in hiding, either intending to escape shortly, or holding themselves in reserve to fill up the ranks at *Appell* when others escape.

WEDNESDAY 20 AUGUST
Fifty-four Yugoslavian troops are quartered at the *Schützenhaus*, the building in which the baronial militia of the *Schloss* were housed in the days of ancient splendour. The news of their arrival there reached us by underground about a fortnight ago, but today open intimation of their presence came by way of a letter to the Colonel. It was from the Yugoslavian senior officer, *Oberstleutnant* Serg M. Altuhov, asking if the British officers could relieve their necessity in the matter of food. For four months, the letter said, they have existed solely on German rations, and they are in very poor physical condition.

A mess meeting was called, and after Major Cleave — acting for the Colonel — had read the letter, he said that the Colonel thought a gift of twenty parcels out of the fifty we have in the store would be welcome. Someone moved thirty, and finally the whole fifty were unanimously voted to them. A further vote called for gifts of cigarettes and tobacco and any such private stores as could be spared.

The secretary of the Red Cross at Geneva wrote a letter a month ago (when our numbers were only twenty-seven, and we are now over fifty) saying that we might expect winter delays in the delivery of parcels and should aim at building up a reserve of four parcels per person. Our present total is not one per person, but we knew hunger at this time last year and, though we may know it again, the immediate concern is that our Yugoslavian comrades know it now.

There is one fly in the ointment which has greatly agitated several members of the mess. The *Schützenhaus* is reported to be a collaboration centre. The French officers here are the ones who seem to have this information. There are no British at the *Schützenhaus* and, before the Yugos came, it was solely a French camp.

Seven new orderlies arrived last night from a camp in Sudetenland. They say they have been working eleven hours a day in the coal mines. They have eaten us out of house and harbour this morning, and almost as thoroughly denuded our wardrobes. Three of them were entirely without underclothes and socks.

FRIDAY 22 AUGUST

Major Cleave announced at breakfast that he would receive private gifts for the Yugoslavs at 11 a.m. I asked if the fifty parcels had been sent. 'No,' he replied. 'The Colonel decided to send twenty only.' And in answer to persistent protests he said, 'Anyway, the parcels aren't yours.'

'Oh yes they are,' several voices cried. 'Our people pay for them, and we can dispose of them.' The resolution to send fifty was restated.

Later in the morning, after Cleave had spoken with the Colonel, he told me that twenty had been sent as a first consignment, and others up to fifty would be sent within the next fortnight.

THURSDAY 28 AUGUST

For weeks Anthony Neave has had no thought for anything but tailoring and dyeing. A month ago he conceived an

133

escape scheme of great audacity. It consisted of passing out of the main gates in the uniform of a German soldier. Since the time the maggot first entered his brain, every minute has been dedicated to 'getting ready'.

The major difficulty was that of getting the German uniform. He might steal it — it could be done at a pinch — but if the escape were to prove abortive, and he was caught wearing it, a very unpleasant situation might arise. So, on reflection, it would be better to take the long route and make it: and during the period of making, nothing else has existed in the world.

With an unethical fertility of invention he got hold of a mixture of several incredible substances which produce a lightish field green if applied to a khaki material. It is not quite near enough for daylight use, but under artificial light it is quite indistinguishable from the real thing. The dyeing experiments have occupied a full three weeks.

His Swastikas, woven on tunic and hat, were extraordinarily well done. So was the belt, a creation in cardboard and tin that deserved a better fate.

He put his wit and audacity to the final test after *Appell* tonight when he passed out of the main gates — jackboots and all — with the duty officers and guards. He looked the part perfectly. Indeed, it wasn't his appearance that gave him away, but the behaviour necessary to getting away. Once outside the gates the guards just stood about waiting to fall in and march back to their quarters. Neave couldn't possibly do that. His only hope for success lay in an unobtrusive disappearance from the immediate scene, and then to walk rapidly down the causeway to the outskirts of the village.

Alas, he was spotted as he disappeared under the first archway, and was called back by the NCO of the guard. He affected not to hear, and perhaps perceptibly quickened his step. The NCO ran after him, shouting excitedly. Neave had not made sufficient distance to warrant making a hit or miss dash for the open country, there wasn't a chance in a million that he would get twenty yards without being shot. So thus failed a very worthy effort.

It is now past 10 p.m. and he has not been returned to us.

## FRIDAY 29 AUGUST

Priem announced at morning *Appell* that the *Engländer* Neave had joined the Germany army and had been given the rank of *Unteroffizier*.

Neave returned to the British quarters at noon. He was detained a long time in the *Kommandantur* last night and told, among other things, that the impersonation of a German soldier is a very serious offence, meriting a court-martial.

## SUNDAY 31 AUGUST

The Queen of the Netherlands' birthday! The Dutch officers were very keen to hold a celebration service this morning, and we were equally anxious to meet them as far as possible. When we were making arrangements for it earlier in the week I found myself responsible for prayers in Afrikaans.* I wrote a special prayer and submitted it, in accordance with the requirements of Camp Orders, to be *Geprüft*. It was returned yesterday with all the references to the Royal Household deleted and forbidden.

I have never, to my knowledge, stood before a so religiously, nationally and socially cosmopolitan crowd: RCs of five nationalities, Non-conformists of three, and C of E; peoples of six nationalities — if Jews can be counted as representing a nation; and two generals, an admiral, titled noblemen of France, Holland, Poland, and all military ranks from general to private. The church was crowded, even to the servants' gallery which is right up under the ceiling of the church like 'the gods' in a theatre.

The service just had to be over by 11 a.m. to allow the ceremonial opening of the International Sports Competition. At a fanfare of trumpets the representative companies, in national costume and bearing national flags, marched out in order: Poles, French, Belgians, Dutch, and British. They stood in double file before the President of Sports,

*Platt had worked for two years in South Africa just before the war.

Colonel Schubert, who had with him as patrons of the contest General LeBleu, General Pishkor, and Admiral Unrug.

Colonel Schubert delivered the introductory oration in Polish, and called upon interpreters to re-deliver the greeting in French and English. There was much clapping of hands and cheering as the national Sports Presidents stepped forward to notify their countries' entries in the events. It was all very Olympic and in the best taste until Bertie, who is the British Sports President, called on the British contingent to dismiss from the playing pitch so that the inaugural game might begin. The other nationalities had been well-rehearsed and dismissed in magnificent style to the quarter of the *Hof* ascribed to them. But Bertie's boys bungled the command 'right turn', some turning one way, some the other, and finally they dismissed in wandering confusion. It all looked so unmistakably like an ill-conceived joke — and of course we had to laugh it off — that some of the other nationalities, the Poles in particular, were a little peeved.

The British Débâcle was the conclusion of the ceremonial opening, and the first game, Poles *v.* French, at volley ball, began. Though set out and conducted in Olympic fashion, all the contests are games played with a ball: volley ball, handball, football. But so as to increase the number of events, teams of different strengths play the same game; e.g. football is seven-a-side, nine-a-side and eleven-a-side. The play was fast and furious all day.

The British position in sports at close of play — four events lost.

MONDAY 1 SEPTEMBER
At 6.30 p.m. the sports were in full swing when Priem stepped through the needle's eye and ordered the *Hof* to be cleared for fire-fighting practice. We dispersed to our quarters and watched the main gates swing open to admit a horse-drawn fire-engine. While the fire-brigade was engaged in winding up the fire-escape ladders and running out hosepipes a second man-drawn engine crawled in. The second brigade got to work winding up their ladders and

paying out the hose. All this, occupying about twenty minutes, was done to the accompaniment of five hundred *Gefangeners'* cheers, catcalls, and imitation dive-bomber roarings.

When the ladders, set in the middle of the *Hof*, were finally mounted, and the firemen swaying like birds in a tree-top, the main hose was passed through the camp kitchen window to connect with the water hydrant. In the process Colonel German, Anderson and Paddon were unearthed; they had been prospecting in the kitchen basement for a possible way of escape. Leaning from our open windows we were astonished to see them emerge, and cheered wildly as they were led away for interrogation. We were all the more amused because a few days ago the Colonel had openly rebuked another British officer for arousing suspicion by unofficially entering the kitchen in pre-arranged pursuit of a tennis ball. 'There was nothing the officer could not be told about the kitchen if he enquired from the proper authority, etc., etc., which would not raise unnecessary suspicion.'

The embarrassed prospectors dealt with, the main hose — which fed the long hoses from a five-point union, was finally connected to the hydrant, and hundreds of gallons of infuriated water shot in twin torrents from the two of the five points that were hoseless. Even louder shouts and jeers came from the *Gefangener* mob and we were quickly chastised. Once in action, the hoses were simultaneously turned on the jeering figures wedged in the open windows. Dozens were well-baptised before they could unjam themselves and get the windows closed.

Then followed a catch-as-catch-can race in which the windows were opened temptingly and remarks hurled at the firemen before the window was slammed again. Sometimes the man at the hose won. By a dexterous switch of the nozzle he would send a spouting stream flushing through the window before it could be slammed to. More often the men at the windows won, and stood grinning through the glass, signalling their triumph with gesticulating hands. On two occasions the impact of water on glass was of such force as to smash the windows and flood the rooms. The humourists were not so taken with that and quickly surrendered the position.

Actually it was a tremendous diversion. The honours were about even, discounting Priem's bag of one colonel and a brace of majors. To me it was a welcome relief from the tension created by the dead seriousness with which the sports contests are being fought.

After two days' play I think that unless radical change of attitude occurs shortly, the Poles in particular, and the French less particularly, will come to regard these sporting events as matters of national honour. It will be unfortunate because allies in a prison camp can't afford to become separate units, and because bloody wars are fought for national honour. When the proposal for the competition was first put to the Dutch, Belgians and British it was accepted as something to enjoy and laugh about.

### SATURDAY 6 SEPTEMBER

A new French officer arrived at noon yesterday, and within half an hour the whole camp was in a fever of excitement. He was recognised by several officers as an undesirable, and was segregated by the French themselves. He was not admitted to the French officers' mess, nor allowed to sleep in either of their dormitories. His bed was carried out into the corridor.

The *Kommandant* wisely arranged his exit at noon today. Most people were eating their midday meal, but a belligerent handful left the table to boo him out of the *Hof*. He smiled his way to the main gates and, before disappearing, sprang to attention and, still smiling, gave the French salute.

His salute infuriated them almost beyond endurance. He was lucky he was out of reach. I have no idea what his offence was or is. He may be a stool-pigeon or a collaborator.

### THURSDAY 11 SEPTEMBER

A Dutch officer was married today by a means entirely new

to me. It appears he wrote out an application and posted it to the Dutch army headquarters stating his wish to marry Miss Someone on 11 September at 11 a.m. He received a notice a week ago saying the necessary arrangements were in hand, and he could consider himself married at that date and hour. And now he is married!

SUNDAY 21 SEPTEMBER

A ceremonial closing of the International Sports Week was timed for 10.30 a.m., but was delayed by a man-hunt for two missing Dutch officers. At eleven o'clock the quest was abandoned, and the Sports Committee very fussily set the stage for the award of diplomas.

Most of the British contingent had not yet breakfasted. From the day of the opening and with increasing determination as the 'national honour' nonsense became established, they have refused to take the contests seriously.

A fanfare sounded at 11.25, and the Polish and French companies marched out in resplendent style to double file smartly before the President and patron.

In our quarters Bertie was making a frantic effort to get his company away from the flesh pots and on parade. The Dutch were five minutes late, and the Belgians and British were ten. Eyes full of displeasure were turned on the ragged, out-of-step British company (three of the twelve were unshaven) as they marched to their appointed stand. As an accompaniment Storie-Pugh, who was an interested spectator seated on a windowsill, slipped the brake off the gramophone he was nursing, and a few bars from a Sousa march played by the Grenadier Guards broke over the *Hof* with a tremendous martial spirit. It brought a roar of laughter from Dutch, Belgian and British spectators.

Under *Sportführer* Boustead's brilliant leadership, the British officers' teams had lost every event. British order-lies who, for obvious reasons, were not told of their officers' attitude to the competition, felt ill-at-ease for Britain's fair name, and went all out to win their own football event: which they did win with a liberal margin of goals. To them fell the only British diploma.

The Olympic week is to be wound up tonight in grand style with an International Concert. As chairman of entertainments, the Olympic Music Festival has been Dick's pigeon.

Last week he threw out the suggestion that eight or nine persons would be sufficient for each choir: they would have the stage for about twenty minutes, and the programme would be arranged accordingly.

The first rehearsal brought trouble. Nineteen young Dutch officers presented themselves. The Poles arrived with seventeen. The French had confined themselves to the number suggested but, on seeing the Dutch and the Polish, they were very nettled and went into a huddle for five minutes. Then they approached Dick and complained heatedly that, by allowing the Dutch a choir of nineteen and the Poles seventeen, Dick was 'besmirching the honour of France'.

I was highly amused. The incident promised interest, for Dick is never in a hurry over words until his usual urbanity is disturbed. He tried to get a quiet word in, but they were all round him, all making their contributions at once.

After a couple of minutes I saw the dark red I was watching for creeping up the back of Dick's neck. Another minute or two, and they would hear things about national honour that diplomats usually avoid mentioning. But another French officer, Lieutenant Lamidet, spoiled my fun by interceding with, *'Qu'est ce que c'est ceci de l'honneur nationale? Les Anglais sont les seuls prisonniers ici avec de l'honneur nationale qui reste, et ils n'ont que quatre personnes à chanter!'**

The discussion was pursued no further beyond an assurance from Dick that they could put the French choir in the body of the theatre and the audience on the stage if they liked.

*'What is this about national honour? The English are the only prisoners here who still have any national honour, and they have only four persons to sing!'

**MONDAY 22 SEPTEMBER**
'Let the people sing', and by Jove they did. Lugubrious national songs — sad as sad can be. The pathos and pain in both words and music was almost unbearable.

Our contribution was very much out of place, though two of the other nationals described it as providing 'comic relief'. We sang for England's honour: 'She was one of the early birds', written by an Irishman; and a sea shanty, 'Spanish Ladies'.

**WEDNESDAY 24 SEPTEMBER**
Reserved accommodation in the cells is likely to be less pleasant as from today. I prepared the 'prisoners' food' (as it is called, as though we were free men) and sent it down to the camp kitchen to be served with rations at 4 p.m. It was returned with the instruction that food can no longer be sent to prisoners undergoing punishment. I went down to the kitchen and was told it was an OKW* order, so there is nothing to be done.

**THURSDAY 25 SEPTEMBER**
Almost a score of French officers left *Oflag* IVc this morning to be repatriated. They stood in their ranks of five, after we were dismissed from *Appell*, for a farewell speech. At the close of the proceedings *Hauptmann* Priem stepped forward with a hand extended to Colonel Marq, and thanked him and them for their *'Mitarbeit'* — with-working, collaboration! There is much speculation as to the significance of that!

**MONDAY 29 SEPTEMBER**
I am making this entry in the midst of fever-heat excitement. In the day room officers are bunched together in anxious conversation. People who think their opinion is important keep up a constant procession from one group to the next, putting forward the important opinion.

The explanation of all this is the theft of a civilian coat.

*Ober-Kommando der Wehrmacht*, the German High Command.

An *Arbeiter* engaged in unloading a piano we were buying for the theatre took off his coat to roll up his shirt
sleeves and, in a trice, the coat was gone. The work of
unloading was suspended at once, and a *Sonderappell*
called. Priem delivered an ultimatum in which he said it
was known the coat was in Dutch or British possession. If
it was not produced in three minutes (he held
his watch in his hand) the piano would not be installed,
certain other musical instruments for which the full price
was not yet paid would be removed, and the theatre
closed.

The three minutes ticked away, the coat was not produced, the parade was dismissed, and the motor lorry
bearing the piano joggled over the sets in the *Hof* and
disappeared through the main gates while the prisoners
cheered.

Between this and the regular evening *Appell* the Polish
Admiral tore a strip off Dick in true naval style. As theatre
manager Dick had been warned by Priem that the theft of
civilian clothing from the *Arbeiters* concerned would be
punished with the loss of the piano and the closing of the
theatre.

Evidently Colonel German had also been talked to,
otherwise his attitude at evening *Appell* was quite inex-
plicable. He stepped out in front of the British ranks and
said that his request made earlier in the evening was a
military order, and if the coat was in the possession of a
British officer it must be handed to him before *Appell*
tomorrow.

The coat *is* in the possession of a British officer, hence
the anxious discussion of some grave questions. In view of
the Colonel's order on the first of July that a stolen civilian
hat should be returned to Priem on the grounds that it was
personal rather than military property, and the present
order about the coat, what is the Colonel's attitude to
escaping? Why has he bowed to foreign opinion?
Should one, in present circumstances, obey one's country
and do all possible to escape, or obey the officer who —
perhaps temporarily — is in British command? And if one

should disobey the order and escape successfully wearing the coat, would one get an MC or a rocket on arriving in England?

## TUESDAY 30 SEPTEMBER

At about one o'clock this morning an almost unanimous agreement was reached. First, it was thought that the Colonel's order was a mistake; but it had been given in the presence of other nationalities in whose eyes, if it were not obeyed, it would cast a serious reflection on his senior-officership. Second, disobedience would reduce the officers to the level of certain orderlies who, knowing the Colonel could not punish them, refused to honour their own oath of service or his position and authority as senior British officer. Third, but it should be pointed out to him that the order is obeyed under protest, officers having it specially in mind that the order was given in the presence of other nationalities who would observe the course of British military discipline.

The officer who is the British escape *chargé d'affaires* was instructed to convey coat and message.

But the affair is settled very amicably!* Everyone is satisfied — I mean prisoners, of course: except perhaps the Admiral.

Most people are concerned about the loss which the *Arbeiter* (a quite innocent person) has sustained, and trust some way might be discovered in which he can be compensated. All escapers would gladly subscribe *Lagermarks,* but such action would introduce a state of things the German authority could never concede. Such an agreement would mean that an actual purchase of civilian clothing had been allowed.

## MONDAY 6 OCTOBER

Storie-Pugh (the Germans pronounce it 'Poog', a pronunciation we have been quick to cotton on to) went into arrest

*This sentence conceals a mystery, for the coat was not returned: see diary entry for 7 October. Perhaps it merely passed voluntarily out of *British* possession?

for twenty-eight days. At the bottom of his bunk he chalked 'Flat to let. Owner back in 28 days'. The sentence is punishment for an attempted escape over the roof that he and a young Dutch officer failed to bring off.

TUESDAY 7 OCTOBER
Yesterday the beginnings of a tunnel were discovered in our lavatory-wash-house. Six weeks ago the concrete floor was neatly cut through at a point near the outside wall and a slab, about 2 ft x 1 ft 6 in, taken out in a single piece. It made a perfect lid for the hole, and when operations were not in progress it fitted snugly in position. With dust brushed carefully into the crevices at the lid edges, it looked innocent and natural.

However, a civilian who evidently knew his job was engaged to go round with Priem, testing walls and floors. His test on the lavatory-wash-house wall revealed the presence of a hollow somewhere nearby. Finally he located the exact spot, and the lid bounced merrily. When it was lifted a gaping cavern was revealed, and also the much-quested civilian coat and a number of tunnelling tools. They were taken out and placed at the side of the hole while further investigations were made. The hole was found to contain nothing more, and the booty was gathered up to be removed — but the coat had gone. It was a slick piece of work right under their very noses and Priem himself, though the loser, could not fail to admire it.

(The point that gives me pause is how all this acquired skill may be expected to react when the war is over and first-class *Gefangener* crooks are turned loose on society.)

As a result of the discovery of a further tunnel, a search was made in the subalterns' dormitory at midnight. I woke to the noise of rending timbers and wondered what on earth was afoot. A small band of *Soldaten*, under the direction of *Hauptman* Priem, were ripping up floor boards to expose a tunnel several feet long. Exactly eight feet away a British team has a working, perhaps half as far advanced as the one found. Today they are cursing themselves for not having prospected more carefully and thus made use of what may easily have been an inheritance from the last war.

## THURSDAY 9 OCTOBER

Two RAF officers, Squadron-Leaders Lockett and McCohn, were marched through the gates and taken to be searched while we were on *Appell*. They had an interesting story to tell about trying to get to Sweden from the German wharf at Lübeck. They succeeded in finding Swedish ships — colliers — that were homeward bound, but were unable to bribe the captains or mates. There are heavy penalties for neutrals who help POWs get away.

Under cover of darkness they stowed away on different boats, and Lockett had the bad luck to be discovered before his boat left the wharf. McColm was about eighty miles out of Lübeck when he could stay awake no longer and began to snore audibly. He was uncovered and told — apologetically, he thought — that he would be handed over to the German pilot when he came aboard in the morning. Swedish ships plying between Germany and Sweden are under German pilotage and escort because of the mine-fields, and they only travel by daylight.

## FRIDAY 10 OCTOBER

The rumour giving four years as Micky Surmanowicz's sentence for the bottle-dropping affair was confirmed by official notice at morning *Appell*.

'It is a bit of very bad staff work that got Micky four years' . . . 'It was the Admiral who ordered him to plead his guilt to the *Kommandant*' . . . 'You can't blame the Germans for imprisoning a stormy petrel. Blame those — or him — who made Micky confess.' That was courtyard gossip during the day. There is a strong courtyard rumour that the Admiral will resign as Polish senior officer in favour of General Pishkor. The only comforting thought is that the war is unlikely to last the sentence out, and a general amnesty to all POWs is likely to be one of the first evidences of peace.

MONDAY 13 OCTOBER

We had notice to parade in the theatre at 8.15 a.m. for a speech from the *Kommandant*, Colonel Schmidt. He arrived at 9.10, accompanied by *Hauptmann* Priem, and Dr Eggers who acted as interpreter.

'Your senior officer,' he began, 'has some days ago submitted to me some wishes and I will answer them and make a declaration.

'At first I want to give you the declaration of the position here. You have fought against Germany as our enemies, and done your duty as soldiers against Germany. You have had the misfortune to become prisoners of war and are now in the power of Germany. Now you are here you form a new community of *Oflag* IVc of which I am *Kommandant*.

'Until now I have always taken you here as comrades, and I have softened the hardship of your stay here as far as possible, and I will do so further. My first duty as *Kommandant* of the camp is to keep order. I expect you to understand fully the difficulties of this duty. There are special difficulties in the camp because of the different elements composing it, and it is very difficult to keep order.

'Now I will speak of the special difficulties your *Oberstleutnant* has submitted to me. I was compelled to forbid the daily walk because some officers tried to escape during the walk. I would like to state that this is no collective punishment, but only taking from you a special favour I had granted you. You have missed the favour for a time, but now I am ready to allow the walks to you again. I expect you not to escape, otherwise I shall be compelled to forbid them again.

'The second wish of your Lieutenant-Colonel was to give you more room in the castle here. To this wish I have to say that all the rooms in the castle are in use. A year ago more than a hundred more prisoners were in this camp and we had no complaints about room. Besides this, there were less rooms in use at that time. I do not know where to get more room for you. Besides this, I have to tell you that, since we have in Germany some millions more prisoners of war, so it would be quite useless to ask for more room for you.

'The other wishes your Lieutenant-Colonel has submitted to me are of less importance, and on the whole are now fulfilled.'

Colonel German, invited to affirm this, said, 'No, they are not fulfilled. It is an accumulation of smaller grievances that is causing so much dissatisfaction among British officers.'

The *Kommandant* replied by Dr Eggers: 'If you will formulate the complaints, I will hear them in the *Evidenz-Zimmer* at ten o'clock.'

WEDNESDAY 15 OCTOBER
For weeks we have been hoping that someone would fetch up here who was taken prisoner in the Middle East. He arrived today in the person of Lieutenant-Colonel G. Young, a short, live man with a searching eye and quick smile. He has the news we have long wanted: the British version of Greece and Italy, Yugoslavia, Crete, and North Africa.

FRIDAY 17 OCTOBER
A new departure in 'reserved accommodation' was made this afternoon. It is the town lock-up, or gaol, or something of the kind. The Colonel has seen it, and has agreed to its suitability. It is in the village and appears to have been requisitioned by the military authorities. Storie-Pugh was the first British officer to give it housewarming.

TUESDAY 21 OCTOBER
A mess meeting was called by the Colonel to decide how many, if any, of the 500 parcels we now possess should be given to the Poles.

The mess has undergone a marked change of feeling about giving away parcels. There was a suspicion that some may have been promised before the meeting was called, and several people of some influence in the mess spoke against giving parcels away to anyone at the moment. It

147

was suggested that, since there was a need of food among the Polish officers, a meal should be prepared in the British quarters, and those who were well known to have special need could be invited to eat it. Otherwise we had no control over the disposition of the food once the parcels left our hands.

The Colonel suggested that seventy-five parcels should be given to the Polish senior officer, General Pishkor, for distribution at his discretion. A narrow majority finally carried an amendment giving fifty.

It is interesting to observe officers' attitude to food now that we are no longer hungry. The experience of hunger makes most men warm-hearted towards the need of others. But in the case of a number of British officers in this camp, it has not had the effect of making them careful about wastage. So far as the communal drawing of foods from the stores is concerned, reasonable care is taken to avoid loss of any kind. For instance, food of one kind — bully beef, meat loaf, or fish — is drawn daily in just sufficient quantity for the day's needs. But when food is issued to the tables, waste that could be avoided does occur.

Things might be different — but I doubt it — if there were cupboards for each table instead of a shelf on which to keep partly eaten foods like jam, margarine, a cut loaf, etc. The bare boards of the day-room give off clouds of dust when they are swept or during horseplay, and all this settles on the food. In consequence the fly-walk is cut from the loaf — often far too thickly — and discarded. And jam and margarine collect a lot of dust which is skimmed off, again with no small loss.

An attempt at a remedy has been to make it one person's definite responsibility to clear the table after meals, and now each table has a roster for a daily table-stooge. In the absence of anything more hygienic, a sheet of newspaper can cover the jam plate, margarine and loaf. But some officers find the duty irksome — as indeed do we all — and do as little as possible.

I submitted an *Antrag* requesting permission to buy some means of heating the small room (Hobling and) I

148

occupy. 'I will gladly purchase an electric fire or a stove, and will pay for all fuel or current used.' It is a cold, damp room in winter. There are windows on three sides, and it sits like a box nailed to the exterior wall.

## SUNDAY 26 OCTOBER

On *Appell* last night Priem was overheard saying that Churchill's nephew would arrive in the camp *'Morgen früh'*. We wondered which of the great War Premier's nephews it would be. There are two in captivity.

It proved to be the *Daily Express* correspondent from Narvik — Mr Giles Romilly. He is a civilian of course, and his position in the *Oflag* is unclear. The ostensible reason for his detention in a military *Sonderlager* is his escape in female attire on visiting day from the internment camp at Tost in Czechoslovakia. But it is still highly irregular, unless IVc is a port *en route* to another civilian camp.

From our point of view he is a very welcome guest. He was put to eat with us at No. 1 table. There is a restless look in his eyes, and a droop of discontent at the corners of his mouth: he is by no means a complacent young man. The relationship with Churchill is not of blood, but marriage. General Romilly and Winston Churchill married sisters.

## MONDAY 27 OCTOBER

At morning *Appell* Romilly submitted a written complaint addressed to the *Kommandant* asking for a clarification of his position as a civilian in an *Oflag*. Later today the *Kommandant* made an order to the effect that Romilly would have private sleeping accommodation — in a cell that he would enter each night at 10 p.m., to be released at reveille. Romilly is greatly displeased, and has replied that he will not go to the cell voluntarily.

## TUESDAY 28 OCTOBER

Another midnight *Appell*. At 10.30 p.m. *Hauptmann* Eggers and two *Posten* came to our quarters and called for

149

Romilly. He did not rise or step forward, and they failed to recognise him (he is in RAF uniform) sitting among half a dozen subalterns. A search of dormitories, lavatory-washhouse and kitchen yielded nothing, and they left to report his absence.

An *Appell* was called at which there was much hilarity. The guard was called out, and had the British contingent covered with rifles while the other nationals were dismissed laughing and shouting, and kept up the laughter and shouting in their quarters. Romilly was finally put in a cell, and we returned to our bunks about 12.30.

## MONDAY 3 NOVEMBER
Storie-Pugh came out of arrest at noon. He likes the new cells.

## FRIDAY 14 NOVEMBER
Rehearsals, rehearsals, rehearsals! Mealtime conversation at No. 1 table has been exclusively 'show' for three full weeks.

It is what one might expect since the producer, Teddy Barton, and Anthony, the author of a public school farce, and Hobling, curtain-raiser-in-chief, and Geoff, an actor in three scenes, are all on No. 1.

Anthony provided a little comic relief at tea. While discussing certain obscurities of the histrionic art, Mr Neave of the Middle Temple, barrister-at-law, did cut himself a slice of rye bread little over half an inch thick, and plastered the same with margarine while further elucidating his point. He piled jam on the margarine, and held the thus completed work midway between table and mouth; but being contradicted at that moment he hurriedly thrust it into his trouser pocket and addressed himself to the contradiction.

Typical of Anthony!

## TUESDAY 18 NOVEMBER
The Colonel and Rupert (who has just done twenty-one days for entering in his diary remarks that were insulting) came out of arrest today in time to see the extension

presentation of 'Ballet Nonsense'. As a revue it has proved
a roaring success. On the first and second nights packed
houses demanded another performance, and Priem gave his
sanction to it this morning. So the show was put on again
tonight and excelled the two previous nights. Priem himself
was present for the latter half, but the two *Dolmetschers*
were in their seats from the word 'go'.

The opening number was the title piece: a ballet in
which five strapping fellows of muscular hairy limbs were
dressed in ballet skirts of crinkled paper, and each with a
blazing red brassière on a brawny bear-like chest. Three of
the five wore moustaches. The curtain lifted on kneeling
figures, bare backs to the audience, and arms engaged in
sinuous graceful movement. A crashing swell from the band
brought them to their feet dancing, and face to face with
the audience.

The second number had somehow been mislaid *en route,*
and there was a blank in the programme; number three was
a comic acrobatic turn from Don Thom on 'How not to
play an instrument', and then followed a melodrama in
which Jim Rogers, a South African, won universal favour.

After the interval Anthony's public school farce delighted
the British and fogged the foreigners. It was followed by a
telephone scene, a Highland dance, an Indian dream, and
finally a pub scene at the Rose and Crown in which old
English songs were sung, solo and chorus.

There was a good deal of over-acting, but each scene
was thoroughly alive. It was primarily the production of
sex-starved, virile young men whose minds — perforce —
inclined towards abuse as an antidote. The public school
farce was redolent of masters' perverted interest in small
boys, though one could plainly see that the intention was
a take-off of a well-known headmaster. Paris came to
Colditz in the persons of Peter Allan and Alan Cheetham:
at the wooing call of French costumiers and make-up artists
two striking females were born (though — despite their skill
— Errol Flynn remained at best a hermaphrodite) and in
all the scenes in which their glamour was displayed, they
filled the role of the oldest profession in the world.

151

The Lord Chamberlain would have prohibited it without finishing the script. But values are different in *Gefangenschaft*. This fight against nature, against tortured bodies, and imagination that has become fevered with longing, is a battle no young man should be required to fight. The presence of three padres — two of whom are church-made bachelors — perhaps tones down a little; but small groups meet in the absence of padres, while a smaller group blatantly ignores their presence.

## FRIDAY 21 NOVEMBER

How flat the post-Revue days are. All yesterday the tide was at a very low ebb.

Today the pulse quickened a little in anticipation of Christmas. At a lunch-hour meeting under the Colonel's presidency a 'religious service' on Christmas morning was called for. The *Saalhaus* officers — the colonels and officers of the three services with the equivalent rank of major — said they would like to eat Christmas dinner with us in our quarters.

Last year we were the delighted guests of both Poles and French, but it is agreed by all nationalities that numbers are now far too great to allow any real international gathering.

## SATURDAY 22 NOVEMBER

Escapological activity gave zest to the day. Geoff Wardle once again justified his soubriquet 'Stooge'. In company with a Polish officer he made another abortive attempt. The scheme was good enough, though a trifle desperate for a winter effort.

By a pretty piece of cunning he managed to get out of the main gates with the Poles and Dutch going for exercise. The idea was to get into a water-control man-hole which has a surface outlet in the exercise enclosure.

While a boisterous crowd sought to distract the guards, and a smaller one gave cover, the iron lid was lifted, Geoff and his Polish ally descended, and the lid was replaced. The little effort appeared to have gone well. The crowd dispersed, leaving the two escapers down the hole with their feet on one slimy girder, their hands gripping another, and water swirling below. It was an uncomfortable position they must maintain for three hours until darkness allowed them to lift the lid (if they were not too stiff and cold) and clamber out.

But after five minutes the two-foot square lid was prized up, and they were ordered to climb out. No one seems to know quite from what point the operation was seen, but it is generally supposed to be binocular observation from the *Schloss* windows.

Geoff is back with us now, waiting his turn in the new cells. Everybody who has done a period of *Stubenarrest* in the town gaol considers it a great improvement on cell life in the *Schloss* itself. The place is spotlessly clean, and they are allowed to take a Red Cross parcel with them when sentence begins.

A strange thing occurred this morning, and yet not so strange really. There was an announcement in the German press of the death on the East Front of *Oberleutnant* von Werra, the holder of the *Ritterkreuz* since his escape from Fort Henry, Ontario. He was the first German escaper to make a home run from an Allied POW camp, and we read his story with considerable interest and admiration in the German newspapers some months ago.

Peter Allan called the attention of the mess to the notice of his death, and there was a momentary silence. 'Poor devil, he deserved to live!' If anyone knows the danger and difficulty of making a successful escape, it is every officer in *Oflag* IVc.

SUNDAY 23 NOVEMBER
The Protestant service was at 8 a.m. At nine o'clock I went to the French mass with Pat. There was something very ease-giving about it.

A black night for the British *Gefangeners*, and a bright one for the Germans. They had six in the bag between 6 and 7.30 p.m. Two Canadian Dons, Don Donaldson and Don Thom, were caught scaling the roof; and Geoff,

Anthony, Jim Rogers, and Cyril Lewthwaite were caught in the Polish orderlies' quarters on top of the old *Revier*. Their presence there was believed to have association with the praiseworthy attempt of the two Dons. Actually they were pursuing interests of their own.

## MONDAY 24 NOVEMBER

The four officers who were caught in the Polish orderlies' quarters were released today. Lewthwaite occupied a single cell in the *Schloss*, but the other three were together in a double cell. It was not heated, and their cigarettes were confiscated, and they thought themselves to be holy innocents exposed to the harsh winds of a cold, hard, and unjust world. They decided on the following protest:

> *Achtung!*
> *Dieser Tat ist eine Schandtat.\**
> *Unterzeichnet:–* Rogers, *Hauptmann*
> Neave, Lt.
> Wardle, Lt. RN

It was of little use to write out so high-minded a notice unless it could be suitably displayed, so they picked the lock of the cell door, pinned the notice at eye level on the outer side, locked themselves in again, and went innocently to sleep.

## TUESDAY 25 NOVEMBER

*Appells* have not been characterised by happy relationships lately. For weeks past the *Lageroffizieren* have been trying to give them a more military character, but with little success. POWs regard *Appell* as a German parade called for the purpose of enumeration, not military drill.

The order of count is usually French, Belgian, Dutch, British, and Polish. With the exception of the Poles and Dutch, most prisoners are always late on parade, and deliberately behave in a most unmilitary fashion. I would

*\*'Attention! This is a scandal!'*

write the following of the British only, but it is equally true of the French and the Belgians. Improperly dressed, they arrive late and stand in little knots chatting, laughing and smoking while the count of preceding nationalities is in progress. When the British turn comes, Harry calls us to attention, but by this time the French and Belgians are at ease again and playing high jinks.

Things now appear to be coming to a head. It was several minutes past nine-o'clock this morning before *Appell* was assembled, and after the count an order was made that everyone except the Dutch would parade at 10 a.m. Four British officers who were not out of quarters at the stroke of ten were shut inside by the sentry on the door, and later had their names taken.

The beginnings of a tunnel were found in the end room in our quarters immediately after lunch.

## WEDNESDAY 26 NOVEMBER

A notice this morning at *Appell* that in future all quarters will be locked at the precise moment of Appell. Officers found locked in will be punished by the *Kommandant*.

## SATURDAY 29 NOVEMBER

Someone was afflicted with a brainwave three weeks ago. The idea was to set a watch on, and make a record of, all German activity in the *Hof*. Once all German movements were timed and entered in the book it would be easy for the escapers: everyone would know the best times for working, how much interruption might be expected, etc, etc.

The big boys of British escape frowned deeply on the notion, but they finally yielded to pressure and set the watch going. It was to be an hourly duty undertaken by everyone who would want to have access to the data collated, and for a week or more a non-stop night and day record was made. Then it was confined to waking hours, but extended to two other places of interest, so we had A watch, B watch, and C watch.

This afternoon Colonel Mackenzie was doing his hour on C watch when he was surprised (it is difficult to see how) by Dixon Hawk who confiscated the book. Mackenzie is far from popular tonight — 'What, hadn't he wit enough to save the book?' Each watcher, before handing the book to his relief, had signed it, thus laying claim not only to his part in the scheme, but also to any facetious remarks he felt like entering.

## SATURDAY 6 DECEMBER

For the past few weeks life has been Novemberish, flat and barren. The French are rehearsing a revue which occupies and interests them; but of the old vitality and tenseness, of the old dynamic atmosphere, there is none. Officers have drawn up their stools to the chess board, and — a new departure — a high-stake poker school is flourishing. Teddy was winning Rm1700 the other day. I suppose there is a thrill in winning £113, and something the reverse of monotony in losing it; but neither excitement contributes much to communal life beyond the opportunity to rag one another.

A small mutual masturbation group hold what they hope are secret sessions. Occasionally they are absent at meal times or from a lecture that most other officers attend. Secret gatherings are quite impossible in these crowded conditions. With two exceptions, there is not a British officer in the camp who is not fully aware of the existence of such a group, or who could not name each member.

Two of our number, on several nights since the 'Ballet Nonsense' revue have sat up after all the others were in bed discussing Plato's acquiescence in the homosexualism of his disciples. At one of these late-adolescent discussions they foresaw themselves as founders of a Platonic cult. But actually homosexualism has advanced little since March. It is still in the coarse humour stage.

The fact is that the true life of IVc is in a state of hibernation: the escape season is virtually closed.

## MONDAY 8 DECEMBER

The chief item from the 6 a.m. radio news bulletin trickled into the *Schloss*, and the dormitories were a-buzz long before *Appell*. Japan has declared war on America and Britain; while Britain has done the same in respect of Finland, Hungary and Rumania.

## THURSDAY 11 DECEMBER

Shortly after tea the Poles and Dutch were in hot water. Some unauthorised person had removed the electrician's kit of tools, and the bunch of keys with which he admitted himself to various store rooms.

The loss had happened in the Polish quarters, and while they were being searched a parcel was seen being dropped through a window into the *Hof*. A guard hurried down the staircase to seize it, but arrived only in time to see a Dutch officer disappearing with a bulge under his coat. The two nationalities were called to a *Sonderappell*, and were warned they would be kept standing in the *Hof* until tools and keys were delivered up. Standing in the *Hof* is a double-edged sword: it means the *Lageroffizieren* have to stand there also.

An hour passed this way, and then the Appell was dismissed with the warning that unless the keys were returned '*morgen früh*' no Christmas privileges would be allowed. The keys were obviously thought to be of less importance than an extension of lights and the use of the theatre at Christmastime, so the keys were returned.

## SUNDAY 21 DECEMBER

At an after-lunch meeting we decided to play Santa Claus to three hundred Russian POWs who are quartered somewhere in the village, and presumably are working on nearby farms.

The original motion before the meeting was to make a Christmas gift of one quarter of a parcel each — 75 parcels. An amendment invited the mess to give one whole parcel to each prisoner — 300. A further amendment, the one finally carried, gave half a parcel each for Christmas, and provided for a review of the situation at an early date, with the possibility of making a second gift of a similar number.

In addition to the food parcels, half a consignment of

75,000 Turkish cigarettes was also donated to Russian cheer. These were the princely gift of a number of British ladies living in Ankara.

Our actual parcel position has never been so secure. Our weekly consumption is 0.7 of a parcel each, instead of one full parcel, which is the aim of the Red Cross. So, before any Christmas gifts are made, we have about 680 food parcels, and seven cigarette parcels each of which contains about 1300 cigarettes and several ounces of tobacco. What wealth compared to last year!

## MONDAY 22 DECEMBER

The Colonel was told by Priem this morning that our proposed gifts to the Russians were '*verboten*'. This is a new development since Saturday when Priem said such gifts might be made. The principal reason he gave was that the Russians had typhus and could not be contacted; whereupon the Colonel said the British officers would undertake transport, and would risk infection if permission was given.

An *Antrag* enquiring further into the matter was put in at evening *Appell*.

## CHRISTMAS EVE

Number 6 table held its private Christmas party last night. It was boisterous and loud, which speaks volumes for the quantity and potency of Pop's home-made raisin and prune wine. He was able to procure a little yeast and, with the help of Red Cross treacle, golden syrup, a little sugar and glucose, produced a brew that cost them a pretty dismal hangover this morning.

All seven tables have addressed themselves to the task of producing wine for Christmas, but last night's party has, I think, assured festive moderation. Drunkenness is anti-social at any time, but in crowded community life like this drunken regurgitation is to be deplored.

Our decorations are almost complete. Paper garlands are festooned across the centre of the day room, while the walls are an academy of regimental badges done in watercolour by John Watton. A yew-tree branch stands in the window recess, and is decorated with celluloid dolls and novelties, many from America.

The Christmas present from the Germans was an addition to rations of tinned herrings in tomato sauce. They were the product of an Italian cannery, so for supper on this Christmas Eve we ate two herrings each that had been tinned by one enemy and were the gift of another.

A large consignment of blankets and chocolates is reported to have arrived from Canada. A splendid gift to receive on so wet, cold and blustery a day.

There was some little carolling — not very enthusiastic — when we came off *Appell* at 10.20 p.m. The French had a Nativity play to precede Midnight Mass. I went to the latter and was most struck by the opportunity for quiet thinking while mass is in progress.

CHRISTMAS DAY
Breakfast at 9 a.m. And what a breakfast! Since the end of September all Red Cross tins of bacon and sausages were put in a Christmas cache. At the divide-out this morning there were three rashers and three sausages each, and a pot of marmalade to each table.

The insistence of Heard and Hobling on a service of Holy Communion for Christmas morning — although ameliorated by the inclusion of two carols — kept several officers and orderlies indoors. Little would have been said — except in appreciation — if Holy Communion had been 'as well as' rather than 'instead of'; but many who are religiously inclined here hate the thought of the Saviour being chained to the pain and blood of the Cross on the day of his birth.

Officers waited at table for the orderlies' midday dinner. The menu, again saved up from September, suggested happier days: soup, salmon, pork and beans, Christmas pudding, and coffee. There was Christmas cake for tea at four o'clock, and at 7.30 p.m. dinner was served to the officers by the orderlies. The menu was the same as for the orderlies, but GHQ — the *Saalhaus* officers — dined with us. Numerous bottles of home-made wine and a special 'Colditz Whisky' distilled in a home-made still were consumed with little pleasure and a lot of courage.

## TUESDAY 30 DECEMBER

Winter in real earnest! Heavy falls of snow; ten degrees of frost; snowballing and a slide down the middle of the *Hof*. Gephard sanded the slide some time before *Appell* this morning.

## LAST DAY OF 1941

A day of very small interest until *Hauptmann* Püpcke announced that the *Hof* would be open to us until the time of *Lichts aus* at 1.30 a.m., and that the New Year's morning *Appell* would be at 10 a.m. rather than 9.

We spent the last moments of the old year in conversation and thought, and then, when '41 ticked over into '42, we joined hands with centuries long dead and sang 'Auld lang syne'. The national anthem followed, and we were ready for the evening to close when the Dutch officers, led by Major Engels, who bore a symbolic broom-at-the-masthead recalling Admiral Tromp's boast in 1666 that he had swept the British Navy from the sea, roared in and round our day room, hands to shoulders, in a chanting human chain. On their heels came a bellowing Belgian chain, followed by a shorter international one. National anthems were sung, and it was demanded that we sang ours again.

Official greetings now over, two hundred or more linked hands to shoulders in a giant, roaring train, and swept out over the snow in the courtyard, howling hoarsely on a tour of all the quarters of the *Schloss*. Shouting, singing, hand-shaking, well-wishing — a mad, riotous whirl of goodwill and fellowship. After running up and down thousands of steps on spiral staircases, through low, narrow, and pitch-black passages, through rooms foetid with blackout fug, it was a gift of the gods to get our sweating bodies out in the *Hof* and the snow again.

At this point Dr Eggers, who had just entered the main gate, handled a situation that had all the material of mischief with admirable tact. Indeed, it was a tactful move to detail Eggers for this particular occasion.

The different nationalities were all now in the *Hof* in national groups singing such songs as the emotion of the moment suggested; all the others standing silent while one or other group sang fiercely of home, love, and liberty. Many were expecting that he would stop them singing and drive them indoors, and had he tried to do so he would have had to call out the guard, and to have thrust officers indoors under threat of fire — a bad beginning for the New Year. Instead he paced about until each nation had had its turn, and then stepped forward and said, 'Now you have had your songs, it is time to go to your quarters,' and everyone went without incident or ill-feeling.

And so to bed with the New Year.

# *Colditz 1942*

NEW YEAR'S DAY

And a dismal day too. Lights were extinguished at the main switch at 9 a.m. and not reconnected until 5 p.m., and a thaw, accompanied by low cloud and rain, added considerably to the deep gloom in which we moved. Officers were unable to read or play. Most of them were tuckered out after last night's impromptu party, and either drooped about remembering happier New Years, or went back to bed.

The Anglo-Dutch party was originally meant to take the form of a cabaret and running buffet, and was planned to take place in the theatre. But since the use of the theatre was prohibited, it resolved itself into a plain reception and running buffet in the British quarters. Everyone was polite to everyone; small talk about small things; everyone laughing dutifully. Though a trifle prosy it was a good party, and not quite the anticlimax it might have proved after last night's spontaneous success.

FRIDAY 2 JANUARY

Three weeks ago I introduced Dick to an entry I made in November.* He thought there was some mistake and said how hesitant he would be to make such an entry; but our conversation gave direction to his observation.

I have waited these three weeks with considerable anxiety. If he failed to observe, and decided against my judgement, my plan to short-circuit the miserable business (a carefully-thought-out plan, too) would fall to the ground.

*He might mean the entry for 18 November, but more probably that for 6 December.

However, to my intense relief, he came to me this morning boiling with indignation, having proved the matter against his own wish and will.

He has real influence with a more or less central person in the wretched affair, and is prepared and willing to use it to the utmost. I cannot begin my personal contacts until Dick wins his round.

MONDAY 5 JANUARY
Anthony Neave and a Dutch officer, Second-Lieutenant Luteyn, escaped ten minutes ago. It was a scheme requiring the boldest initiative and at least eight weeks' preparation.* It was carried out with the utmost secrecy, and already they are at least outside the castle.

During the whole of 1941 only two British escapers, Peter Allan and Bill Lawton, succeeded in getting clear of the castle. The British are due for a success, and the seven people who so far know of Anthony's break are fairly confident that this is it.

Dick engaged his man in earnest conversation today. The fellow was frightfully ashamed of his conduct and promised to cut it out. At tea time he asked to see me and made a frank but shame-faced confession. So now the stage is set, and I must attempt as difficult a task as has yet come my way.

Some of those to whom I intend to speak will deny all knowledge of anything of the kind; while one, I imagine, will tell me to mind my own business. But this happens to be my business: I wish it were not! The thing I must avoid is direct accusation, at least in the initial stages. I think I will begin by enquiring confidentially of each of the persons concerned if they have observed any homosexual tendencies, and what do they think of such perversion and of the perverts. The answers will no doubt reveal with what deliberateness or otherwise such practices have been indulged in.

*For an account of their escape see *The Colditz Story* by Pat Reid, chapter XIII.

163

TUESDAY 6 JANUARY

Hyde-Thompson and a Dutch confrère, Second-Lieutenant Donkers, followed Neave and Luteyn a few minutes ago. They too have made a clean getaway. But unless they are fortunate enough to be able to travel by train they will freeze to death. The thermometer outside the guardhouse this morning showed 17°C below freezing.

The 'Bishop's Palace' is an ice-box. Vapour from our breath has condensed on the walls and windows and the interior has a thick coating of frost which is added to every day. When the light is on at night it is like a fairy cave, beautiful and painful to the eyes. But it is like sleeping in a refrigerator, and dressing and undressing produces better goose-flesh than geese have.

WEDNESDAY 7 JANUARY

Dr Eggers and *Herr Inspektor* — and presumably the *Kommandant* — refuse to believe that the four officers missing from *Appell* this morning have succeeded in breaking out of the camp. Our quarters were searched in the belief that they were in hiding.

With luck Anthony and Luteyn will cross the frontier tonight, or be shot in the attempt. So far as Anthony was concerned there was to be no turning back.

SATURDAY 10 JANUARY

Hyde-Thompson and Donkers are back. I saw two guards shepherd them into the shower-baths this morning. They were caught at Ulm, about sixty kilometres from the Swiss frontier.

Inadequate preparation led to their failure. The *Ausweis* which they had, declared them to be Dutch technicians — electricians working in Germany for the German government. Quite a good falsehood, since technicians from all the occupied territories have accepted *Mitarbeit* employment in Germany. But Anthony and Luteyn, making for the frontier twenty-four hours earlier, had shown the same spurious *Ausweis* to the same inquisitive *Mädchen* in the ticket office who had called the same suspicious policeman who had listened to the same story. On the first occasion — doubting — he had allowed Neave and Luteyn to pass; the second time — disbelieving — he refused to allow Hyde and Donkers to pass. They were handed over to the *Wehrmacht* until their story could be proved; but instead of proof came the hue and cry for two Dutch and two English officers who had escaped from *Oflag* IVc. Hyde will get twenty-eight days *Stubenarrest* since this is his third or fourth attempt; and Donkers, for his first, will get seven days.

Have been busy at my sermon all afternoon — St Matthew 4.17, 'Follow me and I will make you'. 'Maker of men' is the title history has awarded to the Son of Man. While possibly Pythagoras, and certainly Plato, acquiesced in a certain perversion of proper conduct among their disciples, Jesus permitted no such unwholesomeness, but demanded manly behaviour such as became true man and child of God. In such conditions as prevail in a POW camp, men who have kept their bodies fit but have neglected mind and spirit may be tempted to unman themselves by taking base and perverted interest in their fellows. The British military and civil codes have only one answer to such an offence. After eighty days at sea the Admiralty may take a more lenient view\*, but to Christian teaching such abuse is always abhorrent. Though the indulgent may cover his nakedness under a hedonist's cloak, nothing is contributed to manliness. But self-discipline contributes the first essence of manliness and avoids those excesses which impair balanced judgement, and leave a man open to the reproach of his own best self. Manhood is not manly if it is muscle plus, mind minus, much whim and little will.

I do not remember ever having been quite so cold as I am at this moment.

### SUNDAY 11 JANUARY

Unhappily the time of worship coincided with the distribution of Canadian blankets and the presence of a photographer and so there were fewer British worshippers than

---

\*A common Army myth.

usual. But enough! During the day several points from my sermon were discussed in the day room. Two or three officers, with Nicodemus caution, spoke to me about it, and gave me the opportunity for forthright speech. I have a feeling of something attempted, something done.

## THURSDAY 15 JANUARY

An announcement at morning *Appell* that at 9.30 a.m. the British contingent would parade in the *Hof* and march down to the *Schützenhaus* where they would spend the day.

A march of about a kilometre brought us to the thickly-woven barbed wire fence of what has long been regarded as a *Mitarbeit* camp. The presence of decorative electric bulbs on two Christmas trees; a domestic cat purring and rubbing her neck in a friendly fashion on our shins; a quantity of *Mitarbeit* literature, together with spacious grounds in which to walk, play football, grow vegetables, and keep about forty Angora rabbits, confirmed our suspicions.

The residents of the *Schützenhaus* were occupying the upper portion of the building, and we on the ground floor were prevented from any contact with them by armed sentries posted on the stairway. A wise precaution! Free contact would have resulted in bloodshed at least, possibly murder. Few people are quite so detested as *collaborateurs*. The officers therefore had no restraints of conscience in availing themselves of *Mitarbeit* flex, lamps and fittings. An intention to introduce pussy to more of the 'best people' of *Gefangenschaft* was frustrated by a prescient orderly who removed her to the safety of the upper storey.

The march back to the *Schloss* took place according to design an hour before darkness fell. Delay tactics failed in their purpose, and several officers were chagrined to find that, after having been outside this ——— *Schloss*, they were still no nearer to neutral territory than before.

The floor of the subalterns' dormitory had received considerable attention in our absence, and the one remaining tunnel found.

**SATURDAY 17 JANUARY**

An echo of our holiday at the *Schützenhaus*! Half the electric lamps were removed from our day-room this morning. The lighting has never been adequate, but it is now double its former inadequacy. Several members of the mess think it is less of a reprisal than an attempt to conserve electricity — an economy symptomatic of worsening conditions in Germany. A further comment is: 'It is worth a little discomfort to have shown the *collaborateurs* what we think of them.'

Seven months of strenuous and dangerous work had gone into the making of the tunnel that was discovered yesterday. The entrance was in a dormitory wall on the fifth storey, and the shaft went down a buttress to three feet below ground level. From there the tunnel went under the building and into the cellar beneath the church, out again through the opposite wall, under the foundation line of the exterior wall, and under the eastern rampart. The exact spot in the *Schloss* park where it was intended to make an exit would have been reached in two weeks' time. It was a terrific undertaking for, until the church cellar was reached, every ounce — and it ran into tons — of displaced earth and rubble had to be hauled up the buttress. The deeper the hole grew, the higher the climb up again, until a depth of 110 feet was reached. And when tunnelling began at that depth every handful of rubble still had to be carried to the top and then to a further distance where it could be disposed of with some safety.

After seven months of undetected activity a successful conclusion was confidently expected. The tunnel face was already forty-five feet beyond the last sentry, and another fortnight's work would have carried it to the agreed point where, on a rough dark night, escapers would with fair certainty be out of sight and earshot. Hope had soared to dizzy heights that quite a number of prison-weary men would be got out on the first night.

Not least of their many improvisations was the rope ladder 110 feet long. It was made of odd bits of wire, knotted handkerchiefs, old trouser-legs, tunic sleeves, and what not. One weak rung would have dashed someone to his death, and that no accident occurred through the whole seven months of working — though repairs were necessarily frequent — is the best testimony to the makers' skill.

Gephard on one of his perambulations uncovered the entrance and, possessing a suspicious mind, refused the explanations of POWs babbling about mice, or frost cracking things, or the possibility of a dud bomb. Finally one of the electrician's apprentices was lowered down with a rope, and even Gephard's urbanity was shaken to the core when the extent of the working was revealed.

The first consequence of the discovery is the closing of the church for an undefined period — meaning, I suppose, until the tunnel is filled up and the foundations made good.

TUESDAY 20 JANUARY

It was learned some days ago that some British officers were booked for transfer to another camp. Speculation ran riot, but came nowhere near to coupling the names of Guy German and Hobling. At *Appell* this morning they were told they would leave for Spangenberg — *Oflag* IXa — early tomorrow. We were under the impression that Spangenberg was closed and all British Army officers, except ourselves, were at VIb, the RAF officers at *Stalagluft* II in the Baltic, and RN officers at a *Marlag* somewhere between Bremen and Hamburg.

Conversation centres round: 'Is the *Schloss* at Spangenberg being reopened as a super *Straflager*?', if so, 'What has Hobling done to merit it?'

No one is under any misapprehension as to why Guy German is being removed. He is as much a soldier in the field while in prison as before his capture. His almost ferocious loyalty to British escape interests has won commendation from all nationalities.

There was a non-combatant walk today, but Hobling's imminent departure had me separating our private property and dividing the books and accumulated chaplains' paraphernalia. I was the more disappointed at missing the walk when, at 4 p.m., news flashed round the camp that Jean Jean, a French priest, and Leguet, the French MO, had escaped while out walking. I would have given much to have seen Jean Jean's squat figure and Leguet's lean one disappearing in the uncertain quest of liberty.

The *Saalhaus* officers joined us tonight for dinner, making the occasion something of a farewell to the Colonel and Hobling.

FRIDAY 23 JANUARY

Howard Gee, civilian and soldier of fortune, who left this camp in February 1941 and has since done the rounds of several *Ilags* from one of which he escaped, arrived back here this morning. Before leaving a year ago he was in the position of orderly. He has returned to occupy officers' quarters, presumably on the same basis as Red Romilly.

WEDNESDAY 28 JANUARY

An announcement at morning *Appell* shook us rather badly. There are to be no hot bathing facilities for a fortnight because of the shortage of coal. It was not clear whether it was a purely local shortage due to the difficulties of transport in 33° of frost.

The news we have all awaited with increasing eagerness — and with increasing certainty — came this afternoon. Neave and Luteyn crossed the frontier into Switzerland on the night of 7 January. That was good going! I sat next to Anthony at dinner at 7 p.m. on 5 January — his last meal in *Gefangenschaft*.

It has taken the British contingent a whole year to bring off one success. The escape barometer has risen like a hydrogen-inflated balloon. Idle minds that in their idleness were prey to less wholesome pursuits are now escape-minded again — a change that suits me admirably.

THURSDAY 29 JANUARY

A thaw set in during the night and reduced my crystal cave to flooding streams of water. I almost swam out of bed . . .

169

and carried clothes, books, boots etc. into the day room and
waited for the morning.

When the lights came on at 7 a.m. I started de-icing the
walls and windows and mopping up the floor. The day's
bag was four buckets of ice, and three of water that had
dripped from the window sills and been mopped up from
the floor.

After Colonel Stayner took over from Guy German as
SBO, Heard asked permission to move back to these
quarters again, either to the subalterns' dormitory, or to
share the 'Bishops' Palace' (which has been re-christened
the 'Priest's Hole') with me. Stayner promised to review the
matter in a few days, and Biren Mazumdar, an Indian MO,
took advantage of those few days to slip into Hobling's
bed, and now won't budge an inch. Heard has therefore
been given a bed in the captains' room.

SUNDAY 1 FEBRUARY
Sentence of ten days *Stubenarrest* for Jean Jean and Leguet
was notified this morning. It seems they got as far as
Saarbrücken where they were challenged and recaptured.

MONDAY 2 FEBRUARY
Among the new orders announced at *Appell* this morning
was one that it is *verboten* to make rude remarks in letters
about any of the Axis Powers.

Am feeling rather seedy. I have a very nasty cough and
have lost my voice — an entirely new experience. Frost got
into my face after shaving on Sunday morning, and is now
in my eyes. The irritation is almost unendurable. I made an
enquiry tonight about a place in the *Revier* — but all the
beds were full.

TUESDAY 3 FEBRUARY
Lay in my bunk all day except to turn out for *Appell*.
Stood about with thirty others of different nationalities in
one of the Infirmary rooms. Kenneth Lee, who is in like
condition to myself, told me that the barometer (*sic*) showed
minus 20° Centigrade. I think I have a temperature.

**THURSDAY 5 FEBRUARY**

As yesterday and the day before, with the difference that we were hustled out of the Infirmary room at morning *Appell* and ordered to stand in the *Hof*. The British and Dutch were dismissed to their rooms after a moment or so, but the other nationals were kept standing. The reason for all this was that the German dentist's civilian greatcoat disappeared yesterday. He evidently found it an encumbrance while dealing with a wayward tooth and removed it for a moment — only a moment: the temperature is much too low to be without one — but long enough for some *Dummjunge* to remove it. The French, Belgian and Polish quarters were searched, but without success.

**SATURDAY 14 FEBRUARY**

Dr Eggers announced at morning *Appell* that he has taken over the Senior-officership of the camp from *Hauptmann* Priem.

Scorgie Price's sentence to three days' *Stubenarrest* for kicking a football when the *Stabsarzt* was near enough for the ball to pass over his head was also notified. Three days is an irritating sentence. The person concerned has all the humbug of pulling up his stakes — bedding, books, etc. — and getting it over to the cells, and he is no sooner settled than he has to uproot again and return to the nuisance of clearing his bunk which, in his absence, has been piled high with other officers' stuff. A fortnight is the ideal sentence. Two weeks out of every five or six spent in the comparative quiet and peace of the cells would make this life bearable.

**SUNDAY 15 FEBRUARY**

At tea time a radio announcement trickled into the camp via one of the *Posten* telling of the capitulation of Singapore. The loss, coming as it does on the heels of British reverses in North Africa, has taken toll of several officers' natural optimism.

**TUESDAY 17 FEBRUARY**

The question of paying for the grand tunnel has been in

171

dispute for several days. Senior officers of the different nationalities have told the *Kommandant* that they thought the demand for payment of the bill for repairs running to 12,000 or 14,000 RM was contrary to the provisions of the Geneva Convention, and have declined to pay it. It has been suggested that the total should be spread out over three pay days at the rate of RM30 for Lieutenants, RM45 for Captains, and RM60 for officers of Field Rank and above. The only suggestion that Stayner felt himself able to make in reply to this was that the *Kommandant* should give instructions that reductions be made from officers' pay, and officers would sign only for the reduced amount. The *Kommandant* could not agree, and so the matter is at deadlock. Meanwhile the Colonel has written to the Swiss Embassy.

## THURSDAY 19 FEBRUARY
One of the first effects of the new regime since Dr Eggers took over from Priem as senior *Lageroffizier* is a marked mitigation of the drudgery of *Appell*. An electric bell, controlled from the guardhouse, rings loud and long at half an hour before *Appell*, and again at five minutes to. On the first morning, a week ago, the regular set of bed lovers were the regular few minutes late. A *Sonderappell* for all but the Poles, who are precision itself in such matters, was called for 10.30 a.m., and the Colonel addressed several admonitory remarks to the unpunctual which were fruitful. Dr Eggers now wastes no time in numbering the five parades, and so eight or ten minutes — instead of twenty or twenty-five — sees us all dismissed; except, of course, on those perfectly righteous occasions when something of escape value has been stolen, or one or more officers have actually escaped.

## SATURDAY 21 FEBRUARY
Last Wednesday half a dozen officers were stricken with a bright idea. The echo of the impact was audible to all and sundry — why hadn't they thought of it before?

The 'thundering good thing they were on to' was made

possible by the thickness of the snow. They would saw through the window bars from the subalterns' dormitory, and thus gain access to the roof of a loft built over the *Evidenz-Zimmer*. Several feet along the roof are two dormer windows almost buried in the snow, and it would be a simple matter to burrow along under the snow to the slated side of the first one.

By Friday they had reached the window, were through the slates, and inside the loft. The wall at the far end of the loft is the back wall of the German living quarters, and the next intention was to bore through the wall at the least dangerous point — into a corridor or store room. Once through the wall the escapers would lie up until nightfall when they would watch for the right moment to walk out.

Well, the balloon burst at three o'clock today. Four officers were at work in the loft when Dixon Hawk suddenly bounded through the subalterns' dormitory, out through the window, along the snow tunnel, and surprised them at their job. The stooges had given the signal, but too late to be of use.

One of the four rushed to the dormer window, succeeded in opening it, and in a fraction of a second went tobogganing down the roof and flapped over the edge into the *Hof* ten or twelve feet below, landing — fortunately — in a sitting position on a four foot cushion of snow. Priem and the *Hof* sentry had ordered him to stop — the sentry had his rifle trained on him, but did not shoot — but, encouraged by our cheers, he sprang up unhurt and made a dash for the French quarters and went in. But before one could bat an eyelid he was out again looking more of a *collaborateur* than Petain himself.

In the meantime Dixon Hawk had drawn his revolver and, lest the others should similarly try to avoid detection, fired a warning shot which zipped wickedly between Scruffy's legs and stopped the scramble. Scarlett's conversational German is never very good even in calm moments, and being covered with an already-smoking revolver in no way improved it.

173

'*Scheissen Sie nicht mir!*'* he cried.

*Schiessen* — to shoot — was the verb he wanted.

## FRIDAY 27 FEBRUARY

A camp order at *Appell* on Wednesday morning, applying
to British officers only, listed the personal clothing that we
may have in our own keeping after 2 p.m. today. The
permitted articles are: two sets of uniform, one greatcoat,
two pairs of boots or shoes, three changes of undergarments,
and toilet necessities. Only two books may be kept for
personal use.

This morning the dormitories looked like a battlefield
with everyone combing through their stuff and throwing
this here, and that somewhere else. Someone threw an old
trouser leg at someone, and caught someone else a swipe
across the shoulders, and a first-rate pillow fight was at once
in progress — rough and tumble, roll and bang! O-o-o-h!
that's my head, that was — and with a few towels and
shirts torn and trampled, and after a general sorting out of
scattered clothes, the excess was packed into Red Cross
cases released for the purpose by the Germans.

Most officers have packed their summer wear and many
of the unnecessary but pleasant things that have from time
to time arrived with tender touch in next-of-kin parcels.
The impression the order has conveyed is that we are being
made mobile for imminent transfer to another camp,
and our baker's dozen of crack train-jumpers are looking
at their gear and hoping that such is the case. For them
there is no way of escape quite so good as leaping from a
moving train. A further suggestion is that it is because all
goods possessed by POWs are potential hiding places for
escape gear, and the larger a prisoner's personal baggage
the greater the difficulties of search. And now a real hum-
dinger search is expected.

A very promising tunnel leading from the Dutch quarters
and down a buttress to ground level was discovered this
afternoon. From the decided way in which the Germans

*Translation: 'Don't shit on me!'

searched, they knew what they were looking for. A quantity of our spoil from the *Schützenhaus* which had been used for lighting the tunnel was lost, also a fairly large kit of tools.

## WEDNESDAY 11 MARCH

Under a new order all requests of a general nature are submitted to four representatives of the *Kommandant* who sit in the *Evidenz-Zimmer* on Wednesday afternoons. I went today with Colonel Stayner to ask about the stopping of non-combatants' walks. As an answer I was not told that they had been stopped because Jean Jean and Leguet had escaped from one, but that a recent OKW order declared that British chaplains were now to be regarded as other officers.

But that ruling surely awards to weary chaplains the privilege and excitement of engaging in escape rackets. I think it is rather a good exchange!

## MONDAY 16 MARCH

Four new officers have arrived within a few days. Two have been at liberty for several months. Lieutenant Michael Sinclair, 60th King's Royal Rifles, won through from the reprisals camp at Posen on 28 May last year, and made for the Russian frontier; but inopportunely for him and his companion, Major Littledale, the East Front conflagrated, and they found themselves still some distance behind the German lines and had to strike south. They were at liberty five months and were finally taken by the Bulgarian police and handed back to the Germans. Littledale is in hospital in Czechoslovakia. Lieutenant Davies-Scourfield, who escaped with them, and has also arrived here, was recaptured in Poland after nine months' liberty.

Flying-Officer Dominic Bruce and Flight-Lieutenant Tunstall arrived this morning from *Oflag* VIb. They are more than welcome for the news they bring. Bruce was captured only nine months ago and had interesting information about new types of aircraft, the battle of the Atlantic, and conditions in England. They also brought news of escapology at VIb that was greatly applauded here.

## TUESDAY 24 MARCH
Yesterday's German press published the rate at which the 'normal user's' food ration will be reduced on 1 April. The 'normal user' — as being different, I suppose, from men in the services and those engaged in heavy work — will lose one-sixth of his bread ration, one-fifth of his fat, and one-quarter of his meat. His cheese will be increased by one-half It is probable that a similar rate of reduction will apply to us, but our margarine ration was cut by half this morning.

## WEDNESDAY 25 MARCH
Admiral Unrug and General Le Bleu are bound for a Generals' camp somewhere, and were expected to leave shortly after *Appell*. The Polish and French officers remained in the *Hof* to God-speed them on their way.

Alas, alas; as they waited the *Stabsarzt* (Surgeon-Major) arrived and looked upon a *Hof*-ful of potential salutes. But at once everyone turned and walked away like dust before a wind. He watched for a moment, looking very fierce, and then disappeared into the *Revier*. When he came out the same happened, so he walked rapidly towards the end of the *Hof* where the officers had all bunched together, and stepped in front of first one and then another, waiting to see if they would salute. So far as I know, no one thus confronted failed to do so; but from the windows all around were catcalls, loud laughter, and shouts of *'Tierarzt, T-i-e-r-a-r-z-t!'* It was a most unhappy incident, and to no creditable purpose.

## THURSDAY 26 MARCH
The first result of the demonstration against the *Stabsarzt*, Dr Rahm, was the curtailment of official exercise yesterday. Major Engels for the Dutch, and Colonel Stayner for the British, made a joint complaint that their officers were not in the *Hof* at the time, and the exercise ban should not therefore apply to them. The *Kommandant* agreed.

When, however, Stayner told the British officers, it was

176

pointed out that some of the British had shared in the demonstration from their windows, and had no wish to receive treatment discriminating them from their fellow-prisoners. So the Colonel drew up another *Antrag* informing the *Kommandant* that British officers had shared in the demonstration, and that he wished to withdraw his complaint.

He then repeated to the mess his disapproval of shouting and booing, and hoped that officers might not be found doing so again.

WEDNESDAY 1 APRIL
The last of the stacked snow, dirt-encrusted and ugly, was flushed away this morning with pick, shovel and water-hydrant. While it was going on Black Campbell availed himself of one of the hydrant keys — a T-shaped bar — and dashed up the Anglo-Dutch staircase hotly pursued by Dixon Hawk. The key was safely concealed, but Black was taken to the *Kommandantur*, and on the way, at the bottom of the staircase, he slipped his wallet to Romilly, but not unobserved.

Dixon Hawk made a grab at it, whereupon Romilly threw it towards a group of officers. It opened in mid-air, and the contents scattered far and wide. Some of the papers were retrieved by officers who at once disappeared, and some were caught by the representative of the *Wehrmacht*.

After examination at the *Kommandantur*, Black was brought to the cells under armed guard. Later in the day he was visited in his cell and the two counts on which he was to be charged were read to him. They were: 1) assaulting a German *Obergefreite* while in the course of his duty; and 2) taking an iron key which was part of the camp-fire-fighting equipment, thus endangering the lives of people living in the camp and sabotaging the *Schloss* itself. Both charges, he was assured, were punishable by death, the second of the two having a minimum statutory punishment of one year's imprisonment.

Black pleaded guilty to having taken the key, but denied all the implications involved. At this point Priem gave an undertaking that, if the key was returned, the matter would be dealt with summarily by the camp *Kommandant* rather than by courtmartial. Black, who in civilian life is a barrister decided to accept the undertaking, and was released pending sentence.

## GOOD FRIDAY 1942

At 5 p.m. a lightning search descended upon us. There had been more than usual traffic by the Germans in the *Hof*, but the stooges had failed to notice that when four or five soldiery went into the *Evidenz-Zimmer* one less came out, though each time the door was locked as though the room was empty. In that way a search party was collected right at the bottom of our stairway.

At five o'clock they rushed in upon us, the *Posten* taking up their places, and the search party getting to work. The proprietors of 'Fools' Deep' had disliked the movement of so many Germans in the *Hof* and had called off work early in the afternoon; but the 'Dead End Kids' who had just begun working on another tunnel were less cautious, and kept on working with the result that Errol Flynn, who came out of arrest yesterday for a three days' break before beginning a further twenty-eight days on Sunday, was caught at work.

Errol is fast approaching the IVc record. When going down to the cells on 2 March to serve twenty-eight days for an attempted escape in mid-January he made a break, but was recaptured within an hour and sentenced to a further twenty-eight days. The sentence beginning on Sunday will bring his total since he has been here to 142 days, and that will be followed by the sentence for today's episode.

## EASTER DAY 1942

Easter morning service at 11.15., followed by Communion, was well attended. I think it was our record congregation since we united forces.

This has not been an easy day to live. Spiritual joys were great enough, but Red Cross food is in less than adequate supply, and there are complaints of physical hunger. Tobacco and cigarettes are scarcer than for a year past, and there is an atmosphere of lethargy and disappointment.

WEDNESDAY 8 APRIL
Five medical officers — French Jews — were sent from
here this evening to work in Russian POW camps in
Poland. Serious outbreaks of typhus and cholera are said
to be the reason.*

THURSDAY 9 APRIL
A spate of private parcels have banished dull care and
smothered the contents thereof — as they lie on the tables
— with a yellow blanket of tobacco smoke. Tonight the fug
in the day-room is reminiscent of the luxurious days of over
a year ago when the first tobacco parcels began to arrive.

After being without pipe tobacco for a few weeks, Eric
Way's parcel to me containing sixteen ounces of Cut Golden
Bar is a gift to be appreciated. A food parcel from France
was a greater surprise and as great a pleasure. I don't know
the donor, nor she me; but after Anthony Neave's escape
I drew one of his parcels from Mlle Louise Willems, Mons-
en-Peville, Nord, and acknowledged it. Whether Anthony
wrote to her after arriving in England asking her to transfer
the adoption, or whether she has done so out of the goodness of her heart, I have no means of knowing. But it was
welcome indeed.

Sent diary from 1 January — 7 April to be *Geprüft.*

FRIDAY 10 APRIL
The two officers who appear to be getting most out of
*Gefangenschaft* are Monty Bissell and Don Middleton. For
several months past they have worked unceasingly at a
self-set university course. Quite apart from the academic
value of their studies — languages, maths, history and
English literature — their personal conduct and their im-
munity from camp panics and insanities are an example to

*According to the official War Office records, during the winter of
1941–2 typhus, thought to have been brought in by Russian
prisoners, broke out in six POW camps where British prisoners
were held.

179

us and a terrific relief to themselves, for neither of them found imprisonment easy.

TUESDAY 16 APRIL
We got our spring search over today. Officers were under guard in the day-room by 6.30 a.m. while the effort to (spring) clean us of all useful escape gear was in relentless progress.

At 10.30 the stage was all set for the search of our persons. Each officer was taken separately to the kitchen and stood there resplendent in his nakedness until each garment had been thoroughly fingered, seams examined, and pockets turned out. It must have proved extremely distasteful and unsavoury to the searchers, for it is a fortnight since baths were available.

After socks, underpants, vests, trousers etc. were all thoroughly examined, attention was turned to the naked body. By aid of an electric torch, hair, eyelids, ears, mouth — dental plates had to be removed — the interstices of the toes, soles of feet, and every other conceivable place of hiding was closely scrutinised. Then the subject was allowed to dress quickly, and ushered down into the *Hof*. By midday we were all in the *Hof*, and the day-room was under devastating inspection. Books, suspected of concealing escapers' treasure in their binding, were opened up, a window-recess platform was torn up, and tables, stools and benches were carefully examined for any appearance of having been tampered with.

At 2 p.m. the all clear was given, and we trooped up the stairway and into the dormitories to learn the extent of the deprivation. A small quantity of stuff had been found and confiscated, but on the whole it must have proved a very disappointing search — as, indeed, any search of these quarters is likely to do. The eight or ten books that were found to contain maps and money are not regarded as a dead loss because no one had the remotest idea that they held any other secrets than the germs of thought their authors had striven to make clear.

The day was not without its humour. A *Posten* was overheard complaining to an *Unteroffizier* that his relief had not arrived and he had missed his food and was very hungry. Tunstall, thinking it a good joke since they had spent the day searching primarily for money, offered the *Posten* a German coin, saying, 'Here you are, my man, go out and get yourself a good meal.' Covered with confusion the guard replied, '*Nein, nein, danke!*' and refused the coin.

It would be interesting to know how the *Offizier* in charge of the search regarded Monty Bissell's request — whether he regarded it as the observance of some religious discipline. Monty declared that he could not undress except when in the presence of a doctor or priest. No priest was available, but Mazumdar was called, and the search proceeded.

*A month of little interest.*

MONDAY 18 MAY

A three-or-four-days-old rumour that seventy Polish officers would shortly leave this camp became an official announcement at morning *Appell*. They are leaving at 4.30 a.m. tomorrow. They are mostly senior officers and captains who have not attempted to escape; but about forty junior officers and captains — the escape-residue — will remain.

After evening *Appell*, before ranks were broken, three reverberating cheers were given as a mark of general respect and goodwill. Afterwards private gifts, tokens of good friendship, were thrust upon them, and we gave a reception and running buffet for all who are leaving between four and six o'clock. The Poles were more than good to us during the winter of '40–'41 when Red Cross supplies had not yet begun to arrive.

A party of about two hundred Indians were brought to the *Schützenhaus* in January. This morning, while I was out for exercise, they recognised me for a British officer and gave me their smartest salute and a gleaming smile.

**THURSDAY 21 MAY**

A dull, threatening morning, humid and thundery, and full
of the promise of much-needed rain. A steady downpour
set in at noon and has continued all day. Beautiful rain,
falling softly brisk, and giving the *Hof* a much-needed
wash. I could have enjoyed standing idly at the window
watching it and dreaming, but at the 2.30 p.m. *Appell* it
was announced that the *Engländer* would change quarters
between 4–6 p.m.

The Polish orderlies helped us carry palliasses, bedding,
clothing, books, food, etc. across the *Hof* and up the spiral
staircase — eighty-four stone steps making three complete
spirals — to the top storey. Like all mountaineers, our
compensation for trembling thigh muscles, aching biceps
and bursting lungs is the view. It is no sylvan glade or
expansive grandeur, just a bush and scrub-tree covered
hillside that rises sharply at the rear of the *Schloss* not
more than a few hundred yards away. But how marvellous
a change from having one's eyes continually on the prison-
weary, milling herd in the *Hof*.

The accommodation consists of two dormitories, a day-
room, wash-house, lavatory, and small kitchen. In the
captains' room I share a bunk with George Skelton. He
sleeps on the lower deck and there is evidently considerable
life still in the severed nerves of his left arm and leg for,
when asleep, the mutilated limbs spring and leap like
nobody's business — except, of course, the sleepless wight
in the top bunk. In the several operations he underwent
after being shot down various sutures were made, but certain muscles are still atrophied, and he is a bad enough case
to have been recommended for repatriation.

**TUESDAY 26 MAY**

At morning *Appell* 125 French and Belgian officers were
told they would remove to another camp on Thursday. I
think all the French Jews are going, and *Oflag* Xc at
Lübeck is believed to be their destination.

*Hauptmann* Priem told me that the *Kommandant* has
decided to permit British chaplains to take parole walks.

182

The parole would require that we did not use the walks to escape ourselves, or to help others to escape. If the privilege to take a walk denies me my new-found liberty to escape, I don't want a walk. Heard is not frightfully concerned: he has no wish to walk or escape.

D———'s condition has become grave. Periods of deep melancholia have become more frequent and of greater intensity, and for two or three days he has been in deepest despair. This afternoon, when most officers were sunbathing in the *Hof*, he slipped into the wash-house and opened his wrist with a razor blade. Fortunately he was found only a minute or two later. He was sitting on a stool dangling his wrist in a bucket of water placed between his legs. The bleeding had not been severe, and Doc Playoust drew the three cuts together and applied a bandage. D——— was thoroughly resentful at having been frustrated, but was docile enough within half an hour, and amenable to doctor's orders.

Yesterday he thought it would be a good idea to throw a bottle or something through the window at a *Posten* and thus get himself shot. His great obsession is a letter that he must write to his wife releasing her from their marriage. It is evident from her letters that no wish is further from her mind.

Don Thom and I sat with him this evening trying to guide his thought and give some cohesion to the letter in the hope that it might not give his wife cause for alarm. But it is obvious that this is no very temporary derangement. He made an attempt to slash at his throat when we ventured to point out that his wife is worthy of his respect and love.

## WEDNESDAY 27 MAY
By order of the *Kommandant* D——— slept in a cell last night and, when permission was obtained for another officer to stay with him, Don Thom volunteered at once.

*Stabsarzt* Rahm examined D——— this morning, and took down the history of the case. It is thought that an effort will be made to get him into a mental hospital. In the meantime Norman Forbes, who is now the Adjutant, has prepared a list of officers to do hourly shadow duty.

THURSDAY 28 MAY
The party bound for Lübeck left at 4.30 a.m. Throaty farewells came in a sleepy chorus from dormitory windows, and a reverberating reply from the departing host.

The transfer of the sixty-three Poles and four Serbs last week offered an irresistible opportunity for a schoolboy prank — a ludicrous impersonation. Bertie Boustead changed places with Second Lieutenant Count Feliks Jablonowski. They are as unlike in appearance as two men can be — Feliks is short, Slav-featured and past middle-life; Bertie is six-feet-two in his socks, and wears the nonchalant air of an undergraduate. But to our utter amazement he passed muster with the others and was taken to Lübeck with everything, except the clothes he stood up in, belonging to a man half his size.

From the moment of their departure we were constantly on our toes expecting every second moment would bring news of Boustead having been identified, or that Feliks had been spotted — particularly since Feliks has been a not insignificant character in this camp for two years. But he stood on *Appell* with the British company, took exercise with them, and generally passed off as a British officer.

Yesterday, however, he was obviously sought after and, when found, the immediate certainty with which he was accused of changing places with Lieutenant John Boustead was sufficient evidence that Bertie's presence had been established at Lübeck. Feliks left with the French this morning.

Lieutenant Ian Scorgie Price thought the trick worth a second trial and changed places with Lieutenant Louis Fleury. They are much alike in age and appearance — tall, slim, light moustache, and they were able to change dress. Scorgie answered to Fleury's photograph at the identification parade at the *Schützenhaus*, and all was set for the march to the train when one of the English-speaking censors passed along the ranks. He stopped to look twice at Scorgie and exclaimed, 'You cannot do this again! I know you! I was looking at your photograph yesterday. You are Lieutenant Mackenzie!'

Though still leaving much to be desired, the recognition was near enough to get Scorgie bustled back to the *Schloss* and Fleury hustled off to the station.

## ROYAL OAK DAY 1942

D——— was taken to the *Lazarett* at Elsterhorst this morning. While two soldiers of the parcels staff searched his baggage, he made an effort to grab a guard's bayonet from the holster on his belt. The guard had been warned about D———'s condition and did not shoot.

When they were crossing the bridge over the river on the road to the station D——— again tried to provoke the guard to shoot by vaulting the low parapet of the bridge as though he meant to drop into the river and escape. By a miracle that would be impossible to a circus acrobat he gripped the rim of the parapet as he went over and hung suspended above the water. Cyril Lewthwaite, who was also en route for the *Lazarett* helped to haul him back. Poor old D———!

## MONDAY 1 JUNE

The day's major excitement was Boustead's return from Xc. His prank was revealed at an identification parade on his fifth day at Lübeck. When Feliks' name was called Bertie stepped forward but, alas! there was not a single point of resemblance between man and photograph.

Now, in the little prep school preceding the parade, masters and pupil had agreed that if the pupil was questioned it was probable — judging from precedent, that the first request would be for his name, and the second for his number. If those two were satisfactorily answered and the photograph not looked at too closely, he might pass muster. So a few Polish phrases were taught him parrot-fashion.

The first question put to him sounded like a broadside from Nelson's flagship in the Battle of the Nile. But it was question no. 1 and Bertie gave answer no. 1 — 'Second Lieutenant Count Feliks Jablonowski.' The identification officer raised an eyebrow and loosed off another round of grape. It was question no. 2 so Bertie gave answer no. 2 and faithfully repeated Feliks' number: *'Trzy tysiacy siedem diesiat piéc.'* (3075). But the IO appeared not to have heard, so Bertie pronounced his number with confident deliberation. *'Trzy ... tysiacy ... siedem ... diesiat ... piéc.'* A fourth question followed, by which time it was very obvious that the German officer was not playing to prep school rules. But Bertie, with the patient persistence of the British race, went on repeating Feliks' number with unmistakable clearness. *'T-r-z-y ... t-y-s-i-a-c-y- ...'*

Later the Poles told him that the second, third and fourth questions were: 'Where were you born?' 'What was your mother's maiden name?' 'Where were you captured?'

TUESDAY 2 JUNE
'Errol' Flynn came out of arrest this morning after three consecutive months, having had a break of three days between each month. He was desperately hungry as no supplement to bare German rations is now allowed to officers undergoing punishment. But it was fortunate for him that several food parcels were issued this morning, and his friends, one and all, fêted him. A crowning ecstasy came with the news that Mike Sinclair had escaped. He was taken to Leipzig on the early morning train for treatment for sinusitis, and he escaped from the hospital.

WEDNESDAY 3 JUNE
*Hauptmann* Püpcke visited the subalterns' room this morning and expressed disapproval of the way the bunks were arranged. When they came to these quarters a fortnight ago, little groups of close friends arranged their bunks in a rectangular fashion and hung blankets on the outside, thus making a small shut-off cubicle in which to sit in a pitiful privacy. This was the arrangement called in question. The

order desired was the schoolboy-dormitory order, with bunks in severe serried rows.

Colonel Stayner was at once told, and asked to appeal to the *Kommandant* who, after visiting the quarters this afternoon, ruled that the bunks might stand as at present, but during the day time the blanket curtains must be rolled up or drawn aside.

### SUNDAY 7 JUNE

Mike Sinclair was caught yesterday and is now in a train on his way back to IVc.

Three hundred and sixty Red Cross parcels and a large consignment of uniform were delivered at noon. For the first time in the history of British prisoners at IVc we are able to have one whole parcel each in one week — next week. After that we drop back to three-quarters of a parcel, and then to half.

### MONDAY 8 JUNE

Mike has not arrived! Rumour has it that he jumped the train and is away again.

### TUESDAY 9 JUNE

After tea Dick, Scarlett, Rex Harrison (a mountain of a man) and Dickenson gained access to the attic immediately above our quarters. There is only one door to the attic, and it is doubly secured by a large padlock covering a cruciform lock.

The stooges fell down on their job and the four were caught. A *Sonderappell* was called, and they were marched to the cells. An hour later they were released pending sentence, after which they will take their place on the priority list for cells.

### WEDNESDAY 10 JUNE

Mike Sinclair is definitely recaptured. His toilet-bag and a few books were sent down to the town gaol this morning. When Boustead came out of arrest at noon he hadn't seen

Sinclair but knew of his presence in the next cell, and learned that he was caught on Cologne railway station and taken to a nearby *Stalag* from which he escaped again and was recaptured.

MONDAY 15 JUNE

Fire! Fire! They cried; and we turned our heads while standing at ease on evening *Appell* to see dense clouds of smoke issuing from the small stone entrance hall at the base of the British staircase.

Three weeks ago a supply of wood-shavings for our palliasses was dumped there, and after our needs were met a considerable remainder — about two hundredweight — lay in an untidy heap in the far corner.

Nasty eye-stinging smoke filled the staircase and the dormitories, and poured out again from the open windows. *Leutnant* Winze postponed Appell for half an hour while *Posten und Unteroffizier* raced hither and thither. Their scurryings to and fro were greeted by such wisecracks as *'Haben Sie Feuer, bitte?'** etc., etc.

The glass in the window at the end of the entrance hall splintered and fell as the leaping flames reached the small panes. Reports like pistol shots told of explosive specks in the stone walls and floor answering the touch of heat; and plaster that had been used to round off the ceiling cracked and fell like hail.

*Unteroffizier* who ran out a hose were encouraged by the whistle of bombs and the mournful chanting of an appropriate French song. The order, however, was for some reason countermanded, and the hose did not come into action.

*Appell* reassembled at 9 p.m. with the fire still burning fiercely. *Leutnant* Winze, a man of pleasant manner and soft voice, counted the ranks off and, before dismissing the parade, walked round to the British rank and asked the Colonel if his officers would go straight to their rooms and promise not to interfere with the fire (by which he meant, I

*'Have you a light, please?'

188

suppose, not to add more fuel to it). The alternative was to be kept in the *Hof* until it had burnt out.

The Colonel put the question to the officers who said they had no wish to make the promise. The *Posten* on the doors were thereupon ordered to let no one pass, and *Herr Leutnant* walked to the front of the parade to dismiss it. But instead of the usual salute and '*Danke*', he called '*Achtung*', which usually precedes an announcement, and then in his soft voice said, '*Guten Abend*', and walked away. We felt, as he intended we should feel, like small boys left in the nursery.

Brucie got into trouble through slipping in at the Infirmary door, along the passageway and tip-toeing behind the sentry's back up our stairway to continue the water-throwing trick which began last week when the sun was shining and the *Hof* a mosaic of sweating, naked bodies. Water bombs and finally buckets of water were poured on them from the upper storeys.

The laughing crowd, standing round the sentry who blocked the doorway, were an easy target, and Brucie poured on them a drenching bucketful.* The excitement and laughter were as spontaneous as that of small children, but an *Unteroffizier* dashed up the staircase and, since there was no way of escape, Bruce was brought down and presented before *Leutnant* Winze. He had his name taken and may or may not receive disciplinary punishment.

It was nearly ten o'clock before the pile had burnt through, and the little French-Jewish orderly was able to quench the embers with buckets of water. The staircase stank with the acrid smell of warm, wet ashes, but the dormitories cleared quickly with a stiff breeze sweeping through the open windows.

And so to bed — but Lord! how empty of amusement life must be for grown men to welcome fire as a diversion!

*Remembering that these diary pages were eventually to go to a censor, one wonders if the crowd — or the sentry — was really the target.

**SATURDAY 20 JUNE**

The water-throwing joke reached its peak of entertainment this evening and most unhappily came to a miserable climax.

Half an hour ago we were all laughing uproariously at half a dozen each of Polish, French, Dutch and British subalterns who were fighting a water battle in the *Hof* in the same spirit of good fun as the snowball battles in the winter. Buckets, bowls and tins had all been requisitioned, and the players were dripping, their bodies red from the glow and fierce impact of a well-aimed bucketful.

The *Unteroffizier* and *Posten* who were in the *Hof* were laughing as heartily as we were ourselves, and it was good fun. But twenty minutes ago the *Postoffizier*, who is evidently the duty officer tonight, rushed an armed company — about fifteen strong — into the *Hof*, and ordered the players to stop.

There was not the faintest sign of mutiny, rebellion, or illwill; only the continued laughter from the game. But, in a trice, rifles were raised, and a French officer, Lieutenant Fahy, a spectator leaning out of a third storey window, was shot through the neck.

It was an unhappy incident, and will be long remembered.

**MONDAY 6 JULY**

A real stool-pigeon — at least, so the story goes.

Rysard Bednarski claimed to enjoy the rank of lieutenant in the Polish Army, but for some time it has been doubted if he ever were a Polish officer or ever served with the Polish forces. His escape interests and his visits to hospital have been under closest observation.

At *Appell* this morning his presence among Polish officers was complained of. After counting the British *Hauptmann* Thomann passed to the Polish and Colonel Kowalczewski gave the customary call to attention. He then turned to Püpcke and gave the number present as 'Forty-seven officers and one traitor.'

Bednarski was removed from the ranks at once and taken — perhaps for his own safety — outside the camp.

SATURDAY 18 JULY
Three weeks ago Lieutenant Kenneth Lee and Flight-Lieutenant Tunstall were given notice of court martial. They are both on the same charge, that of resisting with force the execution of an order given in the course of duty. The incident arose when *Hauptmann* Püpcke ordered *Unteroffizier* Mudroch to confiscate a trumpet which — it is said — was blown as part of a demonstration. The hearing is fixed for 25 August at Leipzig.

Lieutenant Alan Campbell of the Inner Temple has prepared the defence which is to the effect that when, on the evening of 9 June, four officers who were caught in the attic above our quarters were marched across the *Hof* to the cells, certain commiserative exclamations issued from the open windows of the British quarters. But the trumpet was not blown at the time complained of by either of the officers who have been charged, nor in any connection whatsoever with the four officers under arrest. The trumpet-call that is mistakenly said to have been part of an alleged demonstration was the customary 'Cook-house-door' call sounded by Lieutenant Geoffrey Wardle RN in his capacity as kitchen orderly officer. It was sounded not at the wash-house window where the alleged resistance took place, but outside the kitchen door.

After using the trumpet for this purpose Lieutenant Wardle returned it to Lieutenant Lee's bunk. Between the actual sounding of the supper-call and the serving of food on the tables there is a time lag of ten to fifteen minutes while the table stooges collect the food and apportion it. It was during this period that Kenneth Lee picked up his trumpet, went to the wash-house to which budding instrumentalists are banished, and invited Tunstall to play over a new piece of music he had learned.

While Tunstall was doing so *Hauptmann* Thomann accompanied by *Unteroffizier* Mudroch entered the wash-house and, saying something in German, seized the trumpet.

191

Tunstall did not understand the German sentence spoken to him, and did not withdraw his hand from the trumpet. He asked for an interpreter that he might know what it was all about, but no German interpreter was present, and no explanation was offered. Lee, at this point, wished to indicate that the trumpet was his private property and, in illustration of his meaning, placed a hand on the trumpet and pointed to himself. The trumpet bears no evidence of strain or indentation such as would result from undue pressure of hands or pulling. That is a measure of the resistance upon which they are charged with an offence that is punishable by death.

There are signed statements by the witnesses, and Colonel Stayner has repeated his plea that — *vide* Article 20 of the Geneva Convention — military orders should be given in a language POWs understand.

The defence in a nutshell is that prisoners cannot be expected to obey orders that are given in a language they do not know, and in this case they would not have disobeyed a military order if they had understood it to be one. They should therefore be acquitted of a) failing to obey a military order, because no such order was properly given; and b) resisting with force, because no resistance was offered in any true sense of the word.

### TUESDAY 21 JULY

Two Polish and one Belgian officer are in the cells awaiting sentence. Their tunnel, a really good one and in quite an advanced stage, was discovered at about 2 a.m. on Sunday. They were at work at the time and think it not improbable that a sound detector had amplified their gentle tapping and led to their discovery.

*Hauptmann* Priem assured us on *Appell* that Bednarski (the Polish stool-pigeon) had not disclosed anything. He would have been a clever man if he knew anything to disclose for every effort was made to keep him in the dark.

### FRIDAY 24 JULY

Good old Paddy! He has made it! The fugitive look that

was an integral part of his every movement betrayed us
into imagining he would be arrested by every person who
had ever heard that POWs sometimes try to escape. The
route he intended to take is as difficult and dangerous as
any, and he is — or, rather, was — a notorious prisoner.
Well, the findings of courts martial do not matter now.
How nice to sit in a comfortable chair in England, replete
with good food and surrounded by good company, while
under sentence of four years in a German prison.*

A sad day for Scarlett. In the town gaol, serving twenty-
eight days, he received a letter from his wife with the news
of his small son's death.

## SUNDAY 26 JULY

Bad luck! It was a good hole and promising . . . leading
from our day-room through the south wall, and into the
attic above the German quarters. The exit was near completion — near enough to allow immediate use — and only
one small thing remained to be done. Captain Van den
Heuvel, Lieutenant Kriuming of the Dutch Navy, and
Storie-Pugh were working on it — more carefully and
silently than usual. But a faint sound fell on the quick ear
of the patrol *Gefreiter*, and he reported it. Result: three
officers caught working for escape, and will be punished;
one *Gefreiter* to be rewarded with three days' leave.

## WEDNESDAY 29 JULY

At half an hour after midnight only the bushwackers were
awake, sitting in the day-room smoking, drinking each
other's private coffee and cocoa, and talking of tanks,
fighters, bombers, morale, submarines, tactics, invasion,
and policing Europe after the war.

Suddenly the half-hour *Appell* bell woke those who had
turned in early, and those who rang it were colourfully

---

*Squadron-Leader Brian Paddon escaped on his way to a court-
martial on a charge first made in a previous prison camp, and on
which he had been ably defended first by Lieutenant Airey Neave,
and then by Lieutenant Alan Campbell.

described. Jim Rogers facetiously announced it was the end of the war, and was the only one who saw the joke.

Two *Posten* ponderously climbed the stairway, blowing like a pair of grampuses, and calling '*Appell . . . ein . . . Uhr*'. Greatcoats over pyjamas were sufficient dress when, at one minute to one, we stumbled down the stairway and into the *Hof*.

Half a dozen German officers were present, and the close scrutiny of our lines as we were counted, and the way they all bunched together to see if the total tallied with the British total in their books, showed at once that they thought a British escape had taken place.

We knew, as all the other nationalities knew, by '*Hof*-telegraph' that no escape had been attempted by anyone. So the process of the counting was enlivened by animal and bird calls from the lines of those already counted, and answered by those still waiting. An owl hooted, and was answered from a score of places. A rooster joined the chorus, and so did a bellowing cow, a plaintive calf, and a choir of cats. Authority began to take a poor view, and after the general dismissal, when sirens had begun to wail, accompanied by the sound of falling bombs, the French officers were called out again for a *Strafappell*.

The commiserative callings that then broke out from the windows of the other nationalities were as a sharp breeze is to a lively flame. Armed *Posten* were rushed into the *Hof* — about twenty of them — and fanned out in front of the French lines with rifles at the ready. The rifles were sighted on the Polish, Dutch and British windows, and pseudo-barnyard cocks crowed gaily, their raucous cry mingling unmelodiously with the bawling of a very male cow and the yowling of cats. As a sort of side-line, Allied sentiments, expressed in indifferent French, were released from the corners of the thick walls at the side of the windows. (A small handful of our masters of front-line-talk-and-tactics — as is ever their practice when rifle fire may be expected — fled to the security of the thick-wall enclosed recess we use to stack books in, known euphemistically as the library. Only a thousand-pound bomb could imperil them there.)

Bullets hissed over the heads of the French standing in their lines and zipped through the windows on our side of the *Hof*, burying themselves in the rubble and plaster of the ceiling. It was a regular fusillade. Vandy, in pyjamas, went down to the *Hof* to protest against the use of firearms on unarmed and good-humoured men, but he was ordered back to his quarters as soon as he was seen.

The shooting stopped, the French were dismissed, and in a few minutes the firing party marched out of the *Hof* to an unmusical *Gefangener* accompaniment. The front-line-men emerged from the library, and soon we were all abed.

This morning, at *Appell*, the Senior Officers of the five nationalities made a joint complaint to Priem about the shooting. He disowned responsibility, saying that he had at no time given the order to fire, but a French officer, talking to his neighbour while standing in line, used the word '*Höhe*', and one of the *Posten* who overheard mistook it for the command to fire, '*Feuer!*' The other *Posten* followed the example of the first.

An enquiry was held during the morning at which the *Kommandant* presided, and that was repeated as the official explanation. The *Kommandant* added that another midnight *Appell* would be called tonight and, if another demonstration took place, midnight *Appells* would continue.

At noon Stayner came over to our quarters to tell us what had happened. He and the French colonel had met after the *Kommandant*'s enquiry and, in what some officers described as a 'heart failure conference', decided to ask officers to desist from vocal exercise at *Strafappell* tonight.

THURSDAY 30 JULY
We had no opportunity of showing how silent we could be for the *Appell* was not called. Some thought wiser counsels had prevailed and that the clause in Article 47 of the Geneva Convention, 'collective penalties for individual acts are also prohibited', would be observed. But at evening

*Appell* Priem announced an *Appell* for 1 a.m. No sound of any kind greeted the announcement.

FRIDAY 31 JULY
The bell rang at 12.30 a.m. and at a few minutes to one we trickled down the staircase in stony silence. Priem counted the five companies and his usual dismissal, '*Danke, mein Herren*', echoed hollowly on the huge walls. With soundless tread we glided back to quarters in a silence as solemn as a funeral.

During the day numerous small groups discussed this latest breach of the Convention, but few people — after the *Kommandant's* undertaking on Wednesday that correct behaviour at the *Strafappell* last night would end the matter — were expecting another one tonight. However, *Hauptmann* Püpcke saw the Senior Officers at midday and told them the *Kommandant* had ordered another *Appell* at 11.30 tonight, and whether there would be more of the kind would be left to his, *Hauptmann* Püpcke's discretion. Colonel Stayner is very hurt that the *Kommandant* should have broken faith with him.

SATURDAY 1 AUGUST
The second *Strafappell* was called, not at 11.30 p.m., but at eleven o'clock. It was as silent as the ghostly muster of long dead warriors on a forgotten Waterloo! From the time of assembly to the word of dismissal was two minutes seven seconds. Püpcke did not count, he just walked along the lines of each nationality, then along the orderlies' lines, and signified by a salute and '*Danke*' that he had finished.

Stayner is still hurt, and has drafted a letter to the Protecting Power setting out his complaint.

SUNDAY 2 AUGUST
Communion service at 9.15 a.m. I wrote my weekly letter to Maisie this afternoon, but when it will reach her is very uncertain. A reprisals order, directed against our mail, came into operation today.

A translation of the order has not yet been given us, but

we understand that incoming and outgoing mail will be suspended for a fortnight, and in future, on the 10th of each month, the OKW will issue an instruction to each British company stating the number of letters that may be received by each prisoner, and what proportion of his three letter-cards and four post-cards may leave the camp.

The trouble has blown up, it seems, because German families have complained about the length of time taken to convey German prisoners' mail from Canada. Our Canadians grumble that on average their mail is six months old by the time it reaches them.

THURSDAY 6 AUGUST

Dickenson, who was one of the four caught in the attic and completed his four weeks' arrest on Sunday, was yesterday sentenced to a further ten days. Despite his denial he is charged with having made a drawing which represents three highly placed personalities hanging on a scaffold. 'Adolf', 'Hermann' and 'Josef' are said to be the names written beneath the figures. The offending sketch is said to have been found not in the cells, but to have been picked up by a small boy in the street (albeit close to the cell windows) who handed it to his mother, who reported the matter to the appropriate authority.

E———, who did three consecutive months' *Stuben-arrest*, is in a poor way. The German MO was called to see him this morning, and at once ordered his removal to the *Revier*. He is suffering, among more minor complaints, from deep melancholia.

SATURDAY 8 AUGUST

E——— made an attempt on his life by means of a skip-ping rope at 1 a.m. McColm, who is in the *Revier* with an ulcerated stomach, noticed that he was absent from his bed and, going to the *Abort* in pursuit, was just in time to avert the final tragedy. At 3 a.m. he woke out of a doze just in time to avert a second tragedy, himself the victim. E——— had pretended sleep, and the French orderly put to watch him had disappeared. Suddenly E———'s hands

197

were constricting McColm's throat. McColm gurgled as loudly as he could — loudly enough, happily, to summon fellow-patients to his assistance. Preparation is being made for E————'s removal to hospital.

Tail piece! *Die Geschichte der Kaninchen der Gefangenen.* Eighteen months ago Authority interviewed the Senior Officers of each nationality and said how nice it would be for the prisoners to have a hobby — not a silly hobby, but a money-making hobby.

'How nice!' said the Senior Officers.

'Would you like to keep some really nice rabbits? We can purchase a fine strain for you which will prove a good investment for your Lagermarks.'

'How nice!' said the Senior Officers.

The purchase money, RM400, and the monthly maintenance would be a charge on canteen funds.

'How long the rabbits will they be before they are ready for eating?' asked *Monsieur mon Colonel.*

'Oh, but they are not that kind of rabbits at all. They are beautiful wool-producing rabbits, and twice each year at the proper time the wool will be gathered and sold, and all the gross profits, receipts and dividends will be credited to your canteen funds.' Thus would we prisoners accumulate by the end of the war large sums of money with which to buy ourselves motor cars, steam yachts, aeroplanes — all from our own rabbit farm.

The air was electric when Authority told us that RM400 from our canteen funds had bought a number of rabbits (we didn't know how many), and housed them strongly and hygienically on the farm. Colonel German interpreted our enthusiasm to Authority and was solemnly assured that the lovely little dears were all safely housed in the *Schützenhaus*, but prisoners mustn't be naughty and ask to see the rabbits. The OKW had not issued an order providing for prisoners to pay visits to their rabbits. But on Thursday 15 January we saw them! That was the day we were ordered to the *Schützenhaus* while our quarters were searched, and we talked to our rabbits and offered them bits of snow to eat (the grass was frozen), and came back to the *Schloss* fired again with our dreams of luxury yachts.

We have at no time received information about wool-gathering, but have no doubt it was all duly gathered. We heard on one occasion that a stock sale had been scheduled to take place. We never saw the purchaser, nor the auctioneer; but we learned that we had sold for considerably less than we bought — which only goes to show what terrible business heads we have. After all, we are the best soldiers in the world, and simply brilliant prisoners; and therefore may be excused if we are not quite princes of commerce.

However, we are not easily dismayed, and a lapse of a few weeks saw us again embroiled in the treacherous waters of rabbit-farm-high-finance. Our broker — we don't know his name or where he lives — saw some rabbits which were so good he cornered the market at once without suffering the time-lag needed to consult us about breed and price. So we were all set again to get back those gross profits, dividends and receipts we lost on our last excursion into the rabbit-rearing wool-producing industry.

All that was six months ago, and we are now wiser but sadder men. Colonel Brigant has kept himself *au fait* with the international enterprise by occasionally enquiring on behalf of the six nationalities about the virility of our stud and the fertility of the does. But an interim balance sheet is to hand this week — or, at least, Brigant has been told how matters stand.

It seems that our rabbits, that were thought to be such excellent rabbits, have been found guilty of incorrect behaviour. Our rabbits are escapers! Think of that! After being strongly and hygienically housed, and having a monthly maintenance bill paid for them, the wretched creatures gave themselves up to the sin of ingratitude. They began to dig holes, shafts and tunnels from their strong, hygienic hutches. They escaped and dug more tunnels in a farmer's field, and their depredations among the crops were such that a large bill for damage was immediately drawn up. Of course the rabbits are ours, and quite properly the bill for damages was handed to us — or rather we were told that the Germans who hold our canteen funds for us had paid the farmer on our behalf.

This last blow has shattered our confidence in ourselves as rabbit-farmers. We now fear that, owing to our lack of commercial acumen, when we come to selling this lot of rabbits — those of them who were recaptured and brought back under escort — we may have to recompense the buyer for buying them by giving him the strong, hygienic hutches, and a small bonus from whatever canteen funds are left.

FRIDAY 14 AUGUST
I may be mistaken, but I see it as one more sign of prison-weariness. I cannot imagine the British officers who were in IVc twenty-one months ago giving their parole for anything. They were escape-minded, hating enemy detention and discipline as a wild bird hates the bars of its cage. This was the tough guys' camp, and to escape was the first and last duty of a British officer POW. 'No trucking with the enemy so long as a state of war exists' was the oft-repeated maxim.

Parole was first given for certain additions to theatre equipment; next for Red Cross cases in which to store clothes. Today about twenty-five officers — some belonging to the original seventeen of the early days — have given their parole to play football on a piece of ground outside the *Schloss* boundary.

MONDAY 17 AUGUST
Wing Commander Bader — the legless air ace — has arrived. He is as vital as a naked electric wire. He walks well without the aid of any stick or crutch. All nationalities are thrilled by his presence, and doubly so when they have felt the pep of his conversation.

Zafouk Jaroslav gave me an apple today. He had received three in a parcel from his people in Prague. I ate it half an hour ago while thinking of our first stop at Bala on our honeymoon trip through Wales.

TUESDAY 18 AUGUST
There was to have been more football this afternoon. The teams trooped down to midday *Appell* stripped ready for the game. But there was no football. Dickenson has escaped from the town gaol. This morning his bed was examined and his tunic and boots taken away. We wondered and hoped, and the cancellation of football suggested that every available *Posten* was scouring the countryside. No hopeful footballer expressed disappointment, or anything other than good wishes for Dickie.

Days are so much alike that I, who keep a diary and am constantly asked for the day and date, mistook today for Monday and failed to appear at my Dutch Bible Class.

WEDNESDAY 19 AUGUST
Bader gave an after-lunch talk today. The day-room was crowded with interested foreigners as he detailed the rumours picked up in recent weeks, and the probable course of the war.

We received letters today for the first time since 3 August. I was more than a little disappointed that at least one of my two was not from Maisie.

I asked Dixon Hawk this morning, when the new *Kommandant* visited our quarters, if there was any news of Flying Officer Dickenson. He said he was caught this morning at Chemnitz.

Pat and Rupert were caught searching for gold in the delousing shed an hour ago. The *Duschemeister* discovered a shaft in his domain on 10 July and was rewarded with a period of leave. The shaft was filled in and concreted and the team — none of whom were caught — wrote it off as a lost hope. But the team of which Pat and Rupert are members thought the scheme still had possibilities: which were explored and the work begun — with the result as stated.

THURSDAY 20 AUGUST
Representatives of the International Red Cross visited IVc

today. Requests were made for first aid supplies and medical equipment, sent from time to time by the British Government, to be available in British quarters; and for large-size battledress. Consignments so far have been for small and medium-sized men.

A report was made to them about the inaccessibility of our canteen funds, and about the RM12 that had been paid for damage done to crops by an escaping Angora rabbit.

FRIDAY 21 AUGUST

E—— arrived back last night en route, he said, to another camp. For four days he has been with D—— in the hospital at Schmorchaw where, including himself, there were five Britishers. Two were soldiers, one with rheumatism, the other with pneumonia (strange cases for a mental hospital), and one was a naval rating, a survivor of HMS *Courageous*. He was one of three who were picked up from a small boat after being adrift for several days. His two companions died from exposure, and he is just an unnamed and unknown lunatic beating his life out on the strong walls of a padded cell. D—— is considerably better, E—— says, and may go to any *Oflag* he chooses. E—— himself appears to be very tranquil.

MONDAY 24 AUGUST

Bader continued his talk today when he spoke in the theatre about the Battle of England. The 'Battle of London' he thought would be a better name.

Bader had a command in southern England at the time, and possessed complete information about the strength of the defence. Some of us were almost incredulous when he told us how small the British fighter strength was, and how few the pilots after the losses at Dunkirk.

An early morning rumour that seventeen British officers are expected tomorrow was confirmed at midday *Appell*. Arrangements for sleeping and messing had to be made entailing a changeover of the subalterns' dormitory and our present day room.

**THURSDAY 27 AUGUST**

A bird cage at evening *Appell*! A booted and spurred effigy of Adolf Hitler hanging in a cage! After *Appell* it was collected and borne away by an *Unteroffizier*.

**FRIDAY 28 AUGUST**

Dickenson received fourteen days' *Stubenarrest* for his escape from the cooler. Rumour has it that the *Posten* whose negligence made the escape possible received an exemplary sentence of six months' *Strengarrest*. Poor devil!

Dickie had escaped by leaping the eight foot wall surrounding the enclosure in which he was given daily exercise. And, three hours after receiving sentence, he made another — unhappily abortive — attempt to escape. By a clever ruse, and just under a *Posten*'s nose, he slipped under a motor-van delivering bread, and stretched himself flat under the body of the car, his feet and legs over the covered-in propeller shaft towards the big end, and his hands and head on the back axle. The van drove out of the *Hof*, and we thought he was all set for a rough journey to the bakery and a reasonable chance of escape. Alas! the doors at the rear of the van bounced open just outside the main gates, and drew the eyes of the *Posten* on duty. Dickie was hauled out.

**WEDNESDAY 2 SEPTEMBER**

What a night! The seventeen officers we expected last week turned out to be fifteen. Sixteen Naval officers left Lamsdorf for here, but one — Lieutenant-Commander Stephens, DSC — escaped *en route*.

At midnight they tramped wearily into the *Hof*, having had a personal search at the *Schützenhaus*. We made them some hot cocoa, and while they were drinking it and giving their news we staged the joke we had in mind for them.

Gee, dressed as the Camp *Stabsarzt*, and Brucie as a British medical orderly, came into the day-room. With Jumbo's stethoscope and the French dentist's white overall over a Dutch uniform, Gee looked the part; but how excellent an actor he is, and how fluent his German, we had yet to learn.

His entry into the day-room with Brucie in procession was magnificently done. Tunstall was Adjutant for the occasion, and he muttered a lovely diatribe under his breath as he announced the *Stabsarzt*. Gee shouted at us all to let us know a *Stabsarzt* had arrived, and ordered all the new officers to one side of the room and told the rest of us to get out — which we didn't. The subjects of his inspection did not undress quickly enough and he shouted some more at them and at the Adjutant who remonstrated with him.

Each examination was a prize piece of medical hygiene and etiquette. He touched no part of the body with his hands but with a small piece of wood held in delicately poised fingers. Every fourth man he singled out and shouted at him for suffering from crabs. On each occasion he turned to Brucie and remarked on the filth of these fellows, and had him apply the first treatment. Brucie feigned shyness and bade the patients apply the treatment themselves which consisted of wiping the afflicted part with a piece of cotton wool well-charged with blue dye.

The examination over, Gee departed shouting back at our jeering; but he returned almost immediately to our cheering and loud laughter. The new fellows' eyes popped, and only in a minute or two did they twig the joke. There has never been such hilarity in the British quarters before.

TUESDAY 8 SEPTEMBER

At morning *Appell* there was some little confusion. Brian Armstrong was seen to join the French lines after he had been counted with the British and before the French count had begun. Brian was called out by *Hauptmann* Eggers, and the count proceeded apparently to everyone's satisfaction.*

At 12.30 p.m. a *Sonderappell* was called and, when 'an officer named Bruce' was asked for, a Naval officer bearing

---

*From the way this is written the clumsy movement of Brian Armstrong seems to have been an intended distraction from the real absenteeism.

that name stepped forward. But no! He was not the Bruce required. Where was the other Bruce? Indeed, where? We too would very much like to know.

Later in the day we had a story that he had been seen crossing the bridge in the village, and that the hue and cry is on.

Something also appears to have happened when Rupert and Dickenson, who are in the cells in the *Hof*, were taken for exercise this afternoon. Rupert was brought back alone, and a rumour that Dickie had escaped again had rapid currency. Half an hour later he was found and brought in.

WEDNESDAY 9 SEPTEMBER
They are away! But only four of the six who got out are still at liberty — two British and two Dutch. Stooge Wardle and Donkers were the two to be caught about fifteen kilometres away.

It was a good scheme and cunningly conceived. When it was first discussed it was realised that a tunnel at IVc could not succeed unless it could defeat the sound detectors and the nightly gum-shoe patrol. But no tunnel could be dug with the entire absence of vibration and noise, and stooges could not cope with a gum-shoe patrol. So a daring scheme had to be evolved.*

Gephard and Schädlich have been glutted with success recently, but they lost badly by today's effort because the tunnel entrance was in their office — an office in daily use for several hours a day. The entrance was the very spot where Gephard sits, and the door to the office was secured with a padlock over a cruciform lock.

Authority well knew that work was in progress: detectors and gum-shoe patrol had confirmed it again and again. But repeated searches had failed to reveal it, and we had hopes of using the tunnel a second time. But the entrance was traced through from the exit in the course of the morning.

*A full account of this scheme can be read in Pat Reid's *The Colditz Story*, chapter XVIII.

The *Appells* yesterday, covering up Brucie's escape, were not without interest, but this morning's *Appell* is without parallel. It assumed the character of the declaration of war made by the free town of Berwick on Napoleonic France. Berwick is still at war with France as the authority that declared war never made peace — and our *Appell* this morning was never dismissed, so officially we are still on it.

Authority was in a flap when the bell rang at 8.30 a.m. and everyone trooped down into the *Hof*. After a few minutes the whole parade was dismissed without a count and ordered to reassemble at 9.15. It was this *Appell* that was never dismissed.

It was not possible to rig the numbers; the absence of six officers was something that could not be covered up. While we stood there the *Schloss* was searched and better searched, apparently with the idea that the six had not broken camp, but were lying up in a working somewhere. The look on Gephard's face during all this was that of the RSM who knew better.

Tired of standing we broke from the lines to lean against the wall, but were ordered back again and told the *Appell* was not over. Time dragged on and we broke line again and found entertainment in several ways including an acrobatic display which attracted the whole international circle, followed by a very rough international rugger match in which England lost.

One of the three room seniors who were in the quarters while the search was going on found time to throw a bucketful of water on the general hubbub in the *Hof*. Priem, who was in charge of the search of the quarters, tried to pin it on Tunstall and had him arrested for throwing water at German officers and soldiers while on duty. He said he would be sent to Torgau, the nearest concentration camp. Tunstall was cheered wildly when escorted through the *Hof* to the cells.

We shouted up to the room seniors at the windows asking how the search was progressing, and Priem immediately had two rifles trained on the British windows, threatening to shoot the first person who appeared at a window. Colonel

Stayner protested, and said he would give his officers an order to keep away from the windows if the rifles were removed. Priem answered that he would not accept the word of a British officer.

An identification parade for all nationalities was by this time in full swing. Three British and three Dutch were found to be absent. When the photographs and fingerprints were brought out it was also discovered that one of the orderlies who should have gone to Lamsdorf on 15 July had changed places with Lieutenant Malcolm Keiller. So when Keiller's name was called the orderly, Corporal Hendren, stepped forward. His natural similarity to Keiller had passed in other identification parades, but the close scrutiny this morning was more than he could carry through, and he was taken to the cells where, on the Colonel's advice, he confessed to being who he is.

The officers still at liberty are — Dutch — Lieutenant van Doorninck and Lieutenant Ted Beets; and — British — Flying-Officer Bill Fowler and Captain Bill Lawton.

Dominic Bruce is also still at liberty.

FRIDAY 11 SEPTEMBER
Only Brucie, Bill Fowler and van Doorninck are still at liberty. The other four are in the town gaol. Three out of seven still free after three days is a very fair percentage.

MONDAY 14 SEPTEMBER
A German *Posten* guarding the pay NCO went out of British quarters with a notice, eight inches by six, hanging from his belt at the back. It bore the legend 'Support the Goon improvement drive'. He left behind him a riot of amusement of which he was entirely unconscious.

Malcolm Keiller is back. The escort that brought him took Hendren back to Lamsdorf. Keiller has been impersonating an RAMC corporal, and had not made any attempt to escape.

SUNDAY 20 SEPTEMBER
Bader read the lesson in church this morning. He would

have been more in his element in a dogfight with a Messer-schmitt. I spoke about Harvest. A few Red Cross tins on the altar might fittingly have represented the increase for which we are thankful.

### THURSDAY 24 SEPTEMBER

Dominic Bruce is lying in the town gaol. When he was dragged out of a consignment of hay, in which he had taken cover on the wharf at Danzig, he said he was an RAF sergeant recently shot down. He was therefore sent to *Dulagluft*, but the reception officer recognised him at once and he was unable to contact any of the recently-shot-down inmates for up-to-date news.

### SATURDAY 26 SEPTEMBER

Have been sitting for my portrait for two or three mornings to John Watton. He is a quick and deft worker. I am more than pleased with the result.

### SATURDAY 10 OCTOBER

Seven British parachutists are in the cells under the last archway, hence it has been difficult to establish communication with them. Their first enquiry convulsed us: were they in some sort of detention barracks because they were on half rations? It cheered us tremendously to hear them describe our full rations as half rations, and to hear that bread is still unrationed at home and there is ample food for everyone.

### WEDNESDAY 14 OCTOBER

A very quiet but busy day. An intense, exciting evening.

### THURSDAY 15 OCTOBER

Four British officers escaped between sunset and sunrise: they are Pat Reid, Hank Wardle, Ronnie Littledale, and Bill Stephens.* This is the third try for Pat, Hank and Bill, and the second for Ronnie.

*See *The Colditz Story* by Pat Reid, chapter XIX *et seq.*

208

At *Appell* this morning Priem seemed confident that they were only in hiding, perhaps in the shaft uncovered yesterday in the subalterns' dormitory. It suited us to remain standing in the *Hof* until the investigation showed they must seek in wider fields. Six others, as well as the four escapers, were missing from the identification parade. They were routed out from various parts of the *Schloss*, and so it was some time before the names of the escapers were established.

We were held in the church for about an hour, during which time someone took the opportunity to short-circuit the main switch of the great arc light placed over British lines. It has been a day of very high spirits.

FRIDAY 23 OCTOBER
Hope has passed into confident assumption that the four escapers have safely arrived in neutral territory. Eight British officers out of a *Sonderlager* in six weeks, and five of the eight successful, is indeed an achievement.

The Anthony Neave-Tony Luteyn scheme was attempted again last night, but a *Posten* heard the disturbance and the attempt failed. None of them were caught and they lost only a cap. Authority is reported to have said, 'Now we know how the four British got out!'

MONDAY 2 NOVEMBER
A mess meeting decided to anticipate Christmas and make a gift of Red Cross parcels to the Poles. They are to be taken from current consumption and we will only receive three-quarters of a parcel a week for four weeks. The scheme does not include British orderlies who will receive their full parcel as usual.

Belgian officers are no better off than the Poles, but it was thought that the French would continue to help them.

MONDAY 9 NOVEMBER
News that Hank, Pat, Bill and Ronnie crossed the frontier to liberty on their fourth day. Good boys! — they

met Bill Fowler on their first night and had a celebration supper. For Pat and Hank it was a much-deserved reward.

## FRIDAY 13 NOVEMBER

Tunstall attended at Leipzig for a court martial today. He was charged on three counts: attempting assault on a German officer by throwing water from a window; of endangering discipline, impeding the course of duty, and damaging Reich property; and a breach of discipline in disobeying a camp order prohibiting the throwing of water. The first two charges were dismissed, and Tunstall pleaded guilty to the third and was sentenced to four weeks' *Strengarrest*.

Colonel Stayner and Captain Moquette of the Dutch Colonial Infantry, were the only two witnesses allowed for the defence, but they both said they were impressed by the impartiality and correctness of the officers sitting on the courtmartial, and the gentlemanly way in which they, as witnesses, were received.

## MONDAY 16 NOVEMBER

The Dutch show, *Fata Morgana*, had its first production tonight. It was hugely successful. It took the form of a pleasure cruise from the Hague to the East Indies — an enchanting dream picture of life in the south seas. It was thoroughly clean as no previous show has been. A unanimous judgement acclaims it 'the best yet'.

## THURSDAY 19 NOVEMBER

The mess meeting at noon was presided over by Colonel Young in the absence of the SBO who is doing five days' *Stubenarrest*. Colonel Stayner's offence was providing Peter Tunstall with aids to escape (papers, map and money) on the day of his court martial at Leipzig. They were found by the Germans when Tunstall returned to Colditz as he had had no opportunity to escape.

Stayner is not in the town gaol or the cells in the *Hof*. He has given his word of honour to remain in his private

room in the *Saalhaus* — except for daily exercise of one
hour — until noon on Tuesday.

MONDAY 23 NOVEMBER
'Sheriff' Niederthal came out of confinement today after
sixteen weeks. He was taken to the cells in July for
questioning about the Heath Robinson typewriter that had
been found and confiscated. And thereby hangs a tale!

Sometime about the end of last March a new German
sentry appeared who seemed very keen to talk with us and
declared himself ready to help with our escape schemes if
the pay was good enough. Arrangements were soon made
whereby he would provide tools and equipment for general
escape work and receive a personal rake-off of 100% of the
value of anything he produced. He liked to be paid in
cigarettes, coffee, chocolate, and anything he could get.

There were several things about his dealings that suggested to the oldest inhabitants that his interest was farther-
reaching than personal gain. He was a shade too eager to
know the exact nature of certain schemes that were afoot.
So it was decided, before trusting him with a more serious
commission than the supply of escape gear, to test him in a
decisive way. Authority, we well know, would prefer us
to possess almost anything rather than a radio\*, so we invited him to bring us a radio on the usual terms. But
despite his many promises a radio never came, though his
enquiries about our escape affairs assumed a new eagerness.
Our suspicion was that he was being pressed for results,
and, poor fellow, he had no results!

Suspicion grew to certainty when one day he said that he
knew we had an address in Leipzig from which we received help when escaping, and that it was now dangerous
to use that address, so he would give us his own address in
exchange for the one we were using. And he also advised
us not to use the station at Leipzig, but to get off the train

---

\*The POWs had hidden radios for almost the whole of their time in
Colditz, though throughout the diary what must have been the
news from them Platt consistently refers to as 'rumours'.

at the small station before, and take the tram to his house
— he was a wholesale dealer, he said. Our people smiled
knowingly. Give your friend's address? Get off at a
country station where there would be no more than three or
four other passengers alighting? Travel on a certain tram?
That would be simplification of recapture *par excellence!*
But the sentry was still serving a useful purpose, and it was
decided not to cut down his chocolate and cigarettes until
he had provided a radio. Then he disappeared, presumably
removed for failure.

On 21 July, shortly after the Poles had denounced
Bednarski, a search party descended on the *Saalhaus* and
found a tunnel that was near completion, and in the tunnel
they found the Heath Robinson typewriter. It was an ingenious contraption. The type, supplied by the 'Leipzig
Wholesaler' was fixed on thin wooden stays, all of which
had to be put in position separately by hand, inked with a
feather, then turned on a nail axle and pressed in contact
with the identification paper or *Ausweis*. A word of five
letters might take five minutes to write, but it was precise
clear type, and as good as the work of a Remington.

On 25 July Sheriff was arrested and taken to the cells for
questioning by Priem and a civilian who he thought was
one of the Gestapo. Their idea was that Sheriff should
confess all that had taken place between the 'Wholesale
Dealer' and the prisoners, and the death by execution of
the Wholesaler depended upon whether he confessed or
not. Sheriff had his own ideas about that and confessed
nothing. When he was interrogated again he was told that
certain civilians who had helped the Wholesaler would also
be punished if he failed in his confession, but Sheriff made
it known that he believed the Wholesaler to have been a
stooge, at which the Gestapo laughed rather too heartily.

The interrogation lasted six hours, Sheriff was not court-
martialled or sentenced, but he has been in the cells since
21 July until today.

THURSDAY 26 NOVEMBER
Rupert Barry and Lieutenant Aulard made an unsuccessful

attempt to escape via the German kitchen this afternoon. They had got out of our part of the *Schloss* and were going down to the park gate when the sentry on the gate was not satisfied about their right of entry. The surprise of *Hauptmänner* Eggers and Püpcke who, leaving the *Hof* after midday *Appell*, found themselves suddenly confronted with two prisoners in German uniform whom they thought they had just counted can only be imagined. But so certain were they that no one had got away that a *Sonderappell* was not called, and *Hauptmann* Eggers remarked in the course of the afternoon that it was now impossible for anyone to get out of here, even though they were in imitation German uniform, because an inviolable system of passwords was in operation. So it was not until evening *Appell* that they discovered the absence of Mike Sinclair and *Capitaine* Klein.

## MONDAY 30 NOVEMBER

Early this evening we heard that a telephone call from the Swiss frontier to the *Kommandantur* here had reported the capture of Mike Sinclair. Gephard, when asked, agreed that it was so. I have never known Gephard lie about such a matter.

## WEDNESDAY 16 DECEMBER

We had a pet at IVc — we had! Five months ago a very small bedraggled kitten came under the main gate into the *Hof*. She was an ugly little brute, but was soon whisked away into the French quarters with half a dozen officers following dotingly in her train. Within a week *ma petite* was wandering and wooing in all quarters, taking her pleasures where she found them, and sleeping where last she fed. She grew sleek and strong and full of play, and men who loved cats fondled and caressed and gave too generously of their meagre meat ration and condensed milk.

But this morning nobody could remember having seen her for four or five days. A horrible suspicion quickly hardened into certainty, and Black Campbell went over to the French quarters on a determined investigation. Now

Black is not particularly fond of cats, but he tracked his man down and demanded, *'Est-ce-que vous avez tué et mangé la chatte?'* *'C'est possible, c'est possible,'* said the suspect. Black's next remarks were explosive, but they elicited no satisfactory response.

The French are holding an enquiry tonight; and Rupert, who champions the French but loves cats, is the victim of torn loyalties.

### FRIDAY 18 DECEMBER
The result of the enquiry in the French quarters: a) a large body of opinion held that it was quite a reasonable thing to kill and eat the cat; b) the cat would have been killed and eaten in any case, and those concerned only differed from the majority in that they got in first.

### SUNDAY 20 DECEMBER
Holy Communion at 9.15 a.m. A Carol Service at 6 p.m. took account of all the Protestants in the camp, and officers representing their countries read lessons in Polish, French, Dutch and English. A month ago I was jockeyed into training a number of officers who wanted to sing carols as part songs at the service. To my great discomfort they insisted that I conducted for the actual performance tonight. It was an impressive service that was closed for us by the failure of the lights.

### SUNDAY 27 DECEMBER
'Our third and last Christmas in Germany is over,' so the legend goes. It was as good a Christmas as POWs ought ever to expect . . . good food, good company and good news make an excellent trio, whatever the environment. There were no extra rations from the German kitchen this year, which is regarded as a sign of the times.

*Le vin du Château de Colditz* flowed freely in all quarters. On Christmas morning we ate an enormous breakfast of sausages, bacon, eggs (from Red Cross egg powder), marmalade and coffee; and a Choral Communion Service followed morning *Appell*. French, Dutch and British

Protestants communicated together at a very beautiful and impressive service.

I was under promise to have Christmas dinner with the Poles. The meal started prompt at 2 p.m. and went on to 4.30. I ate sparingly, but was uncomfortably replete before the last course appeared, and the British dinner — whose food and flavours I much preferred — had yet to come.

I walked round and round the *Hof*, but had not succeeded in working up any enthusiasm by 7.30 when the Colonel took his seat at the head of the table and we faced tomato soup, grilled steak and onions, Christmas pudding and custard, sardines on toast, dessert, coffee, and wine — *Château de Colditz*.

Boxing Day was a day on which party-goers recovered from parties.

## LAST DAY OF 1942

Tonight's celebration had nothing new in it: it was just a repetition of last year and the year before — but with more hope. The tide of the war has turned, and a feature of this evening was a sweepstake on the fall of Tripoli, Sfax and Tunis.

The singing of national songs in the *Hof* at midnight was less fierce but more prolonged and harmonious than in previous years. The human crocodile sprang to life, and three hundred men roared through all quarters. The New Year was well and truly let in!

# Colditz 1943

Life in Colditz Castle had little interest or excitement in
the early months of 1943. The prisoners had been warned
at the beginning of January, by the Red Cross in Geneva,
that they could not depend on regular supplies of parcels,
so the distribution was immediately cut to half a parcel a
week each. This quickly meant chronic hunger — particularly among the younger officers — and perhaps it was
because of this that escaping activity fell to a low level, and
no notable break-outs were made. Most of Platt's diary
entries became long accounts of the official wrangling with
the Germans over — often petty — infringements of the
Geneva Convention; synopses of lectures (any prisoner with
a claim to any sort of specialised knowledge was in demand
as a lunch-time lecturer to his fellow-prisoners); and the
constant discussion of the latest rumours about the course
of the war.

By early May the inadequate diet was causing in-
numerable skin complaints among the prisoners, and Platt's
own health deteriorated. The symptoms, as he described
them, almost certainly indicated a vitamin deficiency. His
feet, and later his hands, became swollen and septic, and on
26 May he was given permission to stay in his bunk. His
need was for fresh vegetables, but Eggers, who often visited
him, told him that a wave of vegetable pests had made
vegetables very scarce in Germany that spring. It was 18
June before Platt got 'a dish of lettuce — to last two days',
and it was the end of July before he was well enough to
get up and venture into the Hof again.

The most significant changes in the camp during 1943
were in the personnel. In February a new Commandant,

216

Lieutenant-Colonel Prawitt, took over. He arrived as a new broom, determined to tighten the discipline, especially during Appells, and threatening to put latrines in the middle of the Hof if the prisoners continued to put food waste down the lavatories. He was very given to issuing admonitory Camp Orders and, tongue-in-cheek, Platt recorded most of them in full, and kept a number of the original noticeboard copies in English, French and German among his Colditz souvenirs.

On 22 June thirty-six officers and four orderlies arrived as the first batch of the sixty-seven British officers and men who had taken part in one of the biggest break-outs of the war — the tunnel out of Oflag VIIb at Eichstätt. Most of the rest of the sixty-seven followed a few days later; and then nine more came from another escape attempt at Eichstätt. Among these last was Lieutenant-Colonel Broomhall who, senior in rank to Stayner and to Guy German, who had returned to Colditz, immediately became the Senior British Officer. He was at first suspected of a heel-clicking 'policy of appeasement' towards the Germans, but within a month he had won the camp's respect for the tough stand he took against the Germans on behalf of the growing number of Very Important Prisoners, those peers and relatives of Royalty and Winston Churchill whom the Germans seemed to think might come in useful as hostages, and whom they called the 'Prominente'.

The most radical change began in July. Oflag IVc was to become an all-British camp with a total strength of 520. Most of the Dutch had already gone, and the French (and presumably also the Belgians, though Platt does not specifically mention them) went in two contingents in the second week of July leaving the castle 'so quiet as to be almost deserted'. By the end of August the Poles had gone too; and the complement of prisoners was 228 British and a few Free French.

The departing French had bequeathed one of their hidden radio sets to the British, and all the war news was of the strengthening of the tide in the Allies' favour. In January the prisoners saw and heard their first air raids (probably

*over Berlin) by Allied bombers: 'a strange kind of excite-
ment to hear planes throbbing overhead, knowing that they
were manned by men who spoke our tongue, men who had
enjoyed an English tea and would — at least, most of them
— be back home in a few hours enjoying an early English
breakfast.' The air raids became a regular — and always
welcomed — feature of life. In July Mussolini's fall was a
matter for excited rejoicing; and on 31 August a book was
opened on whether the coming Second Front would be in
Italy or Norway.*

*Then there was another dramatic escape attempt.*

## THURSDAY 2 SEPTEMBER
A day of suppressed excitement, and a very busy day for
the team concerned. The director has a nasty fear that fate
will somehow close in on the scheme.

## FRIDAY 3 SEPTEMBER
Well, the attempt was foiled. Mike Sinclair was shot
through the body, two inches wide of his heart. He was
taken to the hospital at Bad Lausick (?) and Hyde-
Thompson and Lance Pope taken to the cells.

It was a bold scheme. Mike was dressed as *Feldwebel*
'Franz-Joseph' (known by that name because of his
enormous grey moustache). The making of his moustache
was an even more formidable undertaking than the making
of the German uniforms for the occasion*, and Mike had
been practising the stoop of his shoulders, his gait, and his
manner of speaking.

Ways out, after three years, are difficult and hard to
come by, but this one was managed by cutting the window
bars in the *Revier* — an operation rendered thrice difficult
by the continual presence of *Posten* on duty whose attention
had to be distracted. Then 'Franz-Joseph', with Hyde and
Lance dressed as *Posten*, squirmed out of the window and,
once out, made as much noise as any *Feldwebel* with
*Posten* would make. They marched to the first real *Posten*

*See Pat Reid's *The Latter Days at Colditz*, chapter IX.

and ordered him to another point, and one of the spurious *Posten* was put in his place until he was well out of sight. But the second real *Posten* to be displaced refused the order — he was keeper of the gate, and it entailed his handing over certain keys. Franz-Joseph got very fierce in true *Feldwebel* fashion, but to no purpose. The *Posten* knew his job and did it well, and in a few moments he had raised the alarm and brought out the guard.

One of the guard, a *Gefreite* whose conduct has been regarded for some time as decidedly unpleasant, and who is known by the nickname of 'Bigbum', shot Mike with his revolver at point blank range when Mike already had his hands up. That Mike's hands were up and had been for some time is testified by over a dozen officers who were watching from the windows only a few yards away. And after being shot he was left lying bleeding, so the spectators say, for thirty-five minutes without attention to the wound. Doc Dickie, who finally dressed the wound and accompanied Mike to hospital, supports the contention — from his examination of the bullet track — that Mike was shot while his hands were up.

SATURDAY 4 SEPTEMBER
The SBO held a court of enquiry this morning and asked Lieutenant-Colonel Merritt, VC, a British Columbia lawyer, to take charge of the proceedings. No report has come from it yet, though the SBO has made a *prima facie* report to the Swiss asking that the matter be communicated to the British Government, and he has written to Mike's father.

The *Kommandant* held a similar enquiry this morning, and as a result has issued a statement that Lieutenant Sinclair was shot while escaping. The findings of the two courts will at least diverge on that point. The weight of British evidence is that he was shot after capture by *Gefreiter* Bigbum, and that the *Gefreiter's* conduct was supported by the original Franz-Joseph who is reported to have said, 'they should all be shot'.

Mike's condition is said to be not dangerous, though he has lost a lot of blood. Hyde-Thompson and Lance Pope who were captured with him were back in their quarters this afternoon.

The Second Front in Europe at last! It reads as a very minor affair in the German press, as though two men and a boy scout had crossed the Straits of Messina with a toy pistol. However, it does not say that they were at once taken prisoner or driven back across the straits, and after three years we know well how to interpret such reticence.

**TUESDAY 7 SEPTEMBER**
Mike Sinclair is back again. He is in the *Revier* and seems reasonably well.

**MONDAY 13 SEPTEMBER**
The British court of enquiry today published its findings on the shooting of Mike Sinclair under thirteen points. The findings are pretty much the substance of the entry I made on Friday the 3rd, except a) Lieutenant Sinclair was not thirty-five minutes without receiving attention to his wound, but fifteen; and b) the attitude and conduct of the German MO after his arrival on the scene were fully in accord with the highest standards of the medical profession.

The report was signed by the SBO and handed to the Protecting Power.

**WEDNESDAY 15 SEPTEMBER**
All the recent *Antrags* about the non-belligerency of chaplains, and the SBO's pursuit of the matter with the *Kommandant*, had the desired effect today in restoring our walks. Richard Heard and I assembled with Hugh Dickie and Draffin at the main gate at 2 p.m.

I was really not fit for the walk, and at most could not manage more than two or three kilometres. But it was far too attractive an occasion for me to stay behind voluntarily, and the other three almost convinced me that it was I who would be doing them a favour in that my pace would be theirs, and they wanted to walk slowly, and two or three kilometres was all they wished for. All of which I knew was beautifully untrue, but it made me feel their willingness that I should go. It is twenty months since I was last on a noncombatant walk.

It was a great pleasure. Being a typical September day it was cool and sunny, and the woodlands were already touched with autumn colouring. Old men, women of all ages, and numerous POWs were working in the fields. Apart from the POWs, all of whom were quick to offer recognition, some of the villagers nodded in a friendly fashion, and some of the tiny flaxen-haired children, too young to know if their daddies were fighting or not, or to know anything of the artificial barriers between nations and classes, smiled at us and chattered happily.

I resign my escape interests with some regret.

Am almost too tired to keep awake, and am very stiff and sore.

## THURSDAY 16 SEPTEMBER

Quite the largest influx of parcels came today: 2000 British Red Cross food parcels, 45 tobacco parcels, 40 of invalid comforts, 8 surgical, one of 200 tins of tooth powder, one of 144 rolls of toilet paper, plus sugar from Buenos Aires, and coffee from the Venezuelan Red Cross.

We have a store now of 5000 food parcels — five months' supply at one each a week. The impression is that Geneva is expecting a period of disorganised transport in Germany, and have anticipated events.

Another Camp Order today:

Camp Order No 23          Colditz 15 September 1943

By order of the German High Command, Prisoners of War who cause any harm to the German War Economics will be brought in future before a court martial instead of being punished disciplinarily. The following actions will be considered, amongst others, as harming the German War Economics: 1) breaking through walls, floors, ceilings, etc, damages to iron window bars etc; 2) destruction, damage or theft of furnishings and fittings (such as bed-boards, store-doors, electric fittings, etc); 3) altering of uniforms which are not the personal property of Prisoners of War; 4) theft of tools and materials and unauthorised use of electric current when building tunnels, etc; 5) theft and falsification of identity cards, etc.

Offences against these serious war necessities are to be considered a crime against War Economics, and will be punished with severity.

Signed: Prawitt, Lt.Col. and Commandant.

Comment: 'Well, that covers everything, particularly the etceteras!'

## WEDNESDAY 22 SEPTEMBER

Major Miles Reed arrived from Spangenberg this evening. He is a Royal Engineer taken in Greece. The offence for which he is *bestraft* is said to be that he refused to take his trousers down during a search.

## THURSDAY 23 SEPTEMBER

The one bit of disinterested tenderness in this place gathers round the well-being of our two kittens. On fine days their play in the *Hof* is the focus of all eyes, and on wet days, when the Trinity House kitten does not meet for fun and games with the *Kellerhaus* brat, the brat is teased and fondled until from sheer weariness of being passed from one to another, it shows its claws and quarters up in someone's bed.

*The rest of 1943 passed with little to mark it. There were theatrical productions of 'The Importance of Being Earnest' and 'French Without Tears', more lectures, and a number of officers sat various examinations. The library of 1500 books was meticulously reorganised by Major Victor Campbell, and Platt recorded:* 'I glanced through the borrowing lists to get an idea of what officers are reading. Books on sport, hunting, shooting, fishing, the Lonsdale Sporting Library, have rarely been more than twice borrowed. Economics appears to be the pet study of the camp since it became all-British, followed closely by history, especially military history. Religious books are rarely read, except the religious novels of Lloyd Douglas. Detective fiction and sea stories are extremely popular, as are novels like *How Green was my Valley* and *Gone With the Wind*.'

*Two orderlies escaped from a working party that was unloading coal in the local railway goods yard, and were at liberty for four days before being recaptured in West Germany. More tunnels were discovered but, in their surprise searches, the Germans recovered only 'an infinitesimal amount' of escape equipment.*

*The growing intensity of the air raids — the RAF prisoners estimated a thousand bombers over Leipzig and Berlin on 24 December — was a constant encouragement to the prisoners who felt the end of the war was in sight. On 18 November a new senior officer, Lieutenant-Colonel Tod of the Royal Scots Fusiliers, had arrived from Spangenberg, and had at once taken over from Broomhall as SBO. He was immediately respected and popular, and was to remain SBO until he received the surrender of the castle from the Germans at its liberation.*

*Ten days before Christmas the home-made still, constructed from Red Cross tins and stolen lavatory piping, blew up, scalding two de Gaullist officers who were distilling their raisin-prune-apricot-and-fig wine. It did nothing to hinder the Christmas drinking parties which Platt so deplored, with their unpleasant aftermath of vomiting and severe hangovers.*

*There were, by now, too many British in the camp for them to eat their Christmas dinner all together, and so each mess did its own cooking and ate separately. More than anything this emphasised the fact that an era had ended and the British community of Colditz was no longer the close family unity it had been in the international days.*

*On New Year's Eve Platt faced his fourth New Year in Oflag IVc and looked back on 1943.*

But for Jack Best, RAF, and Mike Harvey, RN, the year

is full of escape disappointments.* Heartbreak House indeed! Pat Dickenson broke the town gaol for the second time on 7 March, but was recaptured riding a stolen bicycle on the second day. Davies-Scourfield escaped, and was recaptured on 6 October. 'Scruffy' Orr-Ewing was captured on the same day without getting clear of the *Schloss*. Lance-Corporal Green and Private Fleet, who escaped from a working party in Colditz goods yard, were recaptured at Cottbus (?). The four Eichstätt boys who changed places with four French officers during the exodus of the French in July, and went to Lübeck, found no opportunity to escape. Johnny Rawson, who impersonated Max Aitken, the New Zealand dentist, and went to Mühlberg was immediately given up by the British SBO on the grounds that he was impersonating protected personnel. The *pièce de résistance* of the year — which the patron saint of escapers should have favoured — was the impersonation of *Feldwebel* Franz Joseph by Mike Sinclair on 2 September which led to Mike's being shot at point blank range by Bigbum. That was without doubt the best timed, best acted, best equipped and most richly conceived scheme ever attempted in this camp.

Many other schemes during the year were unmasked before they came to fruition by the multitude of sound detectors, burglar alarms, electric wiring, floodlighting, etc etc; and hosts of *Posten*. It was all too much for our limited equipment and our restricted field of operation.

The *Abwehr* measures are too good for our resources, and the use of German uniform would appear to have served its turn. Apart from the boys of the old brigade — those who came in 1940 — and a few of the Eichstätt boys, and half-a-dozen of the in-between arrivals, the drive has gone after three years of digging, digging, digging, and suffering heartbreak; prospecting, digging, digging, digging, and suffering heartbreak again, and again, and again. And anyway the end of the war has suddenly leapt into sight,

*This sentence was obviously put in for the benefit of the German censors. For the truth of Jack Best's and Mike Harvey's 'escape' see the entry for 29 March 1944.

and betting on the probable date of the end has taken the place of escaping.

Fundamental changes have taken place, too, in the character of the camp. Its most grievous complaint is old age. Young men have grown old from prison-weariness and hope deferred. Occupations of value are taken up in moments of self-criticism and resolution, only to be cast aside again in greater weariness and frustration. Conversation has almost stagnated except for topics of war news, letters, and sex perversion. Talk of 'wimmin' in relation to sex has altogether ceased in some circles.

With the removal of the foreigners *Oflag* IVc has lost its individuality. As an all-British camp it is a psychological mud-flat — no international incidents, no international rub and rasp of political differences, no clash of national hopes, no rivalry between the representatives of conquered and occupied territory, no quarrelling, no language study, no unknown racial characteristic that might at any time leap out to surprise and bewilder, NO NOTHING except British bulldogs in various stages of plethoric and phlegmatic prison weariness.

The coming of the Eichstätt boys marked the end of the British family life as it had been from the beginning. Hitherto newcomers were received into the family and absorbed by it almost at once. But the Eichstätters came in large numbers from a much larger camp, were put in separate quarters, fed and lived separately, and the colonel they brought with them at once succeeded to SBO-ship. They have retained the atmosphere of a large camp and, with a few exceptions, have remained in small friendship circles complete in themselves and almost exclusive.

With the decisive change in the war situation the German attitude to British POWs has changed. Rations are improved in quality (the better cooking is due to Lieutenant Hanney's tireless labour in the camp kitchen, and the orderly, Whittingham's, equally tireless work and skill), the lighting of the quarters is better, some of the rights of non-combatants are recognised, and searches have nothing of the carelessness for private property of three years ago.

H                                   225

Actual discipline is what it ever was, and is fair.

The literary and educational side of camp life shows us to be a good cross section, allowing of course for the banal influence of nearly four years in which high-spirited young men have been shut off from everything that is normal, and subjected to much that is abnormal and sub-normal. A not inconsiderable minority read good literature and work at some serious professional or university study. But it remains a fact that far too large a section of the camp reads nothing but fiction and a little biography.

Camp entertainment has had a rather brighter polish since the Eichstätt invasion; they also contributed a number of good ball-game players, and a high-stake poker school in which no member may continue to play after the end of the month if he has an uncleared debt of £200 or more. A set of hockey sticks that arrived a few weeks ago are in great demand, and so that a dozen teams may play the time in the *Hof* is apportioned. Eichstätt also gave us one or two confirmed gamblers who appear to gamble not to add spice to a game or argument, nor to back a guess or judgement, but simply to gain possession of fellow-prisoners' money. Some of them have sent home cheques for large sums.

Some of the newcomers, particularly from RAF camps, are shocked and pained at the rackets and racketeers of IVc. It has always been a place of rackets. Even in the early days, when Red Cross parcels were few, it was known that certain of the small company would eat some of the communal chocolate while carrying the parcel contents to the British quarters. As the camp enlarged, master racketeers arrived; and soon everyone was driven in self-defence to acceptance or active participation. Nowadays racketeering in high places and low is an unnecessary and unsavoury part of camp life.

There is a decrease in moral resistance and an increase in perverted interest. The general attitude to homosexualism varies from supercilious disregard to mild amusement, from willing ignorance to distress and efforts to resist its development. But the high moral behaviour of the majority is eloquent testimony to the character and balance of fighting

226

men who, after four years of abnormal inactivity and inhibition are as clean of mind and thought as ever.

Of religion one feels that it is moderately patronised by the majority, and to a minority it is vital and real. But it is at a low ebb: not perhaps in fundamental belief, or in the acceptance of its social and political idealism, but definitely so in the practice of worship. The first six months of captivity was very different: consciousness of dependence on some power outside themselves was real, and church service was one of the biggest things in camp life. Some who found a Christian experience then have kept it as the greatest meaning of life.

Pat Reid married an American heiress in Switzerland two months ago!

# Colditz 1944

## NEW YEAR'S DAY

I CREPT UNDER the blankets at midnight wishing to spend an hour in meditation and spiritual communion with Maisie and my people. The New Year arrives one hour earlier here, so she would be listening to the round-the-world broadcast. At that moment I would have given a year of my life to be listening to the same programme.

Barbaric yells issued from the *Hof* at a few minutes to twelve. The orderlies had staged a wild African dance in fancy dress with some of the de Gaullist Africans taking part. After midnight the rest of the prisoners — most of them unaware it was snowing — joined hands and waltzed round — or fell down — singing 'Auld Lang Syne'.

After lights out I dropped into semi-consciousness, and was repeatedly stabbed back to consciousness by the revellers in the next room becoming more than usually vociferous, and by Black Campbell coming to pay New Year compliments, followed by others to assure me — hic — of their pro-hic-found regard f-f-for my good ... work, and to wish me '*un bon neue jahre*'. Rex came with half a bottle of vicious hooch which he knew — hic — would give me a happy new year. He sat on the floor singing while he supposed I drank. He did not see me get out of bed, but noticed my return and insisted on tucking me in, in the process of which he fell across my bunk. He is only six feet six and seventeen stones! It was 2.45 when I got him to the *cabinet* and, mentioning a large piece of fat pork, left him to recover his sobriety.

WEDNESDAY 19 JANUARY

A few days ago a three-minute gap was discovered in the *Abwehr* defences against escape. At 5.10 p.m. today Mike Sinclair and Bob Barnes* escaped. For once, everything was in the escapers' favour.

For a few evenings a time lag in the redistribution of *Posten* had been observed. It occurred a few minutes before the perimeter lights came on, and whoever was responsible had so arranged matters that the western ramparts were not patrolled for a full three minutes. The only gamble was with the perimeter lights. Last night and the night before they came on right at the beginning of the three-minute gap, and the attempt was abandoned. Tonight — the day having been clearer and light for a few minutes longer — the perimeter lights were later coming on. Quick and willing workers did the rest.

The window bars had already been cut where they joined the concrete windowsill. Strong hands wrenched them inwards, leaving a free space of about fourteen inches square. Mike, and then Bob, were pushed through and lowered twenty feet by rope. They then climbed the three-foot balustrade and lowered themselves another twenty feet on to a garden plot next to — but cut off by a barbed wire fence from — the park on the north side of the *Schloss*.

Mike cut through the barbed wire fence and disappeared. Bob followed. The lights came on and a *Posten* wearing thick-lensed glasses for short-sightedness came out of the guard room to see if everything was all right. He saw something which might have looked like a cat, but was Bob's head disappearing beneath the barbed wire as he dropped into the park. The *Posten* shouted 'hello', but seemed quite satisfied until he saw the rope coming rapidly back through our window.

It had been a bare three minutes, but enough to give them liberty. It was audacious and hare-brained but, where

*In fact, Mike Sinclair's companion was Jack Best masquerading as Bob Barnes — which Platt knew very well. See entry for 29 March 1944.

229

escape is concerned, so are they. The ramparts were instantly astir with swarms of *Posten*, but they were blinded by the perimeter lights and it was a full ten minutes before the trail was spotted.

It is now fox and hounds. The fox has fifteen minutes' start, but hounds hunt by telephone, radio, police, and a company of soldiery hot on the trail. How good is the fox?

THURSDAY 20 JANUARY
Hounds have returned to kennels. Fox still running strongly.

TUESDAY 25 JANUARY
Another search. Awakened at 7 a.m. but allowed to wash and visit the lats before being turned out of our quarters. The theatre was opened for those without friends in the *Saalhaus.* This is a great improvement on previous searches, and can only mean that the practice of searching the persons of officers has been dropped after three-and-a-half years. The civilians who directed the last search were present, this time in the uniform of the SS.

Such things were removed as the miserable little fat lamps we use during blackout, and all cooking utensils were taken to the kitchen for checking. Odds and ends of uniform that had been altered in any way were also taken; and Rex's still.

We are told that Mike and Bob will be back at Colditz tomorrow.

FRIDAY 28 JANUARY
Lieutenant Bill Miller, Dieppe-Canadian, has escaped. Authority has not yet decided how. He has not had much start, but a little more than Mike and Bob had — which unlucky pair were brought back to IVc yesterday.

This evening, when the *Prominente* were about to sit down to supper, they were ordered to their rooms to be locked up for the night. They refused, and a few minutes later Püpcke turned an armed guard out and escorted them away in the middle of the meal. The *Kommandant* is evidently very afraid that one of them might escape. The special walks — guarded by tommy-guns — they used to get in lieu of official exercise, have been stopped these two months. The poor fellows get no proper exercise and are now locked up each night at seven o'clock.

TUESDAY 1 FEBRUARY

Became third-floor 'quarter-master' today. It is an unwanted job, hence tables are required to provide an officer for one month each. It consists of receiving German rations in bulk from the camp kitchen, and dividing and serving them. Cutting up German loaves into equal parts is difficult enough, apart from there not being a decent knife in the place. The return of the containers to the kitchen is done by the orderly when he remembers, and by the QM when the orderly forgets. The division of Red Cross cigarettes and tobacco is one of the pleasing duties.

'Wardour for washing!' So ran the legend on the eight-foot banner which was paraded round the *Hof* this afternoon preceded by a band. It was John Arundell of Wardour's retirement from the post of laundry officer, and other placards were carried by sandwichmen. 'Peer's Soap' was a caricature of Lord Arundell bent over a wash tub. Another announced 'Arundell Laundry 1066–1944'. A third, another excellent caricature, showed my lord driving a two-horse fly with great aplomb — his moustache and nose as true to life as life itself — with the caption 'Arundell delivers early'.

After the procession he was chaired and borne round the *Hof*. Bill Burton, the present laundry officer, pretended great indignation, but knew all too well that all the king's horses could not drag John Arundell to the position again.

MONDAY 14 FEBRUARY

A burst of parties. After New Year most tables laid down an invasion-brew, which was ready for distilling at the beginning of this month. The invasion seemed remotely distant, the weather extremely unpleasant and cold, so supplies of hooch ready and waiting seemed very attractive and

231

called for immediate consumption, and the laying-down of more invasion-brew.

## SATURDAY 19 FEBRUARY

An air raid woke us at 3.15 a.m. Most of us dropped off to sleep again, but were wakened later by an enormous explosion which was taken to be a bomb-load released pretty close by a plane in difficulties from German night-fighters. Leipzig appeared to be one of the targets, and the reflection of the fires was a steadily mounting glow.

The German press has been giving publicity to 'reprisal raids on London', which sound very terrible.

## MONDAY 21 FEBRUARY

I was still thirty-nine when I said goodbye to Maisie on Euston Station. Today I am forty-four! And more than ever during this period of separation I am longing to be with her: that is, as different from, and foremost in, the continual longing for liberty.

We had another straw to grasp at today — in a letter dated in London on 24 January which said, 'the London papers yesterday announced that further proposals had been made for the exchange of prisoners who have been in enemy hands for three years or more'. Most officers are expecting this scheme to go on the rocks in the same place that the last one was wrecked.

Dan Halifax, Flight-Lieutenant in the RAF, returned from the hospital at Halle today. He was originally sent to IVc for complaining about the state in which the surgeons had left him after he was shot down. The Mixed Commission recommended him for repatriation long, long ago, and he should have been with the party of repatriates that arrived in England in October last year.

Whether he was overlooked, or kept here deliberately, no one knows. But the OKW suddenly decided to do something about his case, and on 3 December he was taken to the eye clinic at Halle. The eye-surgeon operated at once, and has since done two further operations. The result is a considerable improvement in his appearance: his top and bottom eyelids look natural, though in truth they are the result of manipulative surgery. However, the job is by no means complete: Hugh Dickin describes it as a good beginning.

I spoke with Dan tonight. He said he had been treated by the clinic staff without regard to the fact he was a POW. He had a private room, and at Christmas received the little extras, like chocolate biscuits, that the German civilian patients were given.

## TUESDAY 22 FEBRUARY

A daylight raid. We heard the planes and saw puffs of smoke from the flak, but could not see the bombers. The high revving engines which came within earshot were thought by our RAF officers to be Mosquitoes.

We did not get our fortnightly bath today. Yesterday a shaft was found leading from the shower shed.

## FRIDAY 25 FEBRUARY

Still no bath. Most of us getting high and unpleasant. Thank God the weather is cold!

## TUESDAY 29 FEBRUARY

This is Leap Year's Day, and an excuse for a party. The invasion-brews laid down just before St Valentine's day were distilled during the past week — some of them only having been laid down eight or ten days. Colonel Tod addressed the officers on proper behaviour at lunch time, so the parties did not reach the besotted stage before evening *Appell*. But quite a few bottles had been uncorked, and quite a few were merry.

## WEDNESDAY 1 MARCH

The SBO's speech was not without effect. There was evidence this morning of considerable regurgitation, and of friends and accomplices having done the cleaning up. Many officers did not go to bed — some were recumbent in unusual places. The non-drunks who did go to bed could not get to sleep. Drunken dancing on the wooden floors of the upper stories sounded like thunder. Several parties are still in full swing, and will continue tonight.

There is a notice on the Medical Inspection room door: 'If any British officer thinks he feels worse than the MOs, will he please visit them in their room.'

We had a shortened non-comb. walk again this afternoon. One of the two guards — the same poor fellow as we had one day last week — has been shot up badly in the heel and ankle and wears a surgical boot. He shambles along quite nicely, and is by no means unfriendly, but the pain he has in walking is a source of distress to us. The walk was so shortened today that we were back by 3 p.m. instead of four, and he filled in time by taking us through the streets of the village we had not seen before.

THURSDAY 2 MARCH
A consignment of British matches arrived yesterday. They are Bryant and Mays. Striking one of them is like driving a Rolls Royce.

FRIDAY 3 MARCH
Ernie Champion arrived back from Massfeld last night. He is considerably better and has been on a normal diet for some weeks. The thing he told us that most astounded us — and which we thought to be a mistake — was that an MO at Obermassfeld asked him to convey his condolences to Colonel Tod on the death of his only son. We had heard nothing of such a wartime commonplace affecting the SBO, and his general demeanour had given no inkling of his hearing any such sorrow.

I went over to his room and found it to be sadly true. The news reached him on 18 January that his son (an only child) was killed when a carrier overturned on him. What a courageous man the SBO is.

SATURDAY 4 MARCH
Daylight raid in heavy snow-cloud.

After the parties a general apathy has settled on most people, and the camp is as cold as the weather. Psycho-

234

logically there could have been no better time for the German Ministry of Information to flood the camp with anti-semitic propaganda.

On the title-page of a sixty-four page pamphlet is printed: 'The author of this brochure, which was distributed by a patriotic society in Britain in the year 1938, is a retired captain in the British Army. He has to remain anonymous, he says, "until such time as Englishmen are free to express an opinion on the Jewish menace to their own country without being flung into prison".'

The next pamphlet, *How Odd of God*, bears the name of Douglas Reed, the man who, after graduating to subeditorship of the London *Times* in 1924, was suddenly whisked away to become assistant correspondent to the *Times* in Berlin.

Another smaller booklet, bearing the name of Elma Dangerfield, tells the sorry plight of Estonians, Latvians and Poles who were deported to Russia as workers. The story is reminiscent of some told us by our fellow-POWs before IVc lost its interest and bearableness by becoming an all-British camp.

SUNDAY 5 MARCH 1944
Ralph Holroyd had a visit from his mother this afternoon. She is of German birth and was visiting Germany from Australia when war broke out in 1939. Since Ralph arrived in Germany after his capture in Greece his mother has never ceased her efforts to get permission to visit him. Time and again the OKW has refused her requests, but finally she wrote to Adolf, and on February 18 received his direct approval and the date and time — 3–6 p.m. on 5.3.44 — when she might meet her son. She arrived in Colditz yesterday and stayed at the village hotel, *das Goldene Kreuz*.

Richard Heard, who has gained a not inconsiderable reputation as a pastry-cook, made a cake; and at a few minutes to three o'clock Ralph, laden with tea, sugar, milk, cake, chocolate, bully beef, butter and bread, was taken out of the *Hof* to the German officers' mess. His mother was already sitting in a small comfortably-furnished ante-room, and there they had tea. Dr Eggers was present, but effaced himself as far as he could, sitting writing in the furthest corner of the room. He couldn't accept the gift of a piece of cake and a cup of tea from a prisoner, but was able to do so from Mrs Holroyd, and to enjoy a piece of chocolate.

She was looking older, Ralph said, and was glad to have news from his letters of her husband whom she had not seen for five years. The only correspondence she is able to have with him in Australia is a short telegram-like message once in three months through the Red Cross. If she had not been a German national she would long ago have been interned.

WEDNESDAY 8 MARCH 1944

There was a new arrival this morning: Sub-Lieutenant Purdy, RNR, of HMS *Van Dyke*. He said he was at Spangenberg in 1940, but I did not remember him. All the Naval types were removed to *Marlag Nord* on 24 January 1941 before the March reprisals of that year were taken on the Army.

Nine months ago Purdy was taken out of *Marlag Nord* and, by reason of his having claimed to know the now silent Lord Haw-Haw, was presumed to have gone to the Propaganda Camp at Berlin. His arrival here this morning caused quite a flutter in the naval dovecote. The story of his nine months in Berlin is something more than credible. After five weeks in the Propaganda Camp, during which time he went to the cinema twice a week, and was taken to see the sights of *Hauptstadt*, he threatened to strike a *Sonderführer* (who seems to be an *Offizier* without rank). For this he claims to have been moved to a French *Stalag* in the city.

The French 'workers' received week-end passes which entitled them to spend the week-end in the city. Purdy borrowed a pass and went to a hostel which his French companions were in the habit of visiting, and handed the pass back to one of the workers who came to the hostel to assure himself that it would be returned to its rightful owner.

Purdy was fortunate in having the address of a German girl who owned a chain of millinery shops and was his sister's best friend before the war. He found her at home that night, and lived with her until a few days ago when the block in which they were living was struck by a bomb. They were buried in the débris, but were rescued none the worse for the experience.

He tried to get out of Berlin with the bombed-out citizens, but his papers were not in order: he was not holding the *Ausweis* of the official evacuees. While living with his sister's best friend he had held papers showing him to be 'a British soldier working in Berlin', but he would have had official evacuee papers within a few hours if the Gestapo had not descended on him three days ago and found his *Ausweis* to have one stamp too many. The Gestapo did not bother about his sister's best friend in pre-war days who owned a chain of millinery shops in (war-time) Berlin. After taking Purdy back to — it is not clear where — they sent him under guard to *Oflag* IVc . . . 'and, by Jove, I'm mighty glad to see all you boys!'

Needless to say he is under the gravest suspicion.

FRIDAY 10 MARCH
Sewing number-tabs on laundry has caused more blasphemy than even naval and military circles might deem adequate. In every dormitory officers are stitching inch-square tabs on dirty linen which will have to leave the camp this afternoon. There is much blood on shirt-bands and handkerchiefs, and some on thumbs that have taken the needle so frequently as to be too sore for further operations. It is all an effort to solve a laundry muddle which did not exist when the camp was five hundred strong and of six nationalities. (The present strength is under two hundred, all British.)

Sub-Lieutenant Purdy, RNR, left *Oflag* IVc this afternoon — or, more precisely, was removed from the presence of British officers on the representations of the SBO. The following dialogue seems to have taken place between the SBO and the *Kommandant.*

SBO: 'Purdy must be removed from the presence of British officers. He is a stool pigeon.'

*Kommandant:* 'He was sent here by the OKW, and that is enough for me. I will not have him moved.'

*Kommandant's* Adjutant: 'But Purdy will be safe, will he not?'

*Kommandant:* 'I don't care whether he is or not. He is an enemy officer.'

SBO: 'Well, I'm sure I don't care. Having worked for the Germans he is no longer a British officer. You have been warned of what may happen, and it's your affair now.'

The *Kommandant's* attitude underwent a rapid change. He would have Purdy brought into the *Kommandantur* and, if he told the same story as the one Colonel Tod had told, he would be removed at once.

The story is as follows: when Purdy arrived here on Wednesday, and shot his line as I have already told it, a few of the more senior officers who were not overpowered by his description of his sex life in Berlin considered his story to suffer from over-embellishment. He talked freely to a number of officers who later compared notes and made a report. During the evening he was examined by two of our security officers, and one or two of his discrepancies were pointed out. He was invited to tell the truth.

He tried again, but was interrupted and told what would happen to a stool-pigeon in *Oflag* IVc. His composure was completely shaken, and the second invitation to tell the truth elicited this. He had pre-war acquaintance with William Joyce, and perhaps through his influence was taken from *Marlag Nord* to the Propaganda Camp. After coming to terms with the Germans he allowed himself to be used on the German radio for propaganda broadcasts to England and America. He tried to double-cross the Germans by introducing bits of his own while speaking to England. He was given the proper *Ausweis* and ration cards, and allowed to live with a German woman. He admitted he was a rat, but when asked if he would work for the

Germans again if offered an attractive reward by them he replied: 'I'm afraid I would do it again. I want to get back to my woman in Berlin.'

He was placed under arrest by the SBO, a circumstance for which he should be extremely grateful — unless his shame for his conduct is greater than a natural longing for life.* He is not receiving Red Cross food or cigarettes while here.

It will be interesting to know what happens to the next stool-pigeon who fetches up at IVc: and perhaps no less tragic than interesting!

THURSDAY 16 MARCH

A very quiet and successful search began at 4 p.m. On the second floor they walked straight to what they were looking for — a hide — and found it. It would not have been found thus if they had not known where to look. The fact of its being full of escape gear makes it the richest haul in the history of British interests in IVc. By 4.45 everything was removed, including the still, and typewriter parts. Everyone was exuberant except the POWs.

Yesterday, by order of the *Kommandant*, a Red Cross food parcel was taken from the British store for Purdy who is still somewhere at hand.

FRIDAY 17 MARCH

And so it goes on! This morning it was a tunnel leading from the first floor.

During the search yesterday evening they went straight to the tunnel lid and tapped with hammers, and scrutinised it with torches, but the camouflage was too good for them. However, they knew what they were looking for, and the direction that the tunnel had taken, for, at 8.30 a.m., 'Aunty' arrived at the foot of the staircase with a workman who drove a hole two feet deep in the wall, and entered the tunnel six feet from the proper entrance. Work had been suspended since yesterday's episode, so no one was caught.

*Purdy's final confession was broadly true. A fuller account of his career can be found in *The Meaning of Treason* by Rebecca West.

Purdy need not be responsible for today's affair.* The Germans knew something was going on, but so did Purdy. It was impossible to keep anyone in ignorance of it because the entrance was visible on the first floor and Purdy — very inopportunely for us — passed it when the lid was off within a few hours of being in the camp. He remarked, 'The *Marlag* boys are at it again!'

While the work of driving through the wall at the base of the staircase was going on, someone made off with some of the tools being used — a cold chisel was the most important. After lunch, when the hide that was unearthed yesterday was receiving the carpenter's attention, someone made off with his saw. It was passed from hand to hand, and finally thrust into Bill Scott's hand. Without looking he dashed for the doorway to the first floor and ran into the upraised rifle of the *Posten* who tried to stop him. While Bill was sympathetically fingering his bleeding nose which he thought broken, someone else ran off with the saw. It was recovered by the Germans a few minutes later.

## THURSDAY 23 MARCH
A new arrival was turned in to the *Hof* in the course of the morning. He is Rudi Reichoffen, an Alsatian who claims to have been taken prisoner at Nettuno, and to be an 'aspirant' in de Gaulle's army. He is neither!

## FRIDAY 24 MARCH
Calling from his bed this morning John Penman read aloud the following passage: 'What impressed me most about them was not, I think, their whipped look; not their scowling resignation; not their appearance of being discarded, unusable, unwanted members of society; not the strange rags and ravellings with which their clothes were patched and darned, making them appear like masqueraders in fuzzy caricatures of uniforms. What struck me most was

*At his trial after the war he was acquitted of betraying the Colditz secrets, but condemned to death (the sentence later commuted to life imprisonment) for his propaganda work for the SS.

their noisy and pretended merriment; sudden gusts of mirthless laughter over nothing, almost as if four years of captivity had warped their wits.' It is a descriptive passage from Kenneth Roberts' *Oliver Wiswell* about the remnant of Burgoyne's army who were POWs in a camp at Frederick in the bleak Maryland hills. It was the American War of Independence — but POWs are unchanged in a hundred and sixty years!

The camp kitchen as from today is under British control. The German *Gefreiter* is present only for reasons of security. Lieutenant Edmund Hanney, 2nd Seaforth Highland Regiment, is an admirable kitchen officer who seems to enjoy difficulty.

The series of lectures in German, started for advanced students of German by Dr Eggers, were continued today by one of the censors. The subject was Martin Luther!

MONDAY 27 MARCH 1944

On Friday a Red Cross parcel was taken from the store by order of the *Kommandant* for Purdy. He had also ordered cigarettes to be taken, but the British tobacco officer, Sir Peter Greenwell, who holds the key to the store, was not easy to find. Today, however, he was ordered to open the store and supply 300 Red Cross cigarettes. He opened the door, but refused to hand over any cigarettes, whereupon the *Kommandant*'s representative took the three hundred cigarettes himself, and went off with them.

It is difficult to understand why Purdy is still at IVc. Though living in one of the cells under the archway, he is not being strafed. He goes out of the *Schloss* for walks with an unarmed sentry and, since German rations are obviously insufficient, he has had the Red Cross parcel. A British officer in *Stubenarrest* does not get his weekly parcel.

TUESDAY 28 MARCH

Authority is in something of a dilemma over the identity of one of the two escapers who made the abortive attempt

241

on Sunday night. Bush Parker was recognised at once, and yesterday was turned into the *Hof* to await sentence. But his companion, who gave the name and number of Dennis Bartlett, is the object of some suspicion.

Dr Eggers tonight asked, 'Who is the new-born baby?' It is obvious that they have no idea of his true identity. We think they regard it as a possibility that he is an RAF officer who by freak chance arrived during the last air raid by parachute.

WEDNESDAY 29 MARCH
Identification parade in the theatre at 11 a.m. Dr Eggers asked me if I had ever known of a baby being born without the presence of the mother, and suggested the answer to such a riddle was in the cells.

It was not until I sat at tea opposite to Jack Best that I heard the story of the curtain falling on his and Mike Harvey's little act. He and Mike disappeared from German view on 5 April last year. They were supposed to have escaped, and their names accordingly dropped out of use — among ourselves they were known by a soubriquet.

For the first few days they were kept in close hiding and then, after the hue and cry had subsided and their bedding had been removed, they were only in hiding during *Appell*. It is fairly evident that they were written off the strength of the camp and their identification paraphernalia sent to the OKW. During the fifty-one weeks in which their presence in the camp was unknown to the Germans they have led a charmed life. The test of how well and truly they were forgotten occurred when Jack escaped with Mike Sinclair on 9 January. When caught at Rheine Jack said he was Bob Barnes — a pretence he kept up successfully when they were returned to IVc. He was punished as Bob Barnes and released as Bob Barnes, and then he rejoined Mike Harvey and the real Bob came back into circulation.

When caught on Sunday night Mike Harvey found the impersonation of Dennis Bartlett more difficult than Jack had done of Bob Barnes. How long it took the Germans to suspect his real identity it is difficult to say. But it seems a reasonable supposition that they communicated with the OKW about their mysterious catch, and the OKW sent the papers of identification of all POWs missing from IVc. With the photograph and fingerprints before them, the rest would have been easy.

This morning Dr Eggers visited Mike in the cells and addressed him as Mr Harvey. Deciding that Jack was also in the camp, and with his memory refreshed by looking at the photograph, Fritz came on a round of the camp and, spotting Jack, took him to be interviewed. A comparison of fingerprints established that he was not Lieutenant Barnes, and Dr Eggers said 'I shall have to put you in preventive detention until you know who you are. Now are you Mr Best?' Jack admitted it.

For being late for *Appell* officers are now sentenced to fourteen days *Stubenarrest*. If Jack and Mike get fourteen days for each *Appell* they have not attended they will receive a sentence of thirty years apiece.

GOOD FRIDAY 1944
Only four of us have been at the Holy Week communion services, but fifteen communicated this morning. This is the one day of the year when mass is not said in the Roman Church. One of the things which surprises me is how few of the RCs here are practising.

EASTER DAY
Holy Communion at 8.20 and 9 a.m. There were many communicants, at least half the camp, except the orderlies — none of whom communicated. Attendance at morning service at eleven o'clock was also extremely good, and the choir, collected and trained by John Beaumont, gave a new character to the congregational singing and made it sound like English church worship on an Easter morning. Jack Courtenay had worked nobly, and succeeded in hiding the garish theatre curtain with its griffins, and gave the effect of an unadorned altar with a red cross in the background.

The sun shone and sunbathers were out, and several ball games were played before tea time. Jack's gramophone recital of sacred music was the event of the evening: the uninterested played bridge.

## TUESDAY 11 APRIL

The day's bread ration was not available until the afternoon. At my table we were without breakfast, having had the misfortune this week to draw Canadian parcels that had lost condition. The chocolate was bleached with age, and the usually excellent hard tack biscuits were mouldy.

Jack Best and Mike Harvey were sentenced by Dresden to twenty-eight days' arrest. The findings were translated by a censor: 'because they have hidden intentionally since 5.4.43 until they were found again in *Oflag* IVc intending to prepare an escape, to that they had to be reported as having escaped to the superior authorities, and because they missed in disobeying their orders nearly one year long the daily *Appells* as well as the three check *Appells* every month.'

Purdy is still at IVc.

## SATURDAY 15 APRIL

Had J——— in to see me again. After much soul-searching he has reached the conviction that he must offer himself for the ministry of his church — Church of Scotland. His prospects as a civil engineer are gilt-edged, but he feels he must resign these in answer to his call. I am to start with him on Tuesday evenings a course of such studies as are possible with our limited supply of books.

## THURSDAY 20 APRIL

One of the orderlies claims to have seen Purdy, who is still in the cell under the arch, salute the Nazi flag when passing on his way to or from his cell. Though he was an officer he has also been seen to salute German *Unteroffiziere*! I suppose he has burned his boats with both Germany and England: with England for having betrayed his country, and Germany for having revealed here that he has worked for the Germans.

Dominic Bruce made a brave attempt to escape tonight. He succeeded in getting out of a window and across the rampart on the north side to the first wall of barbed wire. His wire-cutters were home-made, and failed their task. A warning shot was fired, and Brucie was marched off to the *Kommandantur.*

FRIDAY 21 APRIL
The first night of 'Blithe Spirit'. The play is completely amoral as all Coward's stuff is, but it is light and amusing, and the production and acting were extremely good. Wild applause from a very delighted audience.

SUNDAY 23 APRIL
John Crawford came out of the town gaol and told us of a conversation Dominic Bruce had had with Purdy when he was in the next cell to him under the archway.

Purdy opened the conversation through the keyhole. Dominic knew who he was talking to, but gave the impression he had only just arrived at IVc and wondered what the camp was like. Purdy, who said he was Lieutenant-Commander Beale, said he did not know what the camp was like either. He had been taken prisoner, he said, with a fellow named Purdy, and by corrupting the German officers — who were easier to corrupt than the men — with cigarettes, he and Purdy had hoaxed the Germans into sending them to the Propaganda Camp from which they escaped. (The British officers at the Propaganda Camp, he said, were a lot of rats.) After escaping they committed an act of serious sabotage on the German railway and when captured were sentenced to death. He did not know what had happened to poor old Purdy, but he, Beale, had played the Germans along again, and had been sent to IVc instead of being executed. He was expecting to escape shortly and, knowing German and Germany very well, he had no doubt he would succeed.

Dominic was able to tell him where Purdy was, and some things about Purdy which included his being sentenced to death. It concluded the conversation. At least, Purdy did

not answer to such further conversation as Dominic wanted
to pursue.

TUESDAY 2 MAY

X-rays are the order of the day. It appears that the people
with stomach or lung trouble who are to appear before the
Repatriation Board ought to have been X-rayed long ago so
that the preliminary examinations by the German speci-
alists could have the proper aids to diagnosis. They were
hustled off to the hospital at Leipzig this morning.

John Beaumont got away from exercise this afternoon. It
was a clever ruse, cleverly done.* He concealed himself
while on exercise, and was helped to a twenty-minute start
by the rest of the company bungling the count before being
readmitted to the *Hof*. He was recaptured going through
the village about a kilometre away a quarter of an hour
after the *Sonderappell* and identification parade.

THURSDAY 4 MAY

J——— and E——— were hustled off at 4 a.m. to see a
psychiatrist in Leipzig. They are mental cases who are
expected to be passed for repatriation by the Mixed Commission tomorrow.

FRIDAY 5 MAY

At morning *Appell Hauptmann* Püpcke notified the SBO
of a day's delay in the visit of the Commission. It will
arrive tomorrow.

Later he handed the SBO a list of those officers and
orderlies who would be called before the Commission. Six
names were not on the list — all of whom had been proposed under Article 70 of the Geneva Convention. Püpcke
said that an order from the OKW said that the six would
not be allowed to see the Commission. The SBO replied
'either they will all go, or none will go.' And there the
matter rests at the moment.

*John Beaumont who, like his friend Jack Courtenay (see entry
for Easter Day), is now an Anglican priest, hid himself under a
blanket camouflaged as a rubbish heap.

SATURDAY 6 MAY

As is his custom between 8.30 and 9 a.m., the SBO was walking round and round the *Hof* when *Hauptmann* Püpcke intercepted him and asked for the officers and men who were to go before the Repatriation Board to be assembled. Püpcke of course meant all whom the OKW would permit, not the six said to be prohibited by OKW orders. Tod's reply was as yesterday. There was some argument, but no advance; hence Authority had the bugle sounding for a *Sonderappell* for 9.15 a.m.

It was like old times, the golden days of *Hauptmann* Priem. Officers assembled in a party spirit, and cheered happily when an *Unteroffizier* arrived with photographs and the paraphernalia of identification. Eggers and Püpcke held an agitated conversation with Tod who was pointing out that he had been wrongly informed yesterday that two of the six — two badly knocked about de Gaullists — had already been passed for repatriation by the Commission in Italy. This was not so, and he would not change his attitude until he was assured they were to be repatriated at the earliest possible moment.

As a way out of the *impasse* he asked if he could see the Commission himself at once, after which he would order the proposed repatriates to present themselves. Eggers said he couldn't give permission for this, but he would ask the *Kommandant*. After ten minutes' delay the answer was brought. Colonel Tod was not to see the Commission until the authorised list of proposed repatriates had been found, and he was strictly forbidden to mention the two de Gaullist officers or the rest of the six. The SBO did not reply.

*Appell* began. The lines were all counted and a number found to be missing. Heads appeared at various windows, encouraging remarks were made, loud laughter filled the courtyard. Sentries were dispatched to round up the strays, and after a pleasant game of hide and seek — punctuated by more helpful remarks and laughter — *Appell* continued and all were present.

A photograph taken out of the bunch the Germans held

was scrutinised by half a dozen Germans, and then the search began in and out of the lines. Private Brown was the first to be found and marched through the gate. Miles Reid was found next. He side-stepped his guard as they approached the SBO and, coming smartly to attention, asked what he should do. He was advised not to resist.

As he was marched down to the gate a crowd of about a hundred officers flocked behind him wailing raucously and reducing the proceedings to a hubbub. Armed sentries were ordered to thrust them back from the gate, and the whole guard was called out and posted at strategic positions with rifles at the ready.

Now it was really like old times: the guard in position, the prisoners singing, shouting and whistling. 'If only Priem were here!' was the lament of the old lags. This kind of party was right up his street. He would have had musketry loosed off in every direction; but not a shot was fired.

All those on the *Kommandant*'s list were soon found and marched out, and the parade dismissed. When the SBO was taken to the Commission (two Swiss MOs and one German) he apologised for his part in the delay, and explained how the *Kommandant*'s list forbade the presence of six officers by order of the OKW. This amazed the visitors, and there was further delay while their point of view was conveyed to the *Kommandant*.

At 11.45 the Commission began its work, and the six were at once sent for. The two de Gaullists were put under immediate notice to have their kit packed, and by half past one they were entrained for the repatriation centre. Of all the other only six officers and two orderlies were passed. The rest were rejected as being fit.

WEDNESDAY 24 MAY
Brought in a bunch of nettles. Boiled them for supper. Much appreciated.

WHITSUNDAY
At 1.45 p.m. an air-raid warning — a three-blaster notify-

ing that Allied planes have crossed into German territory. I was writing my weekly letter to Maisie, replying to a letter I received four days ago — the first since the beginning of April.

Air-raid warnings are so frequent these days as to make no stir except an odd cheer from the irrepressible. Sunbathers were bathing, letter-writers were writing, readers lay on their bunks in almost complete undress, and bridge-players and poker-players played. Then the Leipzig flak opened up, followed by the detonations of heavy bombs. In a flash the windows on the north and west sides of the *Schloss* were choked three and four deep with watchers and listeners, and wags making unseemly and witty cracks after each fierce detonation, or when the hot blast reached us. And then there was such a crescendo of howling and cheering as I have not heard since I sat with the football crowds at Wembley, for someone at a north window had spotted a formation of bombers with fighter escort that, having passed over the target and unloaded, had turned and were coming in our direction. For fifteen minutes there was such excitement as will only be equalled when the news of the invasion reaches us.

Wave after wave passed over the target. We heard their bombs and then, within a few minutes, they came into view and passed directly over the *Schloss*. Visibility was perfect; even the fighters, at a much greater height than the bombers, could be easily seen.

The bombers were the first Liberators and Fortresses most of us had ever seen, and were certainly the first friendly planes most of us had seen (though we have heard many) since we were taken prisoner.

We saw four men bale out. They were a few miles north of us, and their plane left a smoke-trail as it streaked to the ground. A few stragglers that had either broken away from their formation, or were unable to keep up, or were 'all that were left' of other formations, evoked deafening cheers and some ribald remarks. On our west side we saw several planes crash from a great height to the ground, but could

249

not tell whether they were bombers or fighters, enemy or ours.

The last plane turned west and disappeared in the direction of England. The raid was all-cleared, and the villagers came out of the shelters. But excitement among the prisoners was still running high — as high by contrast as the spirits of the German soldiers on duty round the castle were low. They had had to watch very strong forces of bombers pass in broad daylight over their country with not one German fighter in sight to interrupt the nonchalance with which they were returning home.

After tea one of the unlucky air-crew whom we had seen bale out was now seen to be approaching the *Schloss* under guard. How we all yelled to him! And after he had passed out of sight under the western wall on his way to the entrance we rushed into the *Saalhaus* hoping to see him if he was brought to the *Kommandantur*. His parachute, Mae West, and flying boots were, but not he. Then an ambulance arrived, evidently with the others who had baled out. We had thought at least one of them to be wounded because, when one was descending, he had made no attempt to keep his parachute from swaying.

It is now 9.30 p.m. and we have not seen them. One is certainly an American, and of the other three all we know is that at least one is British and one is wounded.

If ever dull monotony was shattered, it was so today. British air supremacy has passed out of the realm of newspaper reports into mass formations of bombers, with an umbrella of fighters, sailing into our sight as unmolested as though they flew over America, or any country of the British Empire. I have never known this camp so jubilant as on this Whitsunday 1944.

MONDAY 29 MAY
Another raid this afternoon. The details were precisely as yesterday, except that no Allied planes came down in this area. The attacking force was twice the size, and there appeared to be another objective besides Leipzig.

**THURSDAY 1 JUNE**

The millet seed which so often formed the midday (hen-mash) meal is now issued dry, and has become a popular food issue. When crushed with a beer bottle and processed by being put through Kenneth Lockwood's coffee grinder, with the addition of a little crushed biscuit it is capable of becoming — in dexterous hands — a good savoury pastry.

Some of the boys are making efforts to take a holiday. Private arrangements are made for two officers of different messes to change places for a fortnight or three weeks, and then return to their own messes all sun-burnt and hearty.

The beginnings of a shaft in the dental surgery were found this evening.

**SATURDAY 3 JUNE**

Most of the day given up to 'spit and polish' preparation for tomorrow.

**SUNDAY 4 JUNE**

Services as usual. Midday *Appell* was treated as a British parade in honour of the King's birthday. I had almost forgotten that British officers could conduct themselves with military precision on parade.

After the count, and when *Hauptmann* Püpcke was departing, the SBO led three rousing cheers for HM King George VI. It was a very pleasing occasion.

**TUESDAY 6 JUNE**

A rumour this afternoon that the German radio had announced the invasion. It is said to have taken place at 1 a.m. after a hundred hours' bombing, and landings to have been at points on the coastline between Brest and Dunkirk.

A certain agitation was observed among the German soldiers and officers which had earlier been attributed to the *Kommandant* having torn a strip off them. Then the rumour came . . . and a snatch of conversation was overheard . . . and the *Kriegies* needed no further stimulation. Parties are likely to be in full swing tonight.

251

Purdy was seen leaving yesterday.

**WEDNESDAY 7 JUNE**
Never were newspapers awaited with such impatience!
When they arrived they made it quite clear that Rommel
had been taken by surprise. The *Luftwaffe* scarcely figures
in the reports. The German Army doesn't appear to have
been anywhere near. And it is obvious, but not stated, that
the great 'Atlantic Wall' has done little more than
lull the German forces in France into a false sense of
security.

The party men last night touched the high spots; so
much so that at noon today the SBO assembled all officers
and addressed them. No one failed to understand his
opinion of officers he described in language borrowed for
the occasion. Nor will they forget it!

A rumour says that a number of British *Freiwilliges**
who are touring British POW camps were in the *Kommandantur* today. They were seen going in, and to be
wearing German uniform. The *Kommandant* evidently decided that IVc was not a promising field for their propaganda, and did not allow them in the camp.

**THURSDAY 8 JUNE**
Henderson returned from Lamsdorff this evening. He has a

*The British Free Corps, a volunteer unit of disaffected British that
the Germans recruited for propaganda purposes. In his book,
*Colditz: The German Viewpoint*, Reinhold Eggers recorded: 'Just
after D-day we had two visitors to Colditz in the uniforms of the
British Free Corps, whose initials were on the arm-bands they
wore. These two said they wanted a chance to talk to the prisoners,
with a view to getting some of them to join up in the BFC. This
did not seem much of an idea to me, even in my capacity as
Propaganda Officer. It was hardly the moment, June 1944, for the
British to start active collaboration with the enemy. Anyone who
knew Colditz could be certain that, first of all, there would be 100
per cent non-co-operation, plus, if possible, violent reaction against
these two men. Second thoughts, I imagine, might produce a crop
of pseudo-volunteers, whose sole purpose would undoubtedly be to
escape at the first opportunity.'

252

story of shooting at *Stalagluft* III. A mass escape of seventy-seven persons is said to have taken place, and forty-three of them who had Czechoslovakian identity papers are said to have been caught by the Gestapo and taken to Gestapo HQ at Görlitz on the Czech frontier and to have been shot out of hand. The SBO has asked the *Kommandant* to make an enquiry about the matter.

**SATURDAY 10 JUNE**
In such letters as came into the camp today there was an enclosed printed invitation to any British officers and men who wish to join the British Free Corps to fight against Russia. It is supposed to be instead of a visit from the British *Freiwilliges* whom the *Kommandant* did not allow to enter the camp on Wednesday.

**MONDAY 12 JUNE**
Yesterday the SBO addressed the following letter to the *Kommandant* about the *Freiwillige* circular:

'I have received complaints from a number of British officers (POW) that they have received in their private letters pamphlets which insult their honour as British officers. The issue of these pamphlets is of course a breach of Articles 2 and 3 of the International Convention, but presumably the responsibility for this rests with someone who holds a higher position that that of looking after Prisoners of War. As I am desirous of getting my facts correct before writing to the Protecting Power, I should be obliged if you would say if the added insult of placing these pamphlets in private letters from relatives and friends of POWs has been done by your order? I am anxious to get this point settled as I am reluctant to attribute to an officer an action, which may be due to another rank, regarding the code of honour of an officer and a gentleman . . . .'

**WEDNESDAY 14 JUNE**
This afternoon the reply was given to the SBO about the

*Freiwillige* pamphlets. It was all a ghastly error for which some underling was responsible.*

FRIDAY JUNE 16

While walking this afternoon gave the last of Jack Courtenay's chocolate to some Ukrainian kiddies.

There was a *Sonderappell* during the history lecture. Dick Loraine, Boson, and Dominic Bruce were heard tapping at an obstruction in the main sewer under the outer courtyard. A manhole was opened up and they were hoisted out and marched off to the cells. After the *Sonderappell* Bob Barnes, Alan Coxidge and Rex Baxter were detailed to block up our entrance to the sewer down a shaft from the ex-Polish long-room. But the shaft had already been found, and the Germans were down there waiting for them. They also were put in the cells.

The distance through the shaft and sewer to where the first three were caught is roughly a hundred yards. The sewer varies in width from fourteen inches to two feet six inches. The fourteen-inch stretches (one at the entrance to a vertical drain) had to be enlarged. Hence the noise that led to detection.

THURSDAY 13 JULY

Events on the three fighting fronts have turned our hopes into the belief that the European phase of the war is almost over. The Red Armies approaching East Prussia at high

---

*Eggers admitted responsibility in his book quoted in the previous note. While convinced that the two from the British Free Corps had no hopes of success, he felt it his duty to help them and 'we did do them at least the favour, and I don't think it was any more than that, of distributing their leaflets among the PW mail. In these leaflets it was stated that no action was intended hostile to the British Crown. The war was condemned as the work of Jews and international finance, and it was declared to be a betrayal of the British Empire. The pamphlet ended with an appeal for an Anglo-German alliance.

'The prisoners at first burnt all the pamphlets, and then on second thoughts, demanded more as souvenirs. The visitors by then had gone – we had no more of their leaflets left.'

speed, the defeat of Rommel's armoured divisions at Caen, and the rolling front in Italy all seem to indicate imminent collapse.

This is surely a sad stage of the war for a four-year-old-officer-POW to suffer a mental breakdown, but H———'s condition has ceased merely to point that way. He is a quiet man by nature, but he is noisy now. He is immaculately dressed, walks about with a wooden spoon and an iron poker in his hand, demands attention from anyone on whom his eye alights, and discourses unintelligibly on Egyptology, military technique, religion, or going north. Twice today he has set about finding HB whom he wishes to awake from the dead.

### FRIDAY 14 JULY

H——— was astir, shaved and dressed before 0700 hrs *Appell*. He was in a state of great exultation, shouting for different people that he might disclose to them this or that amazing discovery.

The four friends who kept him close company went with him up the stairs, down again to the *Hof*, up again, into this room, into that, down again to the *Hof*, and back up the stairs, *ad infinitum*. His energy continued all day.

### TUESDAY 18 JULY

H——— made a fight of it on Friday evening when he was invited to move into one of the cells in the *Hof*, and his four companions had to carry him there. He remained docile over the weekend, and it seemed as though Hugh Dickin's prescription of a few days in complete quiet might help him. But today he began to smash up his stool and bed and anything he could lay hands on.

### WEDNESDAY 19 JULY

Daylight raid on targets in this area. We saw many planes and heard many heavy detonations.

Could not go for the non-comb. walk today as I was too busy finishing a lecture on the history of the Church in the nineteenth century. Charles Hutt was unable to go for a different reason: he had the unhappy task of accompanying H———— to Schmokau, the mental hospital for POWs.

**FRIDAY 21 JULY**
Rumour of a revolt in Germany and an attempt on Hitler's life! Confirmed at tea-time when the newspapers arrived.

The OKW communique admits that the Red Armies are on the doorstep of East Prussia, and that streams of refugees are coming into Germany.

**MONDAY 24 JULY**
The Nazi salute has replaced the Army salute. German officers and soldiers were seen today to have adopted the order. 'Hal' took *Appell* tonight and gave the Nazi salute as each line was called to attention.

There was a meeting of the Colditz townspeople somewhere tonight, perhaps in the village square. We could see them converging in that direction, and for an hour the streets were deserted.

**WEDNESDAY 26 JULY**
For almost a week the officers and orderlies who are awaiting repatriation have been on the *qui vive* expecting to be moved to Annaberg: a step nearer England. When the order finally came through this morning it concerned only three of them: Harry Elliott, Skipper Barnett, and Louis Esteve. They leave at 4 a.m. tomorrow.

**MONDAY 31 JULY**
For forty-four days — ever since 17 June — the V1 has been front-page news for German readers. Before we knew what it was, or saw a drawing, the creative and speculative brains of the prisoners had produced a rocket plane as the only answer. Today's *Leipziger* heads its front page with '*V1 die wachsende Sorge Londons*'.

Tuesday 1 August
The whole camp is on an unparalleled wave of optimism: 'The war will end in about three weeks.' And from the lips

of military sages: 'If the Germans don't pack it in before, the Russians will be in Berlin by 5 October.'

## THURSDAY 3 AUGUST

While we stood on *Appell* at 7 a.m. a large search party, including members of the SS, entered the *Hof* and took possession of the *Kellerhaus*. We were told that the search on the first floor would be finished by 9.30, and officers living on that floor would at once move into the ex-Dutch quarters.

I felt unfit to move or suffer any kind of disturbance. I had an abscess in my mouth looking the size of a grape and feeling like a very angry Jaffa orange. I had intended to get Eric to lance it when he opened up the medical room at half-past eight, and then to return to my bunk, I got him to lance it, and it stank abominably.

Geoff Ransom, Jerry Hill and John Penman humped my kit, bedding, palliasse, and locker over — no mean job since it meant going down one flight of a spiral staircase, across the *Hof*, up two more spiral flights, and into a small room peopled by genial Dutch ghosts.

We were all clear of the *Kellerhaus* by midday, and the afternoon was spent washing walls and floors and reassembling beds and kit. I merely assembled my bed (a single one — or, rather, a double one at some time sawn in two: the first single-decker I have slept on since entering Germany except for my time in the cells) and lay down. My general cleaning will have to wait a day or two. Everyone is more or less settled in. I am feeling considerably better with my temperature now normal.

Said goodbye to Charles Hutt. He will leave for the repatriation centre at 4 a.m. tomorrow. If he remembers a twentieth of the messages given him for families in England he will prove himself the best-memoried man on earth.

## TUESDAY 8 AUGUST

It looks as though escaping from IVc is no longer allowed! 'Slim' has spent most of the afternoon putting up a wooden plaque on the wall of the *Kellerhaus*. It is painted white, and in large black letters it proclaims the sad tidings of Camp Order No. 21: 'POWs escaping will be shot at.' Several officers have taken pleasure in informing Mike Sinclair — who was shot at a year ago — of the new order.

## THURSDAY 17 AUGUST

Our wedding anniversary: the fifth since we last saw each other — but happier than the previous ones for this separation is obviously almost at an end. I received a letter from Maisie yesterday dated 16 July. This evening I have eaten with relish half a four-ounce bar of chocolate that I had saved for the celebration.

## SUNDAY 20 AUGUST

Entry made by Jack Courtenay:

'The big event today has been John Beaumont's Chorale and Anthem which was sung at Mattins, the service being held in the theatre for the occasion. A year ago John wrote a voluntary for organ and trumpet with the result that the chapel (containing the organ) was closed! Recently he re-wrote it for piano, two trumpets, and a three-part male voice choir, calling it a 'Conventional Shout of Thanks-giving in the Style of Handel'. He then wrote a slow Chorale to precede it. The whole is extraordinarily effective. It is a very definite piece of work, nothing tentative or half-hearted about it.

'The whole service was arranged and rehearsed by John as an expression of thanksgiving, of which this anthem was the climax, coming just before the blessing. Two order-lies, Bullard and Hull, played the trumpets, John Davies the piano, and the composer conducted. We in the choir were thirty strong and well-sited, being broadside-on to the congregation whom, rather to our surprise, we did not outnumber.

'Three comments are worth recording. Jerry Wood, a tough Canadian mining engineer, hardly waited for the blessing before startling John with "Smash hit, boy! Smash hit!" Penbum How, an ex-cinema manager and a pub-keeper in Oxford, described it as a "good box-office attraction". And Paddy Martin, an Irish atheist who heard it from the courtyard, said, "Och, I thocht it was after being the end of the war!" '

## MONDAY 21 AUGUST
There was no *Leipziger* today. Under the total war effort a law comes into operation releasing more men for the *Wehrmacht*. Among other things, postal services will be curtailed, and newspapers published seven days a week will only appear on six. All but two of the illustrated papers are stopped.

Bets laid on the fall of Paris.

## THURSDAY 24 AUGUST
The longest raid: almost three hours. Formation of bombers thirty-five strong passed over the *Schloss*. No enemy fighters were to be seen.

## FRIDAY 1 SEPTEMBER
The end seems very near! Is Germany capable of resisting until the end of the month? Possibly. But, if wiser counsels prevail, resistance will cease within a few weeks, or — better! — days. We had a rumour at tea-time of a second unsuccessful attempt on Hitler's life. This time he was shot at by a soldier, and the bullet passed through his arm and shoulder. It seems to have occurred within a week or two of the Graf von Stauffenberg attempt.

Destroyed all my family mail — except Maisie's — last night. Some of the letters were over four years old and breathed an atmosphere — not in words — of fear of invasion and an uncertain outlook. The words were brave and confident, but we knew precisely what strength Britain had, and what may have been expected from a well-planned invasion. The navy seemed our only hope.

If the best of the German soldiers in this camp are able to interpret the present situation from their newspapers, and know how near the collapse of their nation's dream is, then they deserve congratulation on the level demeanour they maintain, and the calm exterior they present. A few still remain in the camp who were gloatingly cocksure four years ago; *their* present attitude is not commendable.

This hooch is dreadful stuff! With the onward sweep of Anglo-American forces through France, spirits run extremely high, and nerves are on knife-edge, with loss of appetite and loss of sleep. Hooch parties are frequent; orderly enough and not so rowdy as earlier parties, but the stuff they are drinking is poison.

## FRIDAY 8 SEPTEMBER

'What we are fighting for' is the title of the latest production of Dr Goebbels' ministry. It was released through the canteen this morning and, by noon, it had been read by the majority. It was discussed at lunch-time.

The pictures could be discounted since houses, babies, working men, culture and town-planning are not a German monopoly and might just as easily describe the peace-time life of France, Holland, Belgium or Poland — and none of these countries were wanting war in 1939. In the written matter we noticed the absence of phrases like *Herrenvolk, Aryan, Jüdische Weltgefahr*, which have marked earlier productions; and the presence of a social idealism which is common to all the countries fighting against Germany (except one).

## MONDAY 11 SEPTEMBER

Raid: the bombers were in perfect formation, four threes to a twelve and three twelves to a wing. They sailed through the nearest flak without damage, and then the bombs began to fall. We decided from the sound and direction that the Lenna Petrol Refineries were the target. Columns of black belching smoke supported the conclusion.

Returning from our non-comb. walk we saw a German airman with his wife and child, evidently on leave. He was wearing a wounded medal, a Second Class Iron Cross, and two decorations I was unable to identify. But none of these, nor his pretty young *Frau*, nor the baby in the perambulator prevented the *Fruchtpolizei* from doing their duty.

COLDITZ 1944

He was searching under the state fruit trees along the grass verge on either side of the highway. The pickings of fallen fruit were obviously lean and, coming on a plum tree heavy with ripe fruit, he shook it and stood under a hail of plums. Two *Fruchtpolizei* who had been watching through field glasses descended upon him on bicycles. He refused to give his name, whereupon one of the two rode into Colditz for a state policeman while the other kept the airman under observation.

The *Völkischer Beobachter* has an article in yesterday's issue (the only paper available today) pointing to the grave decline in religion in England. One of the sadly obvious evidences of this decline is the song '*Preiset Gott und reicht die Munition*' — 'Praise the Lord and pass the ammunition';

MONDAY 18 SEPTEMBER

Cyril Lewthwaite attempted to escape while on the walk back from exercise this afternoon using John Beaumont's idea: a blanket so adorned with dirt and dead grass and leaves (the latter stitched to it) as to look like a heap of rubbish when he fell down and drew the blanket over him. He did his part well, and with lightning speed but, since the guards on the march back are only about eight paces apart, and though it was timed to take place on a corner so as to obscure the view of one guard behind, and though he was well-crowded by his friends, the front guard evidently saw a movement out of the corner of his eye and raised the alarm.

It was interesting that, when Lewthwaite was discovered, there was none of the usual abuse or threatening to shoot, even though Franz-Joseph was there.

Cyril was put in the cells, but is out again awaiting sentence. A camp order this evening prohibits the taking of a blanket (to sit down on) on exercise.

WEDNESDAY 20 SEPTEMBER

*Hauptmann* Püpcke, for the *Kommandant*, thought it would be nice if the prisoners had the park to themselves without the presence of sentries — on parole. The SBO thought it

261

would be nice, but also thought the proposal had come rather late in the day to be really nice, and said so.

Cinema performance. The films were borrowed by Dr Eggers from the local schoolmaster. They are the products of the German Educational Film Society, and Saturday's 'big picture' was the 'Life of the Cabbage Butterfly'. The supporting programme was of Alpine life and a cartoon.

At this stage of the war, when everyone's nerves are keyed up, it is very mild entertainment.

### THURSDAY 21 SEPTEMBER

It is Maisie's birthday, and my 1,575th day as a prisoner.

We have begun a lean period. The issue of Red Cross parcels has been cut from one parcel to half a parcel a week each. At that consumption rate the supplies will take us to the middle of January. Most of us are going to bed hungry tonight.

### MONDAY 25 SEPTEMBER

A terrible day! We returned from a non-comb. walk at five minutes before the 4 p.m. *Appell*. Officers were standing about in the *Hof* waiting for the bell. Kenneth Lockwood, as I passed him, asked, 'Has there been any shooting on your walk?' and told me that Mike Sinclair had climbed over the barbed wire at the north end of the exercise ground and many shots had been fired as he ran for the exterior wall. He did not know whether Mike had been hit or not, but knew that he had not got away.

At ten past four the Germans came into the *Hof* and *Appell* was on. Instead of saluting and thanking the SBO when the count was finished, *Hauptmann* Püpcke spoke to the SBO and called off all his guards, who went out through the gate. Püpcke then saluted, and Tod called the parade to attention. His words were, 'Par-a-de 'shun! Gentlemen, I am sorry to tell you that Mr Sinclair is dead. Fall out.'

For a second everybody stood immobile. It was a moment of extreme wretchedness.

Hugh Dickin had been called to the spot, and when he returned I asked him what the situation was. He said (and it was also the opinion of the German MO) that death from the gun-shot wound was instantaneous: the track of the bullet was from the right elbow through the body to the heart.

At tea everyone sat silent, and then tried, with desultory results, to make conversation about anything from the wet weather to war news and peace-time sports.

The SBO interviewed the *Kommandant* later this evening about funeral arrangements, and was promised that Mike would be buried with full military honours, and a wreath would be supplied.

### TUESDAY 26 SEPTEMBER

The SBO and the Brigadier saw the *Kommandant* again this morning about the shooting of Mike Sinclair and the funeral arrangements. The *Kommandant* disowned responsibility for the shooting because it was the custom in the German Army to shoot on any such occasion. The SBO reminded him that the *Kommandant* of a camp had power to provide sufficient exercise and playing time and room to improve camp conditions, and so to make it less likely that young officers would attempt hazardous escapes.

When they talked about funeral arrangements the *Kommandant* said that he now found a wreath could not be supplied, nor could full military honours be accorded to Mike.

Have symptons of 'flu, and so to bed with a glass of hooch and two aspirins.

### WEDNESDAY 27 SEPTEMBER

Scarborough (the RC chaplain) said a requiem mass this morning, a generous thing to do, for Mike was not an RC.

Cinema show: film of central Africa and of the Olympic Games in Germany in 1936.

### THURSDAY 28 SEPTEMBER

Mike Sinclair was buried this morning in the local cemetery. The burial party was not allowed to have more than ten people in it, and it was thought right that the eight members of his regiment, the KRRC, in the camp should all be part of it. Colonel Tod was there as SBO, and Richard Heard officiated. Brigadier Davies was disappointed that he could only have shared in the final leave-taking of a gallant soldier at the cost of displacing one of Mike's regimental friends, and this he would not do.

*Hauptmann* Püpcke and a party of nine German soldiers were present throughout the service in the cemetery chapel and the graveside committal. There were no military honours, but a Union Jack had been provided by the Germans, and a large wreath was already in the chapel.

At 1.30 p.m. a memorial was held in the *Schloss* chapel, which the *Kommandant* had agreed to open for the occasion. 'Abide with me' and 'For all the saints' were the hymns chosen by Mike's closest friend, Grismond Davies-Scourfield. Richard spoke very impressively of Mike's fine soldierly character, and his essentially unselfish attitude to escaping.

'Mike Sinclair came from an Ulster family living in England. His younger brother was killed in Normandy, his older brother is fighting in Italy. He was at school in Winchester, went up to Cambridge, and just before the war joined the 60th Rifles. He fought at Calais, was taken prisoner, went to Laufen, and then Poland. There he made his first big escape which took him across the frontiers of Slovakia, Hungary, Yugoslavia; and he was caught trying to get into Bulgaria. He made another unsuccessful attempt on the way back through the Czech Protectorate, was in Gestapo hands for a time, and then was sent here two and a half years ago.

'Since then his life has practically been one escape attempt after another. On different occasions he reached Cologne, the Swiss frontier, and the Dutch frontier. You know better than any congregation in the world what that means. About a hundred of you have got away from a camp once, and only about twenty of you more than once — let alone have got near a frontier: and this is the Escaping Camp.

'Behind Mike's record is Mike's skill and courage. Whenever the story of escaping is written, Mike Sinclair will hold a place high up among the escapers.

'He has now met up with his younger brother and countless others who, in their country's service, have gone before us on the way that leads through death, but comes out in a brighter, eternal world.'

FRIDAY 29 SEPTEMBER

A Camp Order was issued today announcing the end of the currency of *Lagermarks* in the camp as from 1 October. Canteen transactions will be done by chit through Mike Moran. The same applies to haircuts and laundry.

TUESDAY 3 OCTOBER

We are not making out too badly on half a Red Cross parcel each. I think everyone feels he would like to eat a little more, but we shall probably eat less before we do. The German bread ration is to be cut, and the potato ration reduced. But if it is only for a few weeks it matters little.

MONDAY 5 OCTOBER

I put in an *Antrag* on Monday for the use of my military raincoat which was taken from me when I arrived at IVc. 'Aunty' delivered it to me this morning, still in perfect condition.

The *Posten* here are now mostly old veterans of sixty. The younger ones — many of them had been wounded in Russia — have been sent back to fighting units.

SATURDAY 7 OCTOBER

The Swiss were here today. Four and even three years ago the visit of the Protecting Power was an event of some importance, anticipated and prepared for. But four years have taught us many things. While the American Embassy had the job in hand it was done with typical American vigour — and at a time when Germany was confident of victory. But the Swiss, who took over when America entered the war, though they are both just and conscientious, are no match for the OKW, or for Himmler's organisation since he took over. For some time there has been little enthusiasm for the visits — or the visitors. 'What's the use?' is the general feeling.

When the siren sounded this morning one of the Swiss, M. Deuzler, said to Colonel Tod with his customary assuredness, 'Oh, there will be no Anglo-American planes over here. They have as much as they can do bombing western Germany.' His remark was not challenged; but shortly afterwards, when everyone had flocked to the windows or into the *Hof* to see the formations roaring overhead, M. Deuzler betrayed some uneasiness. Nor did he find the c-r-u-n-c-h of distant bombing reassuring; and when a stick of three bombs dropped only a short distance away he looked like a man who would have enjoyed the discomfort of a deep air-raid shelter.

It was the biggest, heaviest, and certainly the longest raid we have had.

MONDAY 9 OCTOBER
Gave 'Winker' my old teeth. He only wanted the gold backing — to make a wedding ring for the lady who will become his wife. Some of the cooking utensils he has made from old cigarette and biscuit tins are true works of art.

TUESDAY 10 OCTOBER
Geoff received one of his traditional clothing parcels containing a tooth brush, tooth paste, a pair of socks, and over 9lbs of chocolate. Between seven of us it shared out at 1¼lbs each. It was as welcome as the first next-of-kin parcels we received in late 1940, though we are by no means so hungry as we were then.

MONDAY 16 OCTOBER
As from today the bread ration is cut by 200 grams a week, and the potato ration by 150 grams a day. These are to be compensated weight for weight by millet, peas, or kohlrabi. It we get either of the first two it will be acceptable ex-

change for the bread is terrible, and we have learned to do rather wonderful things with millet. But if kohlrabi is the most frequent exchange it will be most unacceptable.

The man who thought of bastardising turnip and cabbage might have expended his genius producing something less tasteless and insipid. A better cabbage or a better turnip would have been a worthy accomplishment, but why the worst of both?

TUESDAY 17 OCTOBER
Scarborough said a Requiem Mass this morning for John Arundell. The first notice we had of his death was in Sunday's issue of *The Camp* in which a report said, 'Captain Lord Arundell of Wardour, Wiltshire Regiment, who was recently repatriated from Germany, died in a military hospital on September 24 after an illness resulting from wounds received at Dunkirk.' Actually he received a minor wound in his arm at Dunkirk and, as far as Hugh Dickie knows, it healed at once and left no trace but a small scar. He was repatriated as a TB patient. He had no previous history of TB, either in himself or his family.

Scarborough did not deliver a funeral oration. I wish he had for the plans John made while he was in the *'schaft* for improving the family estate, and for improving the lot of agricultural workers generally, showed him to be a fine Christian gentleman. His natural courtesy made him one of the friendliest of men. But one of his practices was to invite someone to walk round and round the *Hof* with him and, whatever the victim's particular line was, he would want to know all about it, and after the conversation would go back to his bunk to make notes; and woe to the person who held forth on subjects of which he had incomplete knowledge! He died unmarried and there is no successor to the title.

When the rain stops for a while we can hear heavy artillery fire or bombing. There is much speculation about what it might be.

Today's press reports *'Generalfeldmarschall Rommel gestorben'*. He died from severe head wounds sustained in the west by 'Kraftfahr Zengunfall'.* No date is given. His name has not appeared in OKW reports or the German press for several weeks.

## SATURDAY 28 OCTOBER

The ten who were proposed to the Mixed Medical Commission for repatriation and who attended at Elsterhorst, were returned to IVc last night. Four were passed. It is amazing that Brigadier Davies wasn't included. His stomach wound, for which nothing further is being done, is troublesome and makes any kind of free movement difficult and painful. But he is the cheeriest and friendliest of men.

## MONDAY 30 OCTOBER

Half-term vacation began this morning — seven days' rest from pupils and tutorial work is a great joy.

Lights will not be allowed in the theatre for three nights as punishment for twenty-one officers being late for morning *Appell*. It is amazing that the German mind should expect military behaviour and smartness from officer POWs in a camp of the character of IVc. What they fail to understand is that the majority of their guests are not regular soldiers and are British enough to hate uniform, military drill, and brisk efficiency; and that nothing short of a war which threatened their homes and country could have persuaded them to don uniform and submerge their personalities in military mechanism.

Some of those who were late this morning have been so intentionally for two or three mornings hoping to get a period in the cooler. The mental rest of having a cell to oneself, and not having to attend hateful *Appells*, compensates for the shortness of rations.

Lights were out this evening for an air raid: over an hour's complete darkness. We shall have to make those stinking fat lamps again — though margarine for eating is scarce enough.

*Rommel had been severely wounded on 17 July when, being driven back to his HQ at La Roche-Guyon, he had been machine-gunned by a British fighter-bomber. After recuperating for three months, he finally took poison on Hitler's orders.

**WEDNESDAY 1 NOVEMBER**
Very wet and cold. I have put in an *Antrag* asking for some means of heating and drying the small room I occupy. The reasons I gave were that I use it daily as a lesson room, it is also the only chaplains' room that we have for private conversations, and, also, I live in it!

**FRIDAY 3 NOVEMBER**
Carrot cleaning: they were for lunch, and the kitchen staff is far too small to have time for cleaning carrots — or potatoes.

Potatoes boiled in their jackets are quite the proper thing. The carrots — tiny, dirty carrots and as grubby as all carrots seem to be, were cleaned by a volunteer corps of officers of field rank and below, a Brigadier, two colonels, a lieutenant-commander RN, and a chaplain, all standing in a circle in gusty drizzle, scraping little carrots with pocket knives until their hands were numb with cold, dirt and wet.

**WEDNESDAY 8 NOVEMBER**
Received an answer to my *Antrag*. A small stove has been found and will be installed after the ceiling job in the next room is finished — which, I fear, may be some considerable time.

**FRIDAY 10 NOVEMBER**
Two of the new *Prominente* we have been expecting for a week or more arrived today. They are Captain John (the Master of) Elphinstone of the Black Watch Regiment, and nephew of the Queen, and Lieutenant Max Duhamel, nephew of Winston Churchill.

Yesterday's newspaper had a short article on the appearance of the V2 which is said to have been in use against greater London for some weeks. It is also said to be invisible. The same article reported the complete destruction of Euston Station.

**ARMISTICE DAY**
Private Bullard sounded the Last Post at eleven o'clock

and Reveille two minutes later. Officers in their rooms, or walking round the *Hof*, and orderlies working within sound of the bugle, stood to attention. It was a more real memorial than the service of previous years.

### SUNDAY 12 NOVEMBER

The arrival of two more *Prominente*: Captain Earl Haig, Scots Greys and son of the late Field Marshal Earl Haig; and Lieutenant Viscount Lascelles, Grenadier Guards. We had been expecting Lascelles ever since we read of his capture when wounded in Italy.

I watched them come out of the delousing shed — hot and enervated from the steam of the shower house in which they had bathed and waited until their clothes were returned from the delouser. Their battledress had all the shapelessness of clothes thus treated, with heavy creases running in every direction. They carried kitbags and wore ammunition boots. Old school friends welcomed them as though to a house party.

Churchill and Eden are in Paris!

### THURSDAY 16 NOVEMBER

Pictures of the *Volkssturm* are in the papers almost every day. Since their inauguration in Prussia in July, press photographers have been showing the rapid transformation from men and boys at work to men and boys under arms — the only change of clothes being a brassard when under arms.

An article in the *Leipziger* announced that the great autumn offensive has begun in the West. 'If they have got off on the right foot the war might be over by Christmas,' so runs camp gossip. Psychologically November has suddenly become spring on prisoners' faces, despite the hunger they are feeling.

### SATURDAY 18 NOVEMBER

The first night of 'Jupiter Laughs' by Cronin. Dick Howe was producer, and the play was well cast. Howard Gee in the role of Dr Venner was really brilliant.

270

Peter Tunstall (charged with referring to 'b———
Germans') was notified today that the OKW have not confirmed the sentence of his last court martial, and have
ordered a retrial on 5 January. That will be his fifth
appearance before the court at Leipzig.

FRIDAY 24 NOVEMBER
The Red Cross are here today — or, rather, 'a' Red Cross.
He holds out very little hope of our receiving further consignments of Red Cross parcels. Some camps have been
completely without parcels for a considerable time, and we
agreed that it is right they should be supplied first. But
stocks at Geneva are very low.

Prisoners' reaction to the parcels situation was in no way
excited. The general response was, 'Well, I'm pretty hungry,
but the success of the offensive in the past eight days is very
reassuring — it may only be a week or two . . .' So hope
springs eternal and, though not filling empty bellies, dimin-
ishes the consciousness of them.

I missed my non-comb. walk today because of the
promise of the workmen to fix my stove. Having finished
the ceiling in the next room they took down the scaffolding
after lunch and at 3.35 p.m. came to do my job. It was
complete by 5.20, and I lit a fire of wood and began the process of drying out the walls and floor of my
room.

TUESDAY 28 NOVEMBER
One of the amazing things that have happened recently is
that prisoners have taken over the responsibility for keeping the blackout in order. 'Lulu' Lawton comes on a regular
round of visits to examine windows and blinds.

THURSDAY 30 NOVEMBER
A cloudless day, sunshine, and a raid from 12.30 p.m. to
2.30. It seemed to be the biggest raid we have seen in this
area. A dog fight with German fighters was very exciting.
The graceful sweep of flowing vapour ribbons, touched to
bright silver by the sun, made a scene far too beautiful to

271

be as deadly as the two shot-down planes showed it to be.

The sixteen orderlies, who were expected, arrived this morning, making a total of thirty-two. The ones who came to IVc sixteen months ago have been medically examined and expect to be moved in the next few days — much against the will of the majority. But six of them had applied to be moved to another camp — choosing, evidently, to work in German industry rather than for British officers.

### FRIDAY 1 DECEMBER

I heard today that a bridge four were playing for £25 a hundred. If the story is true it indicates a very high state of boredom. I notice some players have dropped out of the poker schools, and one or two ardent players of *chemin* are not playing any more. In one instance at least the losses in sterling amount to several hundred pounds.

### SATURDAY 2 DECEMBER

Today I enter on my fifth year in this camp. I refuse to permit myself the luxury or pain of reflections. But I do frequently ask myself if what I see and hear is real — or if I have fallen into some kind of topsy-turveydom and what I regard as conscious thought is the chimera of a dream, and vice versa. In a word, am I still sane?

The first night tonight of the instrumental concert, 'Hot and Cold'. Jimmy Yule and John Beaumont interchangeably held the baton or played musical instruments.

The first half of the programme belonged to a generation later than mine — a generation which, so far as its popular music is concerned, sees poetry where I see only execrable rhyme, and hears melody where there is only indescribable — and sometimes disgusting — noise. It may be — as I am constantly told — that I have no ear for music, but I could understand and appreciate the second half of the programme which consisted of light classical music, and ended with a selection from Gilbert and Sullivan. I noticed the most vociferous supporters of part one were the less than half-hearted supporters of part two.

SUNDAY 3 DECEMBER
Services as usual. Found it extremely difficult to write my
letter to Maisie. It is only a few weeks short of five years
since I saw her for just a few hours in London before
leaving for France. Letters have been few, and double
censorship renders them almost impersonal and newsless.
Such letters as have arrived recently were written with the
optimism we felt in September-October and have been read
when that optimism has been proved false. By the time I
receive her letters she no longer feels as she wrote.

Our difficulty is to write in a vein which does not reflect
our present large interest in food, and does not show the
pessimism with which we view another Christmas — and a
hungry one — in captivity. How to make a letter naturally
interesting with such reservations and with double censorship is a problem indeed.

MONDAY 4 DECEMBER
Making my one bucket of coal spin out over the week is
quite a problem in mathematics. Divided equally between
seven days, the ration consists of seven nobs a day: each
nob — it is compressed coal dust — is uniform in size, and
not larger than a small orange.

In the week past I have cleared out the previous day's
ashes each morning and at nine o'clock lighted a fire with
eight nobs. With careful control of the draught it has burned
slowly until ten o'clock when I have dampered it down and
hoped to keep the room warm enough to sit and work in
until my last morning pupil departed at noon. Usually the
fire was completely out by that time, for the compressed
nobs have no residue of cinders, but disintegrate when they
burn, and fall through the bars as powdered ashes.

At 6 p.m. I have lighted the remaining nobs and hoped
for enough heat to make the room habitable for another
pupil. Some heat can be got by collecting the floor sweep-
ings from the orderlies each morning: a very undignified
and dirty way of keeping a comfortable temperature, but
what matters dignity and dirt in the 'schaft'? On two sides
of the room, which is about the size of a box-room in a

273

semi-detached house, windows have been bricked in, and the walls are only about four inches thick. On the third side more than half the wall is window — old and ill-fitting — which I have packed round with crushed paper soaked in water and stirred to a pulp. But if it had been impossible to get either stove or fuel I would still have occupied this small room through the winter, even if it had become an ice-box like the old 'priest's hole' I had in the first two winters here. The little privacy it affords, and the opportunity to give private interviews to officers and orderlies in mental, spiritual, and moral difficulty, are worth the risk of pneumonia. I have found, during this second lean period, that more prisoners than ever are in mental distress, and more than usual are wanting to get a religious perspective on life.

TUESDAY 5 DECEMBER

Yesterday our table took over the cooking for the whole floor — eleven tables with an average of seven at each. The arrangement, which has been in operation for two months, requires the duty table to be responsible for all cooking, heating of water for drinks, and collecting the coal issue, etc, for one calendar month. Each table stooge consults each day with the cooks, and oven space and cooking space are allotted. Table stooges deposit the dishes they have prepared at 4.30 p.m., and at 5.30 the cooks go on duty. The difficulty — indeed, impossibility — is then to keep the food warm until the tables wish to eat.

Dishes consist largely of already-cooked vegetable which the stooge has sought to disguise. Kohlrabi is pretty difficult to disguise. The potato ration is three potatoes per person each day, one of which is eaten at midday. With the other two an inventive stooge will make a pastry dish by adding a little crumbled bread or biscuit, or crushed millet or oatmeal (if there are any of those things), and flavour it with a little cheese, or put a little Red Cross stew or salmon in the middle to make a pie. Sometimes the quantity is halved, and one half is made into a pudding by adding a few raisins or a little sugar.

Since German rations were cut, and Red Cross parcels cut by half, the usual complete evening meal could be put without difficulty into a four-ounce tobacco tin.

Breakfast consists of two very thin slices of rye bread spread with prima fat and a little jam on one piece, with a cup of ersatz coffee. Lunch is one small potato and two or three spoonsful of boiled vegetable, followed by two-sevenths of a slice of bread and one-seventh of a tin of cheese. Once a week (but not infrequently missed altogether) we get one-and-a-half ounces of meat. A cup of Red Cross tea rounds off the meal.

At tea-time we have three slices of bread, one spread with jam, and another lightly touched with salmon or sardine that has been mashed to a paste, together with one cup of tea with a colouring of condensed milk. There are other odds and ends — perhaps one of Morton's terrible meat rolls (ask any recipient of British Red Cross parcels about them!), perhaps some bully beef, or butter, biscuits, tinned bacon, or powdered egg. But in no single week does one get all these.

A table of seven over a period of a fortnight gets three English, three New Zealand, and one Canadian parcel. Most of the New Zealand parcels are out of condition. The four-ounce packet of tea is almost always mouldy, but is usable after being washed and dried quickly. The pound tin of butter is almost invariably rancid — sometimes only fit to be used in the fat lamps, though it has to be very bad not to be eaten. The meat, chocolate, cheese and cocoa are usually all right.

Only old age and long storing seem to affect the British and Canadian parcels, and the recent ones we have had must have been in transit a very long time. The chocolate is often crushed, or has been melted out of shape, and is mouldy — but edible, after being scraped and washed. However, a fortnight tomorrow will be the last issue of Red Cross parcels unless any come from Geneva in the meantime, but no one really expects so agreeable an event. By Christmas even a mouldy New Zealand parcel will have the character of manna!

THURSDAY 7 DECEMBER

A 1938 14 h.p. Renault coupé changed hands today for
5lbs of chocolate and £10 sterling. The car and the sterling
are in England. The chocolate arrived in a next-of-kin
parcel from Australia yesterday.

This morning one British Red Cross parcel is said to
have been bought for RM250. It was a private parcel, perhaps one of several accumulated during a period in gaol
and, I think, the sale was made to help the payment of
gambling debts.

FRIDAY 8 DECEMBER

A mild afternoon and a pleasant non-comb. walk to Lastau.
We went past a bakery where the smell of warm, newly-
baked bread was tantalising. I am glad there are no *delicat-
essen* shops on the three routes we take.

SUNDAY 10 DECEMBER

I took the Presbyterian order of service at 11 o'clock. In the
course of the prayer of intercession I asked that we might
be helped not to make life more difficult for those with
whom we are living. And up to half an ago — it is 9 p.m.
— five officers have so far spoken to me of the tentative
rapprochment they have since made to officers who had got
on their nerves (or the other way round) and with whom
they had been either continuously quarrelling, or only
speaking when speech could not be avoided. Four of the
five essays in good relations had been welcomed and
promised success: only one appears to have been a complete failure.

Each of the five who spoke to me were shy about it. One
of them could not bring himself to acknowledge it was a
phrase in a prayer and substituted — rather inaptly — 'a
remark made in your sermon'. I knew he meant prayer,
and he knew that he meant it. But he preferred 'sermon'.

MONDAY 11 DECEMBER

The orderlies who came to us eighteen months ago are in
the process of being moved to work camps. Most of them

regret the move, and there are several whom officers will very much dislike saying goodbye to. As was to be expected, a few of them got up to monkey-tricks in their efforts to stay behind with 'the experts'.

The new orderlies are mostly regulars from Welsh regiments.

### THURSDAY 14 DECEMBER
Temperatures are much lower and we are all feeling the cold. A few weeks ago I gave my troops' greatcoat to Jerry Hill who had been missing his RAF greatcoat since the summer. I have a raincoat which is proof against storms, but its warming value is very low. At midday *Appell* Elmes-Heale kindly presented me with a Norfolk jacket — a troops' greatcoat cut down.

### WEDNESDAY 20 DECEMBER
Bob received, in the nick of time, a parcel of 500 Craven A. We were completely out of cigarettes.

The whole camp was weighed this morning. Everyone has lost weight. I am down to 11 stones 8 lbs, and on our table we have three officers all over six feet tall and weighing less than ten stones each.

A special issue of Christmas coal today. I did not get any.

Drew our last Red Cross parcels — half a parcel each. A few officers have one or two each in the store — a little hoard saved up while in gaol. Next week our table — and presumably others — will be living on German rations. It is an unhappy prospect.

### FRIDAY 22 DECEMBER
The big event of the day was the Christmas draw. Every ticket in it represented a tin of food. Sardines seemed to be in largest supply, and other tins were of oatmeal, cheese, soup, herrings, etc. They were salvage tins from crushed and broken Red Cross parcels, and from Licensed Victuallers' parcels.

For several messes the luck of the draw will make the difference between a Christmas with additions, and one without. There were several 2lb tins of pork and beans, and five tins of cheese of the same weight. These were, of course, the best value.

We drew three tins of sardines, a 2lb tin of Lyle's golden syrup, a small oatmeal, and a small unlabelled tin.

## SUNDAY 24 DECEMBER
Holy Communion at 8.20 a.m. No Morning Service because of the Carol Service at 5.30 p.m. There was a very good attendance, and the congregation got away to a flying start with *Adeste Fideles* sung very lustily.

It is extremely cold. At 4 p.m. it was −7°C. Later, when it was several degrees colder, Czecho (Flight-Lieutenant Chaloupka, RAF), fulfilled the terms of his bet with Derby Curtis; viz; if the war was not won by Christmas Eve Czecho would run naked round the *Hof* twice; if the war was won by that date, Derby would run naked along Piccadilly. Czecho lost his bet and paid his before a boisterous gallery of muffled-up spectators. I doubt if Derby would have found it possible to pay up if he had lost.

## CHRISTMAS DAY
Five Christmases in *Oflag* IVc is too much!

We started the day with a united Communion Service in the theatre at eight o'clock. There was no heat, and the thermometer registered −11°C. Upwards of seventy officers and orderlies communicated.

Breakfast, consisting of porridge, toast with jam, and coffee, was a happy and good breakfast. There was a good atmosphere, due no doubt to the comparative absence of alcohol and Christmas Eve drunkenness: no filth about, or the foul stench of drunken regurgitation, and no one in that stage of offensive dullness the morning after. Everyone seemed to be wishing everyone else a merry Christmas, and there was a lot of free and spontaneous laughter and badinage.

A large congregation assembled for the United Service at eleven o'clock. It was a congregation clad as for an Icelandic expedition with great coats, mufflers, gloves, and any heat-retaining garments the prisoners possessed. The American battledress top made of leather and lined with the thick fleece of a sheepskin topped the list for beauty and serviceableness.

Dinner was a huge success. Rupert Barry and his kitchen staff (the orderlies were on holiday) did an excellent job. The orderlies and senior officers were served first; those in the ex-Dutch and ex-French quarters second, and the *Kellerhaus* third. Barley soup preceded mashed potatoes with peas, beef and pork. In our case at least (in the *Kellerhaus*) the food was hot and very much enjoyed.

We had Sandy as a guest to tea in my mess, and ate a piece of toast with sardines, and a large cake that Jerry had made and iced with cocoa and condensed milk. Finer cakes would be eaten in England, but none more lavishly praised or more richly enjoyed.

A Christmas pantomime, written by Micky Reviere and produced by Charlie Hopetoun, scored a great success. It was called 'Hey Diddle Snow White', and was Prince Charming's attempt to win the wealthy Snow White, foiled again and again by the bad duke and his wicked henchmen. Charlie Hopetoun's 6 ft 2 in., the lower part in thick winter pants, sought to convey the good graces of the fairy queen. Snow White was not a nice lady, but no nice lady could be a popular heroine in a POW camp. The theatre was very cold indeed, but no audience was ever in better humour or readier to laugh.

We — my mess — had supper at nine o'clock. Jerry had done wonders out of next to nothing, and had produced tasty individual meat pies followed by Christmas pudding. How he made the Christmas pudding so good and satisfying baffles my imagination. It was followed by cheese and biscuit with coffee. An extension of lights out until midnight made it possible for us to sit and chat, reminiscing about men and events in the *'schaft*, and on Christmases spent in the sceptr'd isle.

BOXING DAY
The feeling is generally shared that this has been the best

Christmas spent in the *'schaft*. Even the bottle-party people (though this has been the most sober of any Christmas) were saying this morning that it was their best Christmas in Germany. There was only one small drinking party, and I don't believe they had enough alcohol to get tight, though they were of the type that can pretend a good deal.

I think the fact that everyone has been living on the hunger line for some weeks and on Christmas Day was able to eat his fill contributed in a large way to making it a day of happy memory. But whatever may be the reason — and no doubt the war having reached its final phase is one — it is amazing to hear everyone describing this — the Christmas they most hated the thought of spending in Germany — as the best they have spent here.

A very successful whist drive was organised this afternoon, chiefly, I think, in the interest of the orderlies. The prizes were bars of chocolate taken from the SBO's salvage stock.

We are all eating scraps today; yesterday's leftovers fried or made into a stew. In quantity it is less than half of what we had to eat yesterday. Most people are wishing for a little more.

## WEDNESDAY 27 DECEMBER
Right down at the bottom of the *'schaft* again! We had little food all day, and for supper tonight could raise nothing better or more satisfying than potato-peeling soup. And thereby hangs a tale. The Christmas menu said 'mashed potatoes'. To make this possible a voluntary potato-peeling party of one person from each mess was called for on Sunday afternoon. When the task was complete each worker was allowed to take the peelings from the potatoes he had cleaned for the use of his mess. Hence our supper tonight and tomorrow night. After that we shall eat at supper anything we can save during the day.

Now that we are on bare German rations Jack, Bill and Bob return to their bunks immediately after 8 a.m. *Appell* and stay there until midday, and save their two thin slices of breakfast bread to supplement their lunch. Many other officers are doing the same. In bed they don't feel the hunger so much, and having a little more to eat at midday makes it possible to concentrate on a book in the afternoon. The people who are up all day and eat their two slices of bread in the morning are hungry all day, cold all day, and find concentration difficult. The effect of the Christmas food, its energy and warmth, wore off after about thirty-six hours.

During the whole of December the kitchen milched some of each day's ration of potatoes and any issue of peas, and put them on one side for Christmas. The same applied to oats and barley, hence the porridge on Christmas morning, and the large issue of potatoes and peas at the Christmas dinner. The meat was three rations saved up during October, November and December.

A small percentage of potatoes and turnips are being saved each day now for a New Year's bash.

# Colditz 1945

## New Year's Day

THE RUMOUR OF a New Year's bash was a snare and delusion. No potatoes or turnips had been saved; but we had porridge issued for breakfast — the remnant of the oats saved for Christmas. Several messes — ours among them — kept it for supper. There was no *Appell* at midday, so most officers and orderlies (the latter had a holiday) spent the morning in bed.

I have been hungry every minute of the day since Christmas Day, and that includes the minutes immediately following each meal time. The younger men have their sleep haunted by dreams of groaning sideboards just out of reach, or of being at a feast and nightmarishly unable to unlock their jaws — fingering the food but unable to satisfy their hunger. Homer said, 'the belly is a hard master'.

At supper tonight I mentioned, rather shamefaced, that for the past few nights I have gone to bed in my socks, and discovered to my pride's relief that — far from being alone in my shame — several tough guys have adopted the practice.

## Wednesday 3 January

The issue today of two parcels per five persons gave rise to an illuminating incident. It was the offer of £70 sterling for one Red Cross parcel. The mess of seven officers to whom the offer was made refused to sell and, though the offer still stands, there are no sellers. Though I am not a rich man I would gladly give £15.

## Sunday 7 January

The intense cold and the inadequacy of the coal supply

have driven us into unwelcome crowding. So as to make one room on each floor warm enough to sit in, the dormitories have all surrendered a proportion of each week's issue of coal to be used in the day-cum-dining-room. Our dormitories in the *Kellerhaus* now have a fire once in four days.

The room in which we held church services has been abandoned until the weather improves, and such coal as we have had for it has been pooled with the issue for the small silence room. So the service we had this morning was held in the third-floor day-room, and could only be forty minutes long because the benches and table had to be back in place for the table stooges to do the lunch chores before *Appell*.

After lunch Dickie Heard delivered his second and last lecture replying to Micky Burn's lectures on Communism. At the end a number of questions were put, and some of those of the communist protagonists had rather an edge on them. The audience, which mostly wanted to be convinced of the rightness of capitalist democracy, reacted — silently — against them. Dickie had handled the capitalist democratic principle very ably and very convincingly, and the communist bubble seems to be burst.

Major Miles Reid, Captains Dougie Crawford and Victor Vercoe, and Flight-Lieutenant Halifax were told at noon that they will go to the repatriation centre at Annaburg on Monday.

THURSDAY 11 JANUARY

I seem to have lost all count of time since the last entry. My own teeth in my lower jaw — nine in number — have been very troublesome for a fortnight. There was no accompanying swelling, and I thought it might be due to cold, or was perhaps neuralgia and my nerves were reacting to hunger and the poorness of the food. Eric could find nothing to account for the continual pain, but last Friday decided that I must be poulticed. It was done, but nothing happened out of the ordinary until Sunday when the pain became so distracting as to prevent my taking an intelligent interest in anything. I was also drugged and feeling sick from having taken so many aspirin tablets each day on an empty stomach.

On Monday a mushroom growth swelling appeared, and Eric rubbed his hands with glee. But I had to bear with it another day because the abscess was not quite ripe for opening. Its centre could not be found on Tuesday either, and Eric concluded it must be at the base of a tooth which would have to come out.

He had no cocaine, so Hugh Dickie gave me a general anaesthetic, and I awoke thoroughly drunk. I went to bed at 8 p.m. and woke at 7.30 a.m. and tried to get dressed for *Appell*, but it was impossible. I have never had such a head or such faintness. I tried to get up for midday *Appell*, but it was still impossible. I slept until 2.30, felt a good deal better, ate some cold, boiled turnip and a piece of bread, and drank a pint of cold German ersatz coffee. I went to *Appell* at four o'clock and ate my tea: three pieces of German bread and a cup of tea made from boiled-up tea leaves without sugar or milk. I went to bed at 8 p.m. feeling cold, faint and sick. I had hoped I might be given a cup of milk or Bengers or something from the invalid comfort parcel supplies — but perhaps the need of others is greater than mine.

There are two rumours both concerning food. One is that the Germans are increasing our rations as from next week; and the other is that there are 5,000 British Red Cross parcels on the way, and they will be here any day.

SATURDAY 13 JANUARY
Yesterday and today I have been wooing the divine afflatus, but it is a very flat sermon. What can one preach to men who have been captive for five years and are cold and hungry?

I have returned to an old subject that I have preached on many times in different forms during the past four and a half years. It is against the bitterness that can only fill the heart and mind with misery. Empty bellies are made a worse pain under emotional distress.

'World Première', a play written and produced by

Charlie Hopetoun, was presented for the first of two nights
tonight. The cast, not particularly well-chosen, were under-
rehearsed and not altogether certain of their lines. Nor had
the author done justice to his own philosophical mind; but
there were shrewd prophecies about POW psychology in
the first months at home.

WEDNESDAY 17 JANUARY
We had a red-hot rumour that 500 Red Cross parcels had
arrived at Colditz railway station, and confirmation came
an hour later. The people who had gone back to bed after
morning *Appell* dressed quickly and chattered like excited
children. The dormitories were a babel of vocal anticipation.

During the course of the afternoon Colonel German
went to the station to check the number and at supper-time
— my mess was eating a dish of turnip peelings with two
small potatoes each — the Colonel's assistants came round
the table giving us the times tomorrow at which we will draw
half an American parcel for each officer.

We spent the remainder of the time recalling the contents
of former American parcels, and gloating rather disgustingly over the bully beef, milk, cheese, biscuits, chocolate,
margarine, coffee, prunes, cigarettes (we are right out of
them), soap (and out of this), and sugar.

THURSDAY 18 JANUARY
The Germans co-operated over the immediate distribution
of parcels, and by 9.30 a.m. the drawing was in full swing.
The chocolate — half a bar each and half a packet of
sugar-coated chocolate sweets — was bashed at once.

Tonight officers are standing about in small groups laughing and chatting about the good supper they have had, and
how fine it feels to have had a good meal and a full
stomach. But there is another topic of conversation — a
Russian attack in East Prussia, and a rapid Russian drive
towards the German frontier. And Warsaw! The OKW
communique does not admit that German forces have been
driven out of the city, but the report looks very much like

the preparation for such an admission.

Mixed with the gladness of the food and the hope tha
the eastern front may have collapsed is the deep gratitud
to the repatriates who left us on 7 January for Annaburg
The five hundred Red Cross parcels came from there, and
were no doubt due to the good offices of our friends. Some
one who has twice been at a repatriation *lager* says tha
there is always plenty of food there, and the period spen
in a repatriation centre is definitely a fattening and good
humour period. He said he had seen men put on seven kilos
in one week.

I went to the orderlies' quarters after they had eaten
supper.

'Good supper, sir?' they asked me.

'Yes, a very good supper, thank you. And you?'

'The best supper I've ever had since I was caught ... the
best I've ever had in my life!' roared a deep-chested Welsh-
man. Then one after another they told how Bill or 'Orace
had made this dish or that, had cooked it better than any
London cook, and how they had enjoyed it. It was the first
time they had felt satisfied since Christmas Day.

There are a few unfortunate fellows who belong to tables
that are 'squirrelling', and who are lying cold and miserable
in bed, as hungry tonight as they were last night. Some of
them were not hoarders until this period of hunger, but
now they are so afraid of the wolf that they dare not eat the
food that is in their hands. The general state of mind is
much healthier.

FRIDAY 19 JANUARY
Today four French generals — captured in 1940 — were
brought by car from Königstein. This evening they in-
spected the de Gaullists in the de Gaullist quarters and
spoke a few curious words via the mouth of General
Flavigny.*

The 'curious words' might be a discreet reference to the fact that
one of the *five* generals who left Königstein, General Mesny, was
'shot on the autobahn while attempting to escape'. Fourteen years
later *Polizeigeneral* Panzinger was charged with his murder.

Dan Halifax, amid the plenty of a repatriation camp, has
remembered our poverty and has sent to our table a private
parcel of various tins collected from fellow-repatriates. We
had a bash at supper tonight, and stopped between mouth-
fuls of stew and a second course of prunes and milk to say
'Good old Dan!' Jerry, unhappily, is in the cells and could
not share in our immediate fatness, but his share is being
carefully kept for him. We are only five at our table now.
When Dan left for repatriation, Bob Barnes left for another
mess.

## SATURDAY 20 JANUARY
Read in the German press today that Geoffrey Fisher,
Bishop of London, has been preferred to the Archbishopric
of Canterbury.

The weather is very severe.

## SUNDAY 21 JANUARY
Services as usual. After lunch Howard Gee repeated the
lecture he gave two years ago on broadcasting from Radio
Normandy.

Two rumours enlivened the day. The first says that 120
British Red Cross parcels arrived at Colditz station last
night; the second that the *Volksturm* were today
ordered to make their own way to the East Front on
bicycles or by any means of locomotion available. Later
in the day that was modified to making way under
their own steam to district HQs where they would
be formed into companies and drafted to East Prussia and
Silesia.

The company guards here are changing frequently, and
are now mostly old men about sixtyish. Some look five
years more!

## TUESDAY 23 JANUARY
A portable X-ray was brought into the camp this morning,
and this afternoon all POWs' lungs were X-rayed. German
efficiency was at its very peak. In six minutes I had gone
in, undressed, been measured and photographed, dressed,

and was on my way out. A staff of seven was employed, with two instruments.

The reason for today's event can only be our loss of weight during the winter. It was evidently a search for the cause — but TB is not the cause. There is — amazingly enough — not one person in the camp with TB.

## FRIDAY 26 JANUARY

Being a refugee in midwinter — and a severe winter — is very terrible. It was terrible enough for the people in the warmth of May 1940 when they were fleeing before the German armies; but the refugee train we saw arrive today at Colditz from Breslau (we heard the details of the story later) is too painful to think of.

Women and children had been in the trucks two days and nights without food — except what they had with them — or fire. Some of the small children were frozen to death, and not all of those who survived are expected to recover. Many adults had suffered frost-bite to their face and feet. They looked a heart-rending sight trudging brokenly across the bridge. Some carried small bundles, but some could scarcely carry themselves. I saw several officers turn away from the *Schloss* windows with a pain where fighting men feel most pain. Women and children are women and children — be they Polish, Dutch, Russian or German.

## FRIDAY 30 JANUARY

A day of rumours. 'The German radio failed last night. 'It was not the German radio but Breslau station.' 'Our rations are going to feed the Breslau and other refugees.' 'The one hot meal from the kitchen has been reduced from 1200 grams to 70 grams.' 'There is no coal in the village.' 'The Russians are less than a hundred miles from Berlin.'

In the room which mine leads off there is a spate of haversack-making. Some officers are certain we shall be moved from this camp at an hour's notice, probably to the *Schwarzwald*. Some are certain the *Schloss* will be filled up to over-crowding — and the presence of German officers, 'Aunty' and Reichman, in our quarters today, pacing out rooms and counting beds, lends support to their contention.

Many heavy bets have been laid on the war ending next month. The bookies now refuse to accept any further bets for February, and are offering long odds against any week in April or May. There are only a few takers.

The suppressed excitement in the camp is terrific. Caution still controls most tongues, but the atmosphere is crisp with almost frantic expectancy.

Thaw!

### THURSDAY 1 FEBRUARY
Yesterday's thaw continues: the most rapid we have known in five winters.

A press notice dated yesterday tells of the Mayor of Breslau having been shot for disappearing from his position of duty.

Today's big news is of the *Führer*'s speech on Tuesday. There was no mention of new weapons as the media of of victory, but victory was promised in such phrases as *'Deutschland mit Europa wird siegen'*. They would triumph — a sentiment which was closely followed by a warning to any who should fail in their duty. The way in which victory was to be achieved was not specified.

### MONDAY 5 FEBRUARY
Six Polish generals came to IVc this morning, followed by seven orderlies. One of the orderlies, a tall white-faced pimply boy, is fifteen years old. He lied about his age to get into General Bor's forces. General Bor is the most insignificant and worst clad of all the officers.*

It has been a pleasure to hear Polish voices again. They have the typical military precision of the last Poles, and there is as much heel-clicking as ever: a politeness which palls very visibly with British officers, though the Germans

*In *The Latter Days at Colditz* Pat Reid describes him as 'General BOR Komorowski, the head of that courageous, almost suicidal band of Polish patriots who kept the heart of Poland beating throughout the blackest years of the war.'

seem to appreciate it. The Poles have all been treated well at Nuremberg.

TUESDAY 6 FEBRUARY
The Swiss paid their January visit today — a momentous visit. They took out ten senior officers to a private bash at tea-time. The feasted ones — after the Germans had refused consent for the Brigadier and the *Prominente* — were the SBO, Lieutenant-Colonels Broomhall, German, Stayner, Young and Stirling, Wing-Commander Bader, Surgeon-Commander Gieves, Lieutenant-Commander Stevens, and the Adjutant, Willie Elstob.

After giving their parole they all walked out (only two German soldiers with them) to a roadhouse about a mile away. Two pretty waitresses were at their service in a large well-furnished dining-room, with tables laid with a white cloth and cutlery, and every appurtenance of civilisation. Each person sat down to one and a half tins of meat, with white rolls and margarine ad lib. One fried egg each followed; then *pain d'épice* with butter, and cream cheese with *Brezel*: tea and sugar ad lib., but no milk. There were vanilla and strawberry ices, three bottles of hock and one of Hungarian wine, and cigars.

Needless to say, when the revellers returned and told their story, we were just envious of the stomach-feeling they had: not in a dog-in-the-manger fashion, for the general comment was, 'Well, that's probably the best thing the Swiss have done!'

Before leaving, the Swiss said they would try and get parcels to us from the supply dump at Lübeck, and from Geneva.

THURSDAY 8 FEBRUARY
There is a rumour of a thousand *Prominente* arriving in a day or so. We have been expecting this camp to fill up, but not to that strength. If the Germans have evacuated all the prison camps in the eastern provinces the roads must be choc-a-bloc with POWs and foreign workers, and the railways choked with refugees. The three or four thousand

POWs who have been in Sagan, and the even larger number at Lamsdorff, will provide the Germans with a pretty problem — not to mention the misery of the prisoners themselves.

And when our contingent arrives, will they be weary and hungry? The rumour of their coming is said to be confirmed by a German officer. The questions much debated tonight are: what will conditions in this camp be like when it is 1400 strong; and will the thousand birds of passage, after a few resting days here, continue south, tagging us along with them? We are in no physical condition for marching, not to speak of carrying the amount of kit that would be necessary should the war last another two months. It is a pretty dreary prospect, and is regarded as almost a certainty.

Peter Allan asked Dr Eggers for the first refusal on a small hand-truck on which he could carry his kit if the camp was moved. Dr Eggers replied, 'If the Russians get this far we shall hand you over to your allies!'

SATURDAY 10 FEBRUARY
Priestley's play, 'They Came to a City', was presented this evening to a very appreciative audience.

MONDAY 12 FEBRUARY
The attics appear to be under repair. Evidently the thousand — or the seventy-one, or the 1300, as alternative rumours suggest — are expected. We don't like the idea of the attics being renovated.*

Everyone was weighed again this morning. The Germans had been very insistent that we should be weighed in our clothes, which would have shown a phenomenal increase in our weight since the last occasion, when we were stripped. This was strongly resisted by the SBO, and the point was conceded. A few officers had increased in weight by about one kilo, but none had regained much of

*By this time the famous Colditz glider, built and concealed in one of the attics, must have been nearing completion.

291

the seven or eight kilos lost at the last time of weighing.

Rumours today are about the nearness to Colditz of the Russian spearhead. Bautzen, lying between Breslau and Dresden is mentioned, and from there, as the crow flies, the distance is between sixty and seventy miles. It is hard to believe, unless the news has not been given truthfully, and the Russian penetration into Germany is deeper than we have been led to suppose.

TUESDAY 13 FEBRUARY
For several days we have been expecting each newspaper to have some report of the conference of the Big Three* held somewhere around the Black Sea. The German news announced several days ago that the conference — which aimed at the destruction of the German people — was in progress.

Rumours are our daily meat and drink, and the behaviour of many officers is a perfect mirror of the day's rumour content.

If the rumour is revived that we are to be moved on our flat feet, away go numerous officers to look over the essentials they have already packed, to feel their weight, to try on their home-made rucksacks, to examine boots and shoes, to roll up a blanket and try it this way and that, and to ask old Bill's idea about it. Then some destroyer of images happens along and gives reasons for the rumour being groundless, and the rucksacks are kicked under the bunk, and we are ready for the next rumour. Today's states that two hundred new arrivals are expected this evening. It is a cause for great concern for, if there are no arrivals today, there is half a parcel a head — the last — to be issued tomorrow.

I suspect some bright boy has thought it funny to start such a rumour. One such bright boy conceived the witty idea this morning of altering a very short parcels list on which I had a Danish parcel notified. He added 'zweimal', the way in which the Germans indicate two parcels, and it

*Churchill, Roosevelt and Stalin's meeting in Yalta.

involved the parcels officer and myself in an unpleasant contretemps with the German parcels staff.

The witty one later had a rocket from the SBO. The SBO's rockets are not to be sought after! He does not waste words, nor does he spare them! Only rarely does he have the culprit before him. His usual procedure is to give a notice on *Appell* which begins: 'Gentlemen, some ————————, I don't want to know his name, has done/said so-and-so. Only a ———— ———— would do such a thing, and this person, whoever he may be, can have my opinion of his deed and of himself in the following words, ————————— ————! It is a British order that it will not be done again!

## WEDNESDAY 14 FEBRUARY

Some say it was the largest raid ever, some say it was four successive raids, but bombs were falling from 9.30 p.m. until dawn. The nearest target would have been twenty to thirty miles away, but the blast here was almost unbelievable. The main gates shook as though a giant was trying to get in and almost succeeding in shaking them down. Standing watching at the open windows it was like an idiotic gale in our faces. We saw the fires flare up, making grotesque shadows among the clouds, and followed by columns of smoke glowering angry and red. One stick of bombs fell too close for comfort and the old *Schloss* rocked, dropping dust and plaster. Fires were all round us.

I got into bed at midnight and was out again by 1.30 a.m. Planes were roaring overhead, and RAF prisoners were praying to free pilots not to press their buttons until they got near the fires. Knowing the hazards of approaching the target, the RAF prisoners are always jumpy at such moments.

The headline in today's *Leipziger* runs '*Acht Tage Hasskonferenz*',* and the following article says it is the will and purpose of the Big Three to destroy (*Vernichtungswille*) the German people, and has passed upon them *des Todes-*

*Translation: 'Eight days' hate-conference'.

293

*urteils'*. It seems the meeting was in Yalta in the Crimea, but the article gives no indication of what decisions were reached. What amazes me is that the German people should be content to know so little — indeed, nothing — of the decisions of their enemies about their own immediate future, and the long-term future of their country.

At the *Besprechung* this afternoon the new German second-in-command, Major Howe, was asked by the SBO about our laundry which is three weeks overdue. He said the trouble was the coal shortage, and that a supply from the *Schloss* reserve would be sent to the laundry so that the dirty clothes waiting there could be washed and returned. But no further washing could be done. He also said he would do his utmost to get a supply of Red Cross parcels from Lübeck. He could not say whether we should be moved from this camp, but did not think it likely.

The weather is still very mild with some rain and much sunshine.

## FRIDAY 16 FEBRUARY
Visard, the orderly, did me some laundry, and did it well.

Rumour says that 100,000 people were killed in the raid on Dresden (there has been no statement in the press), and that two hundred prisoners are due to arrive on Monday or Tuesday next week.

I went on the non-comb. walk this afternoon, the first for several weeks. Scarborough, Eric Cooper and Hugh Dickin have proved the stalwarts; the rest of us haven't felt equal to it, nor to bearing with the ravenous appetite we worked up and were unable to satisfy. The last walk I went on several weeks ago left me with an uncomfortable hunger which did not subside for several days.

But today was like a day borrowed from April. Birds have been deceived into thinking it was time for mating. A chaffinch burst into song. Coal-tits, which are legion, were singing their eager, nervous little ditty, and flitting through the apple trees as though it were a summer day. There were many long-tailed tits in colonies of five or six. We walked through Schadrass, past four large hospitals and a mental hospital, and returned along the Mulde valley. Huge ice-floes lay melting in the sun on the meadows where they had been stranded when the flood-waters subsided.

We could not have walked more than five miles, but I was dog-weary and hungry beyond belief.

SATURDAY 17 FEBRUARY

Rumour quotes Dr Eggers as having said that unless/until the Russians make further advances in the East, the two hundred prospective arrivals will not come.

Yesterday, knowing how hungry I would be after the walk, I baked a cake. It consisted of half my day's bread ration soaked in water and beaten with a fork, one potato mashed and stirred in, and half the day's issue of margarine. When baked soggy (and it is impossible to bake soaked German bread in any other way) and eaten warm, such a cake sits more heavily, and for a longer period on the stomach. It has the glutinous virtue of sticking to the ribs.

*This is the last of the 'fair copy' diary. From here on it is written scrappily in minute writing on small sheets of paper.*

*19th Feb. Mon.* A 10% cut in the bread ration took effect this a.m. We now receive 1/8 of a loaf. At 4 p.m. the SBO was called to see Maj. Howe, S-in-C. At 6 p.m. he (the SBO) called a meeting of mess representatives. He said — 'the thing is so bad as to be funny', and smiled in the way we shall all remember him. 1500 French will arrive on Friday — they are on foot from IVd 80 miles away. All the British, including de Gaullists, Czechs, etc., will have to accommodate themselves in the *Kellerhaus*: officers on 1st three floors: orderlies on 4th floor. With no day-dining place, we shall have to live entirely in dormitories. A 12% cut in all rations next week! Rupert Barry, our very able K.O., replied, 'It will make little difference for we are not now getting full rations.' The *Stellvertretender* (said the SBO) was extremely sorry conditions were going to be so bad, but a terrible thing was happening to his country. There was no more about the laundry because the lorry had broken down. No salt was available — the QM must go to Leipzig to find some because he — Maj. Howe — had given his word. The theatre would no longer be available for entertainment, and no room for silence or in which to hold a religious service. The SBO concluded with his infectious chuckle and officers reflected his smile. Conversation: 'Back to Laufen days...or Spangenburg...or *Stalagluft*...or *Marlag*' or wherever officers began their period in the *'schaft*. 'As we began, so do we end.'

*20th Feb. Tues.* The chapel is being evacuated of its benches. The poor wretched French are to live in there also. The SBO and Tom Kimber made a tour of the *Kellerhaus* to allot rooms to the inhabitants of the *Saalhaus*. Most rooms were already too full for comfort, without having to accommodate over 100 additional officers & 40-odd orderlies. Lists were made available to room seniors at 2.30 p.m. Then began the scramble of making exchanges, and private arrangements by Messes who still have a reserve of Red X food & and want to eat together as to the best way of fair distribution. Terrific 'bash' at supper — guest of Lord Welsh's table: soup, toad-in-the-hole — boiled pudding!

*21st Feb. Wed.* My birthday. Began at once to collect kit & dispose of much to achieve a bare minimum should we be put on the road. Was hurt to dispose of my books & notes. Thought to burn Maisie's letters, but cd not. Began carrying across of lunch. Sentries in yard to prevent us carrying stools, benches, lockers or tables. What a mix-up. Beds head to foot, no lockers or anywhere to bestow our treasures. As we jostled each other, trampled on bedding and clothes, the conversation was good-humoured and often amusing. But what will sleeping be like? Our room is a passage-way for the French-Canadians.

*22nd Feb. Thurs.* Slept reasonably well, all things considered. A few bed boards kept clattering down and beds squeaking, but not too disturbed a night. Went on a tour of visitation this morning. What a shambles! Orderlies on the floor made three-tier beds in one room to give space for eating. A load of straw taken into the chapel. Only 500 to arrive as first contingent. Our mess broke up — there were no Red X parcels as from a week yesterday . . . rations are eaten as they are served in the dormitories we are in. There are twelve of us in this small room, sleeping head-to-toe. 4 are Czechs.

*23rd Feb. Fri.* Weighed again this a.m. The scales had been altered and showed 5 kilos increase, but half a dozen officers were checked on the rations' scale in the kitchen.

*Volksturm* battalion passing over bridge on foot, heavily laden. One of the French who escaped *en route* from IVd came by train and is in the cells. Saw refugees in covered wagons, on bicycles, & on foot, travelling west when we were walking this afternoon. Listened to an extremely interesting lecture this evening in room above chapel. It is impossible to work in these conditions. I have tried to make a sermon — but what a sermon!

*24th Feb. Saturday* There were many minor events during the day, but all is lost in the gt excitement — prisoners cd be seen on the move in large columns, none of them ours. At 6.30 p.m. someone said the French have arrived; are in the *Hof*. Immediate rush outside — it was not the arrival of prisoners but news of a sealed truck of Red X parcels having arrived at Colditz. Excitement knew no bounds. Speculation on how many a truck contained — 5,000, 2,000, 3,000? 'Aunty' was reported as having said the truck was registered as holding 200 'centaurs'. Col. German and Lance Pope went down and found 1,064 American (parcels). At lights out it was known that the SBO had decided to issue half a parcel each first thing in the morning — retrospective as from Wednesday — and another half each on Wednesday next. The supply will therefore cover a period of six weeks at the rate of half a parcel. Much talk until midnight — all about parcels.

*25th Feb. Sunday* The French not having yet arrived, H.C.
& Church Service were held at the usual times in room 311.
There was straw on the floor wh Jack had pushed aside.
The dust was like a cloud. It was the first bit of peace we
had enjoyed since Wed.

We had thought conditions to be bad before, but it used
to be possible by a very tiring effort to concentrate for an
hour or two during the day. Now one can only hope to
pass the time — by talking, or lying in a bunk reading
something light and exciting. No games are in favour. A
small poker school functions occasionally, and betting is
pretty reckless. On Friday we were told the Frogs wd be
here tomorrow: on the morrow it was again tomorrow.
Today is the morrow and tomorrow we are told they will
arrive.

A load of straw, dumped in the *Hof* last night, caught
fire this morning 9 a.m. It was a terrific blaze. Everyone at
once became fire-conscious. With loads of loose straw for
bedding in the largest part of the *Schloss* there is real danger
of fire. And the way we are packed in it wd be impossible
to get out of the building. In accordance with SBO's representations, window-bars are to be removed from certain
windows opening on the *Hof*, & a fire-fighting squad of
prisoners to be formed today with Major Cleave as Fireman-
in-Chief. We drew our half-parcel this a.m. & have eaten
well. Cheerful in spite of conditions.

*26th Feb. Monday* Wet dull day. Poor wretched refugees
crossing the bridge continuously. Women moiling with
children, a pair of horses in a rackety covered wagon, with
perhaps aged parents. God, what misery! All this we saw
while on non-comb walk. Passed the *Schützenhaus*: the
frogs had arrived and were waiting behind the barbed wire
until ready to be received in the *Schloss*. Admission, after
cursory search, began at about 7 p.m. They were still
crowding into the *Hof* after lights out. A raid occurred
during the process of admission — fortunately it was not a
local one or bomber pilots might have been attracted to the
dimmed lights. There seemed to be thousands & thousands

of French instead of 1100. Some were limping miserably, some seemed comparatively fresh — they had come from Elsterhorst & had been on the road 8 days.

Weather dull wet & blustery.

*27th Feb. Tuesday* I went across the *Hof* to shave at 7.40 a.m. Never saw such a sight. The more ingenious French had made themselves trolleys, hand-barrows, trucks of every conceivable model. One truck I saw was very ingeniously sprung on two tennis balls. There were three perambulators. Some of the trucks were as rude structures as one can imagine. Wheels in most cases were hand-turned and tyred with tin. We had decided to jettison the kit we could not carry if we had to move but many of these trolley manufacturers appear to have brought all they possessed. Our mass of books which had just been dumped when they were brought over from the library had been attacked by numerous English-reading Frenchmen before the librarian was awake.

I have to think in French again. There are twenty-two Protestants, all of whom sought me out this a.m. Two are preparing to offer themselves as candidates for the ministry of the *Eglise Réformée de France*. I am not able to help them much for there is no place where students could be removed from the incessant racket & jangle of overcrowding and as, in the new conditions, I had no accommodation to keep my books, they were destroyed.

*28th Feb. Wednesday Appell* is a strange phenomenon nowadays. The British are counted in their quarters; the French overflow in the *Hof* and present a real counting problem. One wonders why, at this stage of the war, the toil of *Appells* — from the German point of view — is continued. If the chaos here represents the condition of the nation — & it must from what we can see of the refugees from the windows of the *Schloss* — then the country is completely disorganised and demoralised.

The conditions in which the French are living are utterly appalling & sordid. Lavatory accommodation is totally inadequate, the same for washing their persons, not to speak of linen. And this evening they are to be seen crouching over tin-can manufactured smokeless heaters trying to heat drinking water, or warm up bits of food. Why the German Govt didn't allow the Russians to liberate them instead of bringing them to this increased misery — particularly since the war is almost over — passes my understanding.

It is evident from the press that something has boiled over on the West Front. Anglo-American offensive is not announced, but seems obvious — & as tho' it were the real thing. Tried to write to Maisie on Sunday — cd not — finished half-written letter today.

*1st Mar. Thursday Appells* are 8 a.m. & 4.30 p.m. March has come in like a lion. The north-west wind has huffed and puffed all night & day & is still roaring as tho' it had no intention of blowing itself out. The temperature is considerably lower. Refugee columns evidently from the east of Dresden area stream thro' the village continuously. A *Grossangriff* in the west is admitted. The sickening crunch of bombs is the regular thing now — an accompaniment to most meals. Lights are out each night by about 8 p.m. for an hour & a half. Usually another raid after midnight.

*2nd Mar. Friday* Gale — hail — vast columns of refugees — two heavy raids — still lower temperature. Josephine [a cat?] has disappeared — down French throats we believe. Already French quarters are beginning to get high. I doubt if even in these wretched circumstances they have overcome a Frenchman's natural aversion to sleeping in a room with windows open. In time past there has been much unpleasantness when, as in the *Revier*, French and English have had to sleep in one room. Much trade is in progress for trolleys against cigarettes & tobacco.

The Bandit & I sit together to eat. He has a flair for bright clean things — the Milko tin in which he makes his drinks is polished bright as silver. The only way in wh we can help the French is to invite them to eat some Red X food with us. It means turning other members of the dormitory out for a time — but all are co-operative & all take a turn. Some of the French are pretty ravenous & others have a few kilos reserve of dry food, beans etc.

*3rd Mar. Sunday* Each day is like its predecessor — crowds, smell & cold. The weather has turned to snow! Attended French Protestant service in their dormitory in the old *Revier*. 22 were present.

*4th Mar. Monday* A rumour states that Anglo-American forces have crossed the Rhine! The kitchen is unable to cope with food for over 2,000. The midday soup is pretty terrible. Potatoes are not boiled separately, but in the soup, grit, peeling, sprits & all.

*7th Mar. Wednesday* When the newspapers arrived today — covering several days — there was no confirmation of Monday's rumour about a Rhine crossing, but it is obvious that Cologne is in American hands & that the 6th British Army controls much of the western bank of the Rhine. The German press does not admit it, but names in the news suggest that the German forces west of the Rhine are completely defeated. There are many atrocity stories from the east front — rape, murder, etc. The lights are on to-night, but are winking like stars. How I wish I cd get away from these crowded quarters for a day. Every place is crowded, stairs, corridors, rooms, lavatories, wash-houses, yard; all is jostle & racket & apology & smell. The general forbearance, however, is a miracle of self-discipline & goodwill.

*8th Mar. Thursday* Immediately after 0800 hrs *Appell* the SBO warned me to be on duty for burial of an American at 0815 hrs tomorrow. He had no further particulars.

Cologne has fallen. The Germans say it was not a victory, they were not intending to hold Cologne. Everyone is buying & selling. Cigarettes, food & tobacco are the currency. Money will not buy anything.

301

*9th Mar. Friday* Col Dukes, USA Army, & I presented ourselves at the main gates at 8 a.m. for the funeral of Cpl Caldwell. *Hptmn* Müller & the *Dolmetscher* accompanied us to the cemetery. A guard of German soldiers was also present. Caldwell was taken prisoner in December & taken to Görlitz *Stalag* VIIIa. In January the *Stalag* was evacuated on foot. Four days before reaching Colditz three weeks ago he contracted 'flu & was put in the wagon. He had no greatcoat and, being a Texan, he wd feel the severe cold. After four days in the wagon he arrived at Colditz with pneumonia & died of double pneumonia after three weeks — on Monday last at 5.10 a.m. His friend, Cpl Collins (Virginia) who was also ill, remained in the *Lazarett* here, & was at the funeral. A shaft of sunlight broke through the widespread cloud while we performed the last rites. Caldwell was a Baptist. I have written to his widowed mother.

*10th Mar. Black Saturday* I lost my towel this morning, my favourite pipe at noon, & broke my lower denture this evening. Unless Eric or Julius can improvise something, my denture is a dead loss until the end of the war.

*11 Mar. Sunday* Found pipe & towel. Pipe had strayed to the third floor — towel just returned like a homing pigeon.

Arranged a *Service de Sainte Cène* at request of French — it is the beginning of their church year. Had to be postponed to 2.30 p.m. & was held finally not in the dormitory but in the dressing annexe to the shower room. H.C. also held in shower annexe.

A cut in rations takes effect tomorrow.

*12 Mar. Monday* Started a daily programme of talking Eng & French with Capt Souche. We walked round & round the *Hof*, were jostled & pushed by hundreds of others — some of whom were upon their lawful occasions, most just walking, or rather crushing, to breathe such fresh air as there was. Explaining English in French & having French explained in Eng had the unusual difficulty of not knowing

two minutes together to whom one was talking. Twice we
were separated & continued the conversation with a complete stranger also separated & talking with gesticulations to
a lost companion. The French habit of walking with linked
arms has something to say for it — but is impossible to an
Englishman, as is the daily & sometimes more frequent
hand-shaking.

Newspapers covering five days arrived this evening —
nowhere was there confirmation of rumours re crossing the
Rhine at several places by the American 1st Army. Nor of
today's rumour that the OKW had announced how 20,000
*Volksturm* at Cologne had shot their officers & surrendered,
and that such *Feigheit* wd be rewarded by death, & reprisals
taken on families.

*13 March Tuesday* Refugees still going SW. The branch line
to Leipzig running through Colditz is in use now for heavy
trains — military traffic is quite frequent: much, I should
say, to the distress of a sleepy country-line signalman —
and we fear it may prove attractive to some of the American formations of Fortresses that pass over here. The railway is much too close for our comfort.

*14th March Wednesday* A spring day — sunshine — the
*Hof* crowded beyond standing room. Rumours: 500 French
are leaving IVc; the whole British company is leaving IVc
by train, bound for a castle somewhere in Bavaria. Watches
are changing hands in amazing fashion — direct exchanges
of good watches, for good watches, or cigarettes, or clothes.

*21st March Wednesday* Before dawn an extremely heavy
raid on local targets. Saw a plane burst into flames. The
*Schloss* shook like an earthquake town. All day a dense
column of smoke has spread across the sky. It was still as
dense as ever at dusk.

At 4.30 p.m. a motor wagon arrived with a delivery of
food from the Danish Red X. The description is: porridge
oats, condensed milk, bacon & 2,000 Danish Red X parcels.
The whole is to be divided equally thr'out the camp &

will run out at 1lb of porridge oats, 3 ozs bacon, & a tin of condensed milk each. The whole of the parcels will go to the French.

*22nd March Thursday* The distribution took place this evening — one cupful of either oats or barley, $1\frac{1}{4}$ tins of condensed milk, about 3ozs of smoked bacon — the parcels went to the French. Many officers bashed the milk after lights out lying on a bunk ... two holes in the tin, suck, suck, suck!

*23rd March Friday* We have not had a walk this week: nor a bath since the French came. The standard of living is very low ... we are in slums feeding in worse fashion than slum-dwellers. Scarlett's smokeless heater is a feat of genius — dehydrated jam, said to be supplied to the front-line forces.

*26th March Monday* German press admits crossing of the Rhine by Patton's & Montgomery's forces. Rumours of revolt in Germany. Optimists forecast end of war by Easter Sunday — they envisage the collapse of organised resistance. But it seems impossible that the end should be so near. Tea is 25 cigarettes an ounce.

*28th March Wednesday* Sporadic shooting at 2300 hrs last night. Excitement is tense! No raid at midday hence a noncomb. walk at 2 p.m. A flaxen-haired girl of about 13 spat in unladylike fashion as she passed & if looks wd kill we are all dead. We observed while out that much of land under plough last year has not been touched. There appears to be little land sown. Woodcutting party. These parties are to be regular & twice weekly. Tommy Catlow & George Young lost party & returned alone.

*Good Friday* Communion Service 8.50 — our only preparation for Easter. Impossible to think of it as a holy day. The talk is all about victory, the German collapse, and when will the end be.

*Easter Saturday* Deep penetration of American armies into Germany. Great excitement & much speculation about wh of the armies will release us. The 3rd, 7th & 9th American Armies under Genl Hodges — with Genl Patton in the lead, seem to be headed for us. One or other of them is tonight said to be in the outskirts of Kassel. Does that mean the Spangenburg people have been released? It is generally believed they are on their way home.*

*Easter Sunday* H.C. 8.45 a.m. in the attic up 98 steps. Went to *Schützenhaus* to conduct worship for French Protestants. Was too late returning to be present at morning worship at 11.15. Took a French service with Richard assisting at 7 p.m. Large expectation that hostilities will cease today. Organised resistance has very evidently broken down completely. Victory dinners are being eaten thr'out the camp tonight.

*Easter Monday* Great excitement. Some say they can hear the guns on the west front. Talk is all about the end. This week is a great favourite.

*3rd April Tuesday* A March morning, dull, blustery, cold wind. At noon 80 French officers were given $1\frac{1}{2}$ hours' notice of removal. While they were assembled in the *Hof* for search some British officers looking out over the village saw ten trucks bearing the insignia of the Red X pass over the bridge in our direction. The cry of Red X parcels spread like a cry of fire, and completely overshadowed the departure of the French. It was not until 7 p.m., when Col German & Lance Pope returned from checking the number, that official confirmation was given.

The last consignment, issued at the rate of half a parcel each, gave out last Wednesday. The present supply is for 3 weeks at the rate of $\frac{1}{2}$ a parcel each. The French have received a similar quota. The trucks we saw arriving were like gutted charabancs, hooded & painted white with huge

*They were, in fact being marched eastwards.

305

Rd X on the roof. It wd be impossible, even on a dull day, to mistake them from the air.

The issue begins at 8.30 a.m. tomorrow.

*4th April Wednesday* The pleasure & excitement of drawing parcels. 300 French leaving today were being searched by 8.40 a.m. Whether they are all to be moved is not yet known. They are returning in the direction from wh they came — to the east of the Elbe — to Zeiten. Popular opinion has it that the Spangenburg-Rotenburg people were not relieved & are expected here — hence the clearing. Each day, until all are cleared, the French will be moved in companies of two or three hundred. Only volunteers will march, the remainder will be conveyed by truck. A company of 60 volunteers leave here tomorrow.

We are halfway between two of the greatest fighting armies in history — yet there is no disturbance except that for two days we have been under pretty constant air alarm. The siren no sooner all-clears a raid than it warns us of another.

The parcels situation developed into acrimony today with much waving of arms & shrugging of shoulders & conversation carried on in Eng, French & German. M. Albert Cockatrix, in charge of the convoy of parcels, was completely unaware that *Oflag* IVc also accommodated members of *Oflag* IVd. He said he had ten lorries each holding 960 parcels driven by British POWs. We maintained that, as we had received no direct consignment of parcels since April 1944, we were entitled to one load, 960, & the fact that IVd officers were lodged in the *Schloss* did not materially affect the position. British & French parcels officers had a session lasting about an hour & a half, & *Hptmn* Püpcke, with pencil & paper & many manoeuvres, fought a stout action on our behalf against his opposite number, the *Lageroffizier* of *Oflag* IVd. Result was one & a half parcels all round.

Camp gossip: 'These something something something French are ready to fight hard enough if it is to get a woman or food!' 'The something something tadpoles wanted to take the whole caboodle!' 'All this food-grabbing reminds me of the march into Germany — a man had to be as low as a Frog to get a bite of anything.' In the course of the evening I spoke with several of my French Protestant friends. Their conversation was too rapid for me, but I could pick out *'la perfide Albion'*, and comments that, 'The English suppose they are superior to everyone . . . they want to tell everyone what they shall have & what they shall not have.' 'They shall not decide the future of France!'

The highlight of gossip in both Eng & Fr circles was the interview Genl Daine sought with the SBO which concluded with the Genl remarking with some asperity that 'the English have always been a nation of shopkeepers.' The SBO, who is a Scot, may or may not secretly sympathise with that point of view, but on this occasion he rose &, opening the door of his room (it is one of the cells opening on to the *Hof*) very politely said, *'s'il vous plaît, Monsieur le Général,'* at which the astonished General with great dignity rose & took his leave.

*6th April Friday* Arrival of 2/Lt Winant, USAAF, from a camp near Munich. He is the son of the American Ambassador in London, so he was at once made a *Prominente*. At the camp he has left they are on a whole parcel a week, but are receiving no German rations.

Two British officers, Clive Dieppe & Teddy Barton, & the *Revier* orderly, were in Leipzig today — Clive & Teddy for a medical inspection. Their visit coincided with a heavy air-raid. They were not, as the people of Leipzig are, 'bomb-happy'; they thought they were the most frightened people in the shelter. The man in charge of the shelter had a map showing the sectors into which the town has been divided, & a radio told of the progress of the raid: 'Enemy planes are passing out of Sector P into Sector K,' followed by a snatch of music, & then, 'Enemy planes are passing out of Sector K into Sector L.' Then the radio stopped, the lights were dimmed, and the thud & tremor of distant bombs became the shrill swish & whistle & horrible shattering of heavy bombs dropping near by. The man in charge showed them on the map how the bombing tactics operated. The bombers first passed over the sector in which their target lay, & then turned to release their load. There was a time-lag of about 3 minutes between each wave attacking the target. He was explaining all this while the raid was at its height. Some of the women in the shelter heaved a sigh during the three minutes' relief, but none fainted or screamed.

The sector was all-cleared & the lights restored, & the radio told which of the other sectors were under bombardment. The planes were not out of hearing before the radio issued orders to fire-fighters & medical personnel, & the prisoners who were engaged in clearing the debris. When Clive & Teddy emerged from the shelter the air was thick & acrid. Fires were raging, & in several places horses' entrails, feet, heads and legs splashed about. No one treated them unkindly, or spoke disparagingly of Britain, America, or anyone. They had to walk several kilometres down what had been the railway track from what had been the largest station in Europe before they reached the point from wh a train cd travel.

7th April Saturday The number of French already gone to Zeithin is about 700. Those who remained in the camp chapel were moved — at the request of l'Abbé de Matan, the senior French priest — to some of the vacant rooms, and the straw was cleared from the chapel. But we were told there wd be no time available for Protestant services.

9th April Monday Returning from the non-comb. walk this afternoon we met the three who were in Leipzig on Friday on their way to the Mixed Medical Commission. Most of us fail to understand why they shd be seeking repatriation when the war is only a matter of days from its end. The French who were packed & searched yesterday were packed & searched again today. The train did not arrive. They were turned into the *Hof* again for the night. Must be ready again tomorrow morning.

*10th April Tuesday* Fountain pens, leather straps, pocket-knives with a spike, haversacks, all the things we were not allowed to keep in our possession as POWs were returned to us this morning after almost five years. My money is not yet returned, one penny, half-a-crown, & a 100Fr note. This evening a trail of Fortresses & an umbrella of fighters returned via Colditz from an attack on Leipzig & oil targets in the Leipzig area. It was an amazing sight, they were as free from battle formation as though flying idly over home territory.

The Exchange Prices Board today shows an offer of £100 for 1,000 cigarettes, & a second offer reads £150 for 1,000 cigarettes, French cheque. Other prices are 4ozs American choc for 55 cigs (a reduction from last week when it was 70); Spam, 50 cigs; prunes, 45; 4ozs tea, 60; 2ozs coffee, 55. With the exception of the last item all prices are considerably reduced as the lack of cigarettes increases.

Many claim to hear the artillery on the western front. The French packed & were searched, but no train! Turned into the *Hof* again.

*11th April Wednesday* The SBO had an interview with the *Kommandant* & pointed out that Colditz was fast becoming a battle zone, and asked his intentions. The *Kommandant* said he was awaiting orders from Himmler.

A reduction in rations announced — fat, now ¾ inch cube, is reduced by half; sugar, now 150 grams, also cut by half; and there is a corresponding increase in peas & meat — the joke being that we don't get any peas or meat.

Colditz is evidently in the battle zone. The town is in a general state of alarm. Raiders overhead all day. Artillery is to be heard in the distance, and excitement & tension are beyond description.

*12th April Thursday* Army trucks, armoured cars, armed reconnaisance cars, a few tanks, troop carriers, staff cars, have streamed over the bridge all day towards Chemnitz in the south. They had all the appearance of an army in retreat. By 10 a.m. we had a rumour of an American army having reached the Elbe; by midday they were reported at Halle, & by 3 p.m. to be 12 miles from Leipzig. The camp was a furore of excitement, & every inch of window-space was crowded with leaning, crushing bodies. Artillery has been plainly heard since 1.30. Officers are in a fever of packing & most messes are eating the food wh was to last until Wednesday next. The more prudent are waiting until they see the first Sherman tank coming down the Leipzig road. The army personnel, armour & convoys, were leaving the battle, coming down the Leipzig Rd, and are perhaps making for Berchtesgarten area where, rumour says, the last stand will be made. Tonight we have a red-hot rumour of a large tank concentration at Berner, 4 miles west of Colditz.

This evening, about 7 p.m., 2/Lt Winant was put under orders to leave at 8 a.m. tomorrow. This is most unpleasant for it may mean he is to be held as a hostage. The Brig & the SBO have gone to interview the *Kommandant* — on what subject we do not yet know.

*Hptmn* Püpcke and 'Aunty' were in their best uniform today. It reminded me of France five years ago when we knew we were to be taken prisoner and hence dressed ourselves in the best clothes we possessed, discarding those we could best afford to lose. The latest rumour (it is 8.40 p.m.) is that the *Kommandant* of IVd, Genl Hoffmann, and all the officers' wives of both camps, packed and left this afternoon.

*13th April Friday* Friday the 13th — is it ominous? More happened last night than in most months of our being here. Winant was put in a hide & wd not have been found but at 10 p.m. the SAO [Senior American Officer] sent an order for him to appear in the courtyard. Evidently it was the *Kommandant's* way of discovering how the camp wd react, for at 10.30 the whole of the *Prominente* were put under two hours' notice of removal. Prawitt & most of the German staff were in the *Hof* waiting. There were at least two German officers I had never seen before, and they had a map and appeared to be studying a route. From what I could see they seemed to be indicating a road going east for a short distance, then veering south in the direction of Oberbayern — Berchtesgarten.

Many officers had not gone to bed, the tension & excitement proving the enemy of sleep. Others got up, unable to sleep, & joined the excited groups debating how long it wd be before the 7th Army wd reach here from Leipzig. Wd Leipzig be bypassed as Brunswick & Hanover were? Wd it surrender as Weimar had done? Weimar & Leipzig were both very Red before the Nazi regime. Wd the 3rd Army make a junction, Chemnitz-Leipzig, and thus relieve us, or wd it continue east to Czechoslovakia? Wd the camp be moved? If so they wd not dare to make us 'pad the hoof' or the spearhead of the advancing army wd overtake and release us, and they do not appear to have transport — tho' there are two lorries in the outer courtyard waiting, one to convey the *Prominente*, and one, it is said, to convey certain officers of the staffs of the two camps.

We shouted from the windows to the *Prominente* as they departed.* Charlie Hopetoun looked a little shaky — he had been in the *Revier* recovering from an illness wh had kept him in bed for a fortnight. No sooner had they gone than we saw the true purpose of the second truck. The Polish generals & the whole of the Polish company were ordered into it & rushed away.

The *Kommandant* was reported to have said a) 'that the Americans wd arrive during the week-end, but the camp wd have been moved by then'; and b) 'that no one wd now be moved, and camp administration wd continue in the ordinary way until the end.' Opinion in the camp is very divided. Where can they move us to?

*The SBO had argued bitterly with Prawitt, the *Kommandant*, to keep the *Prominente* at Colditz, despite Himmler's orders. But it was more than the *Kommandant's* life was worth, and his only concession was that some of his staff who were to accompany the *Prominente* should bring back news of their destination and their safe arrival. The *Prominente* had an adventurous and nerve-wracking time. Romilly escaped, and several others tried to. They were eventually taken to Austria and handed over to the Swiss on 25 April.

311

We were all pretty tired at 0800 hrs *Appell* today, having turned into our bunks at 0400 hrs. A day of rumours and high expectation — *Panzerspitzen* at Leipzig. The afternoon appeared to be dead still, no aircraft or anything warlike. Tommy Catlow likened it to the middle of a typhoon. At 3 p.m. a rumour of a five-minute warning to the village of a *Panzerspitzen*. Something is happening under the bridge — a line of people leaning over the parapet — evidently mining it. Vehicles streaming south. It is a rout.

*14th April Saturday* . . .

The diary ends at this point and there is no further account of Platt's own experiences and emotions during the hours that led to the liberation.

On Saturday morning the front-line fighting moved towards Colditz and American artillery began ranging on the town and its castle while the prisoners watched from the open windows.

In the course of the morning panic orders came from the *Generalkommando* at Dresden. The *Kommandant* was to evacuate the castle and march the prisoners eastwards, away from the Americans. The orders ignored the Russians who were advancing at equal speed from the east and would soon be in Dresden itself.

When Colonel Tod was called to the *Kommandantur* he flatly refused to let his officers be taken out of the castle. Their safety lay within its walls and, he told the *Kommandant*, if the Germans tried to force them out the British would resist in self-defence.

*Oberst* Prawitt telephoned Dresden.

'The British refuse to move.'

'They must!' came an explosion the other end,

'I can't move them without shooting. If any get killed, will you take the responsibility?'

'No!'

'Neither will I!' and the *Kommandant* banged down the receiver.

312

Now that his country was collapsing he could defy his *Wehrmacht* superiors. His real fear was of the SS unit in the town who had oversight of the concentration camp for Hungarian Jews. What he dreaded most (and so did the prisoners) was that they might move into the castle for a final and ruthless stand.

In these last hours the British prisoners seemed to be the allies he could best trust for his own future safety and that of his staff. He accepted the inevitable and, in the early afternoon, he formally surrendered the castle to Colonel Tod and the American Lieutenant-Colonel Duke (the French did not take part) on condition that no sign of surrender should be visible in the town. No Allied or white flags must be seen at the windows, and the sentries outside the walls must remain at their posts. He also asked for a guarantee that he himself should remain in British hands and not be turned over to the Russians. Tod promised to see that he was treated with justice, but could make no guarantee beyond that.

Tod now had control of the interior of the castle and its armoury. His cool authority and iron discipline had become the strength on which both the Germans and the now ex-prisoners depended. He kept a rigid control at a highly emotional time, and it was through him that the liberation took place with the orderly smoothness of a well-planned military action.

For safety's sake he kept his men in the *Hof* and on the lower floors of their quarters while the Germans remained in the *Kommandantur*. It was a tense night, and few men could sleep. From the first light on the Sunday morning the windows of the *Schloss* were crowded. The battle for Colditz was on. Shells ripped into the town and flames engulfed familiar buildings. Two shells tore into the walls of the *Kommandantur*, and the blast blew Douglas Bader off his tin legs.

It could now be only a matter of hours before the Americans reached them and ended their years of captivity, the moment they had been dreaming about and longing for since the castle gates first clanged behind them. When they

313

looked back in the years after their liberation, those last hours were a confusion of unbearable emotions. Few could be sure how long the battle went on, or how may hours or days they spent watching at the windows as the Americans advanced on the town. Nor could they remember whether it was the Sunday afternoon or the Monday morning when the first American walked into the *Hof*.

They did know, however, that after the first few shells hit the castle, no more came their way, and though the town was devastated, the *Schloss* was hardly damaged. They learned the explanation later. The Americans had all their artillery ranged on the castle as the stronghold of the town when, just as the order to fire had been given, one of their spotters saw through his binoculars an Allied flag at one of the windows. Memories are confused about whether this occurred before or after Colonel Tod had promised *Oberst* Prawitt that no flags would be shown, or whether in fact it was on the advice of the German officers. But the showing of the red-white-and-blue flag, whether it was French or English, undoubtedly saved the castle and the men inside it.

Among all the conflicting written and verbal accounts of the actual liberation, those by the two German officers, *Hauptmann* Eggers and *Hauptmann* Püpcke are the clearest. While for the prisoners it was the emotional climax of years of waiting, with the crazy excitement of imminent freedom and reunion with their families, for the Germans it was a sombre moment of truth that they now faced imprisonment or worse. Some British accounts say that the liberation took place on the Sunday afternoon, but the two Germans, and the American Commander of the Task Force that took Colditz, agree that it was on the Monday morning, April 16th, that an American patrol first entered one of the outer courtyards of the castle. The *Kommandant* and Eggers, as the best English-speaker among the Germans, were taken down to the American command post across the river while a single GI went on into the castle and through the gate of the *Hof*.

For a moment he stood inside the gate; and John Watton, the artist, remembers how strong, tanned and healthy the young American looked as he surveyed the pink and boney scarecrows that pressed towards him. Instinctively the GI raised his rifle to hold them back as a roar of cheering filled the courtyard. Other GIs came through the gate, and suddenly they were being hugged and grabbed at, kissed by Frenchmen, and wept over. Everybody wanted to touch them to see if they were real.

Colonel Tod retained his cool and rigidly disciplined hold on his men for the next two days. Working parties with the necessary skills were sent out to restore the damaged electricity and water supplies to the town, but the rest of the ex-prisoners were kept within the castle walls, protected from excesses of their own exuberance, and also from the German suicide parties of SS and Hitler Youth who were roaming the countryside.

They were all driven in American trucks to a captured airfield near Chemnitz, and the next day a flight of Dakotas was ready to take them to England.

Padre Platt found himself in a plane which contained many of his companions from the earliest days at Colditz: Dick Howe, Guy German, Rupert Barry, Peter Storie-Pugh, Scarlett O'Hara, Stooge Wardle, and Don Donaldson. It was a terrible journey, the Dakota lurched and fell among the clouds, and everybody was sick. There was a moment when they looked as though they might meet their end head-on against the white cliffs of Dover. But then they were back, and down, and once more on the green turf of England.

# *Glossary of German Words*

*Abort* — lavatory, WC
*Achtung!* — Attention!
*Antrag* — request, application
*Appell* — roll-call
*Arbeiter* — workman
*Arzt* — doctor, medical practitioner
*Ausweis* — identity card
*Besprechung* — conference, discussion
*bestraft* — punished
*Brezel* — pretzel

*Danke* — thanks
*Dolmetscher* — interpreter
*Dulagluft* – transit camp for airmen
*Dumm Junge* — stupid youngster
*Duschemeister* — NCO in charge of showerbaths

*ein* — one
*Engländer* — Englishman
*Evidenz-zimmer* — evidence-room where interrogations took place

*Feigheit* — cowardice
*Feldlazarett* — field hospital, casualty clearing station
*Feldwebel* — sergeant
*Frau* — woman, wife
*Fruchtpolizei* — orchard guards
*Gefangene* — prisoner, captive
*Gefangenschaft* — imprisonment (often shortened to *Schaft* among POWs)

316

*Gefreite* — lance-corporal
*geprüft* — examined (by censor)
*Geschichte* — story
*gestorben* — dead
*Grossangriff* — large-scale attack
*Guten Abend!* — Good evening.

*Hauptmann* — captain
*Hauptstadt* — capital city
*Herr,* — Mr, master, sir
*Herrenvolk* — master race (Nazi term for the German people)
*Hof* — yard, courtyard

*Ich weiss nicht* — I do not know
*Ilag* — internment camp (for civilians)
*Inspektor* — inspector

*Jüdische Weltegefahr* — world-wide Jewish menace

*Kaninchen* — rabbits
*Kellerhaus* — that part of the *Schloss* that included the (wine) cellar(s)
*Kommandant* — commanding officer
*Kommandantur* — garrison, headquarters
*Kriegsefangene* — prisoner-of-war (often shorted to *Kriegie* by POWs)

*Lager* — camp
*Lagernummer* — camp-number
*Lageroffiziere* — camp officers
*Lazarett* — military hospital
*Leutnant* — Lieutenant
*Lichts aus!* — Lights out!

*Mädchen* — girl, maiden
*Marlag* — camp for naval POWs
*Militärgesetze* — military law

317

*Mitarbeit* — collaboration
*mitarbeiten* — work with, collaborate (with the enemy)
*morgen früh* — tomorrow morning

*Nudeln* — pasta, noodles

*Obergefreite* — lance-corporal
*Oberlager* — upper (high) camp
*Oberstleutnant* — lieutenant-colonel
*Oflag* — camp for officer POWs

*Panzerspitzen* — armoured spearhead division
*Pfennig* — small coin, one-hundredth part of Mark
*Posten* — sentry, sentries, guard

*Reich Mark* — the agreed exchange rate during 1939–45 war was 15RM = £1
*Revier* — sick bay
*Ritterkreuz* — gallantry medal, a higher grade of the Iron Cross
*Rittmeister* — cavalry captain

*Saalhaus* — that part of *Schloss* which contained a great hall
*'Schaft* — see *Gefangenschaft*
*Schweinhunde* — filthy fellow; literally pig-dog
*Schloss* — castle
*Schnüffelhunde* — sleuth-hound, tracker-dog
*Schützenhaus* — guardhouse, rifle-range
*Schwarzwald* — Black Forest
*Soldaten* — soldiers
*Sonderappell* — special roll-call
*Sonderführer* — officer on special duty
*Sonderlager* — special camp
*Sorge* — worry, concern
*Sportführer* — sports leader, captain
*Stabsarzt* — surgeon-major
*Stalag* — POW camp for other ranks, not officers
*Stalagluft* — POW camp for airmen, not officers

# GLOSSARY OF GERMAN WORDS

*Stellvertretender* — representative
*Strafappell* — roll-call ordered as a punishment
*Strafe* — punishment
*Straflager* — punishment camp
*Stubenarrest* — confinement to quarters
*Such!* — Seek!

*Tierarzt* — horse-doctor, veterinary surgeon
*Todesurteil* — death sentence

*Uhr* — time, hour, clock
*Unterlager* — lower camp
*Unteroffizier* — non-commissioned officer

*Verboten!* — forbidden
*Vernichtungswille* — intention to annihilate, exterminate
*Volksturm* — people's army, Home Guard

*wachsende* — growing, becoming, increasing
*Wehrmacht* — Regular Army, Armed Services (as opposed to SS)
*Wehrmachtsuppe* — army soup
*Wurst* — sausage